A CHOICE OF POETS

An anthology of poets
from Wordsworth to the present day

chosen and edited by

R. P. HEWETT
Formerly Senior English Master
Northgate Grammar School for Boys Ipswich

Nelson

A CHOICE OF POETS

Thomas Nelson and Sons Ltd
Nelson House   Mayfield Road
Walton-on-Thames   Surrey KT12 5PL   UK
51 York Place   Edinburgh   EH1 3JD   UK

Thomas Nelson (Hong Kong) Ltd
Toppan Building 10/F
22A Westlands Road   Quarry Bay   Hong Kong

Distributed in Australia by
Thomas Nelson Australia
480 La Trobe Street
Melbourne   Victoria 3000
and in Sydney, Brisbane, Adelaide and Perth

© R. P. Hewett 1968
First published by George G. Harrap and Co. Ltd 1968
(under ISBN 0-245-53305-2)
Reprinted 17 times
Nineteenth impression published by Thomas Nelson and Sons Ltd
1984
Reprinted 1985 (twice), 1986 (three times), 1987 (twice)
ISBN 0-17-444112-6
NPN 19 18 17 16 15 14 13 12 11 10
Printed in Hong Kong

Harrap's
New Outlook Series

A CHOICE OF POETS, an anthology of poets from Wordsworth to the present day—*by* R. P. HEWETT

A FURTHER CHOICE OF POETS, an anthology of poets from Crabbe to Ted Hughes—*by* R. P. HEWETT

A CHOICE OF DRAMATIC THEMES —*by* R. P. HEWETT

7 THEMES IN MODERN VERSE— *edited by* MAURICE WOLLMAN

By the same author

READING AND RESPONSE
An approach to the criticism of literature

Harrap's
New Outlook Series

A CHOICE OF POETS

Preface

This anthology is intended mainly for students from fourteen to sixteen. It includes a fairly representative selection of the work of fourteen poets, on the principle that it is often better to study a number of poems by the same author, as they so often cross-fertilize each other. There are plenty of anthologies of *poems* for this age-group and also of collections of modern poets, but this collection aims at offering the whole range that is accessible—and this range, I take it, is from about 1800 to the present day. It is a common experience, I think, that though individual poems from the whole of English poetry can and should be read by these students, the pre-Romantic poets are not accessible *as poets* to students before the sixth form.

The choice of poets is a frankly personal one, and doesn't claim to offer a complete range. Some major poets are omitted on grounds of difficulty (*e.g.* Yeats), some on personal reservations (*e.g.* Browning), some on grounds of space (Clare, de la Mare, Philip Larkin), some because they wouldn't fit (*e.g.* Byron, many of whose lyrics seem to me flawed and the Byron I admire takes too long to make his effects). Only two (Tennyson and Auden) are included mainly because of their representative status rather than any deep personal affection for them. I hope there is a fair range of kinds, and that the presence of Owen, Eliot, and Auden will mitigate the impression that this is an anthology of nature poetry. I have felt obliged to omit some of the greatest poems of my chosen poets on grounds of difficulty, though I wouldn't describe all the poems here as by any means easy. Occasionally I have used extracts from longer poems (Wordsworth and Keats, for example), where it seemed that the poet's individual quality could not be fully shown without it; these I hope may in some cases lead on to reading the complete poems.

This selection unashamedly makes a feature of notes, designed to help in elucidating and appreciating the poems.

I think the loathing we justifiably feel for forcing poetry on to reluctant children has produced an excessive swing of the pendulum—a doctrine that any poem can mean exactly what the reader wants it to mean, and that guidance in the exploration of its meaning is treason. This seems to me nonsense. I have given a very short biography of each poet, and a brief introductory essay, which I have tried to keep fluid and undoctrinal, and which I hope will be used, if at all, as a body of ideas to be challenged rather than final judgements. The poems are followed by three kinds of notes: brief comments on the subject or tone of the poem, references to particular words or phrases which may be helpful, and series of questions (marked with the letter 'A') designed to help student and teacher come to grips with the meaning of the poem, particularly by drawing attention to 'local' effects of rhythm or sense. Some of the notes might well be used orally in class, some in private reading, some might be dispensed with entirely. I hope they will not be used as a drill. Suggestions are made under the letter 'B' for using many (but not all) of the poems as stimuli for personal writing in prose or verse; all English teachers are increasingly restless under the rigidity of the false distinction between literature and language, especially at 'O' level and CSE level, and this is a contribution to blurring that distinction. I very much hope that these will not be used as a penny-in-the-slot exercise that comes up with deadly monotony as the price one pays for reading the poem. So I stress that these are *suggestions*, certain to deaden if they are used mechanically: the expression 'creative writing' is, I think, in some danger of becoming fashionable and therefore lifeless. Lastly, each batch of notes is followed by suggestions for further reading and a very short reference to critical writing about the poet; it would be nice to think that these might sometimes be followed up by the student.

Any anthologist writing mainly for schools is aware of a very fine dividing line between teachers and students who want help and teachers and students who don't want all the work done for them, and especially resent having a particular reading imposed on them. I can't avoid frustrating one or other of these groups, but have tried at least to keep them in mind—that is, not to claim to aim at exhausting what a poem or poet offers, and yet not to assume knowledge or observation or sensibility which can't be guaranteed to be always present. Professor Empson in a recent review wrote: "The person engaged in the large profession of English Literature is expected to be able to make the 'magic' of a poem available to many people who could not otherwise have experienced it." This states neatly the predicament of all of us who 'present' poetry to our classes. The only essential things between these covers are the poems; given optimum conditions, they will in the end make available their own 'magic'.

Acknowledgments

For permission to publish copyright material in this anthology, acknowledgment is made to the following:

For W. H. Auden: the author and Faber and Faber Ltd (*Collected Shorter Poems*).

For T. S. Eliot: the author's executors and Faber and Faber Ltd (*Collected Poems 1909–1962* and *Old Possum's Book of Practical Cats*).

For Robert Frost: the author's executors, Jonathan Cape Ltd, and Holt, Rinehart and Winston Inc.

For Robert Graves: the author (*Collected Poems 1959, Collected Poems 1961, Collected Poems 1965*).

For Thomas Hardy: the Trustees of the Hardy Estate and Macmillan and Co. Ltd (*The Collected Poems* by *Thomas Hardy*).

For D. H. Lawrence: the Estate of the late Mrs Frieda Lawrence, William Heinemann Ltd, and Laurence Pollinger Ltd.

For Wilfred Owen: Mr Harold Owen and Chatto and Windus Ltd. (*The Collected Poems of Wilfred Owen*)

For Edward Thomas: Mrs Helen Thomas and Faber and Faber Ltd.

For R. S. Thomas: the author and Rupert Hart-Davis Ltd (*The Bread of Truth, Tares, Poetry for Supper*, and *Song at the Year's Turning*).

Contents

[11]

Introduction

MAINLY TO THE STUDENT

The fourteen poets represented in this book—and a large number of the poems reprinted—have all been found of interest to some students of your age at some time. But the reading of poetry, like the writing of a poem, is an extremely tricky and above all an extremely personal activity. The ideal frame of mind in which to read poetry is, in D. H. Lawrence's phrase, "a reverent openness"; in other words it is unwise to start with *any* assumptions or preconceptions as to what poetry should be. Poetry is perhaps the most concentrated form of literature, and needs for its full enjoyment the highest powers of response we can muster. We need to bring into play at the same time our highest powers of intelligence and sensitivity; or, to put it another way, poetry at its best works through our hearts and our brains simultaneously. Critics and commentators can usefully point out features, aspects, rhythms, images, and so forth which contribute to the impact a poem makes, and there is often a good deal of hard work in understanding exactly what the poet is getting at. But when all this preliminary study has been done the poem 'works' (or doesn't work) for each of us by means of something beyond the grasp of logic or analysis. Thus every good poem has a paraphraseable meaning, but no good poem *is* its 'paraphraseable meaning'; the language, imagery, and rhythms of poetry cannot be peeled off its surface, as they are not decorative additions but parts of the poem itself. It follows that after the close attention we may give to parts of the poem—to lines, to phrases, to single words—we should always reconstitute the poem as a whole. It is a good practice with a new poem to read or hear it first as a whole, for its general drift and subject matter, and above all for its *flavour*; then to do the detailed study it seems to need (and this varies greatly from poem to poem); then, finally, to read or hear it at least once again. With a little practice you can read poetry aloud silently—that is, with the 'inner ear'—and the *sound* of a poem is always an essential part of its effect. If you like a poem very much you will find that you know bits of it by heart without ever meaning to and that with not much further effort you can commit the whole of a short poem to memory. This experience is very different from 'learning by heart for homework'.

Three final points. First, try not to think of poetry as rarefied or specialized, or "not for scientists (geographers, historians, practical people . . .) like me"; good poetry is addressed directly to the humanity we all have in common. Secondly, you may find that some of these poems set you off on writing your own verse; don't be afraid of imitations or echoes: they are, after all, the way in which you first learned to speak, so why not also to write in poetry? A lot of poetry written by young children, some of it splendid, has been published recently, but this activity tends to drop out in the middle of the secondary school and to be taken up again by only a minority of specialists, in the sixth form, and in between there lies a period of excessive self-consciousness about writing in verse—and, far too often, a violent distaste for poetry itself. This is a sad loss. Try writing in free rhythms, uncorseted by regular patterns or restrictive rhyme schemes—perhaps at first in the manner of Lawrence—the animal poems or the short *Pansies* that end the selection of his poems in this book. You may be surprised at what you find you can do. If you find you can't or won't write in verse at all, some of the poems here may suggest themes for short stories or other forms of imaginative writing. Finally, there is at the heart of poetry a mystery; a good poem seems to work directly on our nerve-ends—a 'taste in the head', a small shudder in the spine. No one can make you have this response, and it can't—or should not—ever be faked. It follows that in the last analysis only you can say whether you like a poem or not. So don't let anyone dictate to you about this—neither teachers nor critics—nor, above all, editors of anthologies.

William Wordsworth

WILLIAM WORDSWORTH was born in Cockermouth, Cumberland, 1770, the son of a lawyer. He was educated at Hawkshead among mountains, and at St John's College, Cambridge. He spent the year 1791–2 in France, and at that time was a warm admirer of the French Revolution, but was recalled to England. In 1795, as the result of a legacy, he moved with his sister Dorothy, first to Dorset, then to Somerset, as a near neighbour of the poet Coleridge; these two had a tremendous influence on him, and he and Coleridge published *Lyrical Ballads* (1798). Before this he started writing *The Prelude*, a record of his childhood and imaginative development, and by far his greatest single achievement. Next year he settled with Dorothy at Dove Cottage, Grasmere, in the Lake District; in 1813 he moved to Rydal Mount and spent the rest of his life there. He married a childhood friend in 1802. He finished the first draft of *The Prelude* in 1805, but went on revising it throughout his life. He led a rather uneventful life, but made a series of tours into Europe. He became Poet Laureate in 1843, and died in 1850.

Wordsworth was one of the first of the 'romantic' poets. His early experiences in France and his support for the Revolution, together with his conviction that much of the poetry of his time was conventional, over-literary and 'dead', resulted in his contribution to *Lyrical Ballads*, in which he aimed to use "a selection of the language really used by men"; thus he initiated a revolt against the conventional language and even subject-matter of poetry. The colloquial simplicity of his language produced at his best a new intensity, though sometimes it became flat and prosaic, and his subjects at this stage were often simple ballad tales of country people—an idiot boy, a beggar, a betrayed woman. This volume was added to and republished several times from 1800 to 1805, and its important preface challenges the conventions of the day. "They who have been accustomed to the gaudiness and inane phraseology of many modern writers, if they persist in reading this book to its conclusion will, no doubt, frequently have to struggle with feelings of strangeness and awkwardness." He went on to write in a wider variety of styles, but his greatest achievement was during the period of *The Prelude* and *The Excursion* (1814). After this time much of his poetry was mechanical, deliberate, and relatively uninspired; he had long been disillusioned with the French Revolution, and became reactionary in his general outlook.

In his great creative period he is above all the poet of man and nature—the emotions inspired by his early experience of nature as an unfailing source of "joy and purest passion" combined with his warm sense of human characters following their natural activities—Michael the old shepherd building his sheepfold, the old leech-gatherer on the moors, the Scottish girl reaping corn; and he remained, in spite of changes in political outlook, a champion of the poor and humble. He thought of his own poetry as originating in "emotion recollected in tranquillity", and though he has often a splendid eye for natural appearances, for him the feelings were primary—even his memories are memories of feelings. Perhaps his most fundamental belief was that the imagination can reach truths beyond the grasp of reason, and his most fundamental contribution to poetry the demonstration that its language must be alive, and therefore come from living people, and that a special 'poetical' vocabulary can only result in the death of poetry.

Behold her, single in the field,
Yon solitary Highland Lass!
Reaping and singing by herself;
Stop here, or gently pass!   4
Alone she cuts and binds the grain,
And sings a melancholy strain;
O listen! for the Vale profound
Is overflowing with the sound.   8

No Nightingale did ever chaunt
More welcome notes to weary bands
Of travellers in some shady haunt,
Among Arabian sands: 12
A voice so thrilling ne'er was heard
In spring-time from the Cuckoo-bird,
Breaking the silence of the seas
Among the farthest Hebrides.   16

Will no one tell me what she sings?—
Perhaps the plaintive numbers flow
For old, unhappy, far-off things,
And battles long ago: 20
Or is it some more humble lay,
Familiar matter of to-day?
Some natural sorrow, loss, or pain,
That has been, and may be again?   24

What'er the theme, the Maiden sang
As if her song could have no ending;
I saw her singing at her work,

And o'er the sickle bending;—   28
I listened, motionless and still;
And, as I mounted up the hill,
The music in my heart I bore,
Long after it was heard no more.   32

from *The Prelude* (I)

One summer evening (led by her) I found
A little boat tied to a willow tree
Within a rocky cave, its usual home.
Straight I unloosed her chain, and stepping in
Pushed from the shore. It was an act of stealth   5
And troubled pleasure, nor without the voice
Of mountain-echoes did my boat move on;
Leaving behind her still, on either side,
Small circles glittering idly in the moon,
Until they melted all into one track   10
Of sparkling light. But now, like one who rows,
Proud of his skill, to reach a chosen point
With an unswerving line, I fixed my view
Upon the summit of a craggy ridge,
The horizon's utmost boundary; for above   15
Was nothing but the stars and the grey sky.
She was an elfin pinnace; lustily
I dipped my oars into the silent lake
And, as I rose upon the stroke, my boat
Went heaving through the water like a swan;   20
When, from behind that craggy steep till then
The horizon's bound, a huge peak, black and
    huge,
As if with voluntary power instinct
Upreared its head. I struck and struck again,

And growing still in stature the grim shape   25
Towered up between me and the stars, and still,
For so it seemed, with purpose of its own
And measured motion like a living thing,
Strode after me. With trembling oars I turned,
And through the silent water stole my way   30
Back to the covert of the willow tree;
There in her mooring-place I left my bark,
And through the meadows homeward went, in grave
And serious mood; but after I had seen
That spectacle, for many days, my brain   35
Worked with a dim and undetermined sense
Of unknown modes of being; o'er my thoughts
There hung a darkness, call it solitude
Or blank desertion. No familiar shapes
Remained, no pleasant images of trees,   40
Of sea or sky, no colours of green fields;
But huge and mighty forms, that do not live
Like living men, moved slowly through the mind
By day, and were a trouble to my dreams.

from *The Prelude* (II)

And in the frosty season, when the sun
Was set, and visible for many a mile
The cottage windows blazed through twilight gloom,
I heeded not their summons: happy time
It was indeed for all of us—for me   5
It was a time of rapture! Clear and loud
The village clock tolled six,—I wheeled about,
Proud and exulting like an untired horse
That cares not for his home. All shod with steel,
We hissed along the polished ice in games   10

Confederate, imitative of the chase
And woodland pleasures,—the resounding horn,
The pack loud chiming, and the hunted hare.
So through the darkness and the cold we flew,
And not a voice was idle; with the din   15
Smitten, the precipices rang aloud;
The leafless trees and every icy crag
Tinkled like iron; while far distant hills
Into the tumult sent an alien sound
Of melancholy not unnoticed, while the stars   20
Eastward were sparkling clear, and in the west
The orange sky of evening died away.
Not seldom from the uproar I retired
Into a silent bay, or sportively
Glanced sideway, leaving the tumultuous throng, 25
To cut across the reflex of a star
That fled, and, flying still before me, gleamed
Upon the glassy plain; and oftentimes,
When we had given our bodies to the wind,
And all the shadowy banks on either side   30
Came sweeping through the darkness, spinning still
The rapid line of motion, then at once
Have I, reclining back upon my heels,
Stopped short; yet still the solitary cliffs
Wheeled by me—even as if the earth had rolled   35
With visible motion her diurnal round!
Behind me did they stretch in solemn train,
Feebler and feebler, and I stood and watched
Till all was tranquil as a dreamless sleep.

The World is Too Much With Us

The world is too much with us; late and soon
Getting and spending, we lay waste our powers:
Little we see in Nature that is ours;
We have given our hearts away, a sordid boon!
This Sea that bares her bosom to the moon;   5
The winds that will be howling at all hours,
And are up-gathered now like sleeping flowers;
For this, for everything, we are out of tune;
It moves us not.—Great God! I'd rather be
A Pagan suckled in a creed outworn;   10
So might I, standing on this pleasant lea,
Have glimpses that would make me less forlorn;
Have sight of Proteus rising from the sea;
Or hear old Triton blow his wreathèd horn.

To a Skylark

Ethereal minstrel! pilgrim of the sky!
Dost thou despise the earth where cares abound?
Or, while the wings aspire, are heart and eye
Both with thy nest upon the dewy ground?
Thy nest which thou canst drop into at will,   5
Those quivering wings composed, that music still!

Leave to the nightingale her shady wood;
A privacy of glorious light is thine;

Whence thou dost pour upon the world a flood
Of harmony, with instinct more divine;   10
Type of the wise who soar, but never roam;
True to the kindred points of Heaven and Home!

Nutting

It seems a day
(I speak of one from many singled out)
One of those heavenly days that cannot die;
When, in the eagerness of boyish hope,
I left our cottage-threshold, sallying forth   5
With a huge wallet o'er my shoulder slung,
A nutting-crook in hand; and turned my steps
Tow'rd some far-distant wood, a Figure quaint,
Tricked out in proud disguise of cast-off weeds
Which for that service had been husbanded,   10
By exhortation of my frugal Dame—
Motley accoutrement, of power to smile
At thorns, and brakes, and brambles,—and in truth
More ragged than need was! O'er pathless rocks,
Through beds of matted fern, and tangled thickets, 15
Forcing my way, I came to one dear nook
Unvisited, where not a broken bough
Drooped with its withered leaves, ungracious sign
Of devastation; but the hazels rose
Tall and erect, with tempting clusters hung,   20
A virgin scene!—A little while I stood,
Breathing with such suppression of the heart
As joy delights in; and with wise restraint
Voluptuous, fearless of a rival, eyed
The banquet; or beneath the trees I sate   25
Among the flowers, and with the flowers I played;

A temper known to those who, after long
And weary expectation, have been blest
With sudden happiness beyond all hope.
Perhaps it was a bower beneath whose leaves   30
The violets of five seasons re-appear
And fade, unseen by any human eye;
Where fairy water-breaks do murmur on
For ever; and I saw the sparkling foam,
And—with my cheek on one of those green stones,   35
That, fleeced with moss, under the shady trees,
Lay round me, scattered like a flock of sheep—
I heard the murmur and the murmuring sound,
In that sweet mood when pleasure loves to pay
Tribute to ease; and, of its joy secure,   40
The heart luxuriates with indifferent things,
Wasting its kindliness on stocks and stones,
And on the vacant air. Then up I rose,
And dragged to earth both branch and bough, with
     crash
And merciless ravage: and the shady nook   45
Of hazels, and the green and mossy bower,
Deformed and sullied, patiently gave up
Their quiet being: and unless I now
Confound my present feelings with the past,
Ere from the mutilated bower I turned   50
Exulting, rich beyond the wealth of kings,
I felt a sense of pain when I beheld
The silent trees, and saw the intruding sky.—
Then, dearest Maiden, move along these shades
In gentleness of heart; with gentle hand   55
Touch—for there is a spirit in the woods.

Composed upon Westminster Bridge

Earth has not anything to show more fair:
Dull would he be of soul who could pass by
A sight so touching in its majesty:
This City now doth, like a garment, wear
The beauty of the morning; silent, bare,   5
Ships, towers, domes, theatres, and temples lie
Open unto the fields, and to the sky;
All bright and glittering in the smokeless air.
Never did sun more beautifully steep
In his first splendour, valley, rock, or hill;   10
Ne'er saw I, never felt, a calm so deep!
The river glideth at his own sweet will:
Dear God! the very houses seem asleep;
And all that mighty heart is lying still!

'Lucy Poems'

I

I travelled among unknown men,
  In lands beyond the sea;
Nor, England! did I know till then
  What love I bore to thee.   4

'Tis past, that melancholy dream!
  Nor will I quit thy shore
A second time; for still I seem
  To love thee more and more.   8

Among thy mountains did I feel
    The joy of my desire;
And she I cherished turned her wheel
    Beside an English fire.   12

Thy mornings showed, thy nights concealed,
    The bowers where Lucy played;
And thine too is the last green field
    That Lucy's eyes surveyed.   16

II

She dwelt among the untrodden ways
    Beside the springs of Dove,
A maid whom there were none to praise
    And very few to love: 4

A violet by a mossy stone
    Half hidden from the eye!
—Fair as a star, when only one
    Is shining in the sky.   8

She lived unknown, and few could know
    When Lucy ceased to be:
But she is in her grave, and, oh,
    The difference to me!   12

III

A slumber did my spirit seal;
  I had no human fears:
She seemed a thing that could not feel
  The touch of earthly years.   4

No motion has she now, no force;
  She neither hears nor sees;
Rolled round in earth's diurnal course,
  With rocks, and stones, and trees.   8

Notes

The Solitary Reaper (p. 21)

l. 6   *strain:* tune, snatch of melody.
l. 7   *vale profound:* here, a deep valley.
l. 9   *chaunt:* chant, sing.
l. 18 *plaintive numbers:* sad verses or rhythms.
l. 22 *lay :* song, lyric.

(A)   Point out four references to the solitude of the 'Highland Lass' in the first five lines, and say why there is this stress. What is meant by l. 4, and to whom is it addressed? Where is the song first described as a sad one, and where is this picked up again later in the poem? What would cause the 'vale' to 'overflow' with her song (ll. 7–8)? With what two 'natural' singers is she compared in the second verse, what is significant about the circumstances in which they are heard, and what have they in common? Suggest what sort of song is hinted at in ll. 18–20, and how this relates to and contrasts with the kind of song described in ll. 21–24. Which phrase dismisses the question of the words and returns to the effect of the melody? What is the girl's posture (compare it with R. S. Thomas's *Soil*), and what is a sickle (l. 28)? What earlier 'instruction' does he obey in l. 29, and what is meant by the last two lines?

(B)   Write in verse or prose about a song heard out of doors.

from The Prelude (I) (p. 22)

The Prelude is perhaps Wordsworth's greatest achievement. Its sub-title, "Growth of a Poet's Mind", gives some indication of its range, and it runs to over a hundred pages in the collected works. Some of the most vivid sections are in Books I and II, which cover the poet's childhood and schooltime. The extract printed comes from Book I (ll. 357–400), and it describes with great power a childhood experience, not then, or even when the poem was written, fully understood by the writer. There is a fine analysis of this extract in an essay called "Wordsworth's Poetry" by R. O. C. Winkler. (See 'Further Reading', p. 38.)

l. 1 *led by her:* i.e., Nature, as the previous lines show us.

l. 17 *elfin pinnace:* small version of a large rowing-boat.

l. 23 *instinct:* charged.

l. 31 *covert:* hiding-place, shelter.

(A) How do you know that his trip in the boat was not planned before? Which lines show that he felt guilty about borrowing the boat? What is significant in this connexion about 'the voice/Of mountain echoes' (ll. 6–7) and what do you imagine them 'saying' to him? How exactly were the 'small circles' (l. 9) made? Describe the effect of moonlight on them and on the 'track' (ll. 9–11). Explain 'unswerving' (l. 13) and why he fixed his eye on 'a summit' (l. 14). What is meant by 'lustily' (l. 17), 'as I rose upon the stroke' (l. 19), and what is the effect of l. 20? Which earlier phrase is picked up in 'the horizon's bound', and is there any point in this repetition? What other repetitions are there in this sentence (ll. 21–24)? Suggest a meaning for l. 23 and for the dominant position of the word 'upreared' in l. 24. Examine the words and phrases denoting fear in ll. 24–29; explain the real reasons why the mountains 'strode after me' (l. 29) or seemed to do so. Point out more words suggesting fear in ll. 29–31; why should we include 'covert'? How does his mood in ll. 33–34 contrast with his feelings on setting out, and why? Which words in ll. 36–39 suggest a kind of haunted bewilderment? What had happened to the 'familiar' and 'pleasant' shapes and images, and why did 'huge and mighty forms' '*move* slowly through the mind'? Finally, try to summarize what you think was the significance of the experience to the child.

(B) Write in prose or verse about something that frightened you for no good reason when you were a child.

from *The Prelude* (II) (*p. 23*)

This passage comes also from Book I, a little after the one above (ll. 425–463) and is chosen both to contrast with it (as it describes a happy and exhilarating experience skating on a lake) and to echo it, since the experience has something in common with the first one.

l. 26 *reflex:* here, reflection.

l. 36 *diurnal:* daily.

l. 37 *train:* procession.

(A) What 'summons' did the lit windows of the cottages make (l. 4), and why did the boy not 'heed' it? Where is this idea repeated? Where is the image of the 'untired horse' (l. 8) picked up and developed? Describe in your own words what kind of game the children played while skating (ll. 10–25). Which lines describe the sound of their shouting, and how do the words and rhythms contribute to the effect? Where is an echo described? Why should the stars be brightest in the east (ll. 20–21)? Where do we learn that the young Wordsworth loved solitude? What is meant by l. 26 and why does the 'reflex' 'fly still' before him (l. 27)? What picture do you get from l. 29, and what effect is described in ll. 30–32? Why is it that the cliffs still 'wheeled by me' though he had 'stopped short' (ll. 34 and 35), what sensation of slowing down is described in ll. 37–39, and what effect is achieved by the last line?

(B) Write about an exhilarating experience of action (skating, cycling, at a fair) and the sensations it gave you.

The World is Too Much With Us (*p. 25*)

This famous sonnet embodies one of the central ideas of the Romantic movement in poetry, of which Wordsworth was a founder—that in our daily life, especially living in towns, we have lost touch with the renewing powers of nature.

If you have read the Hopkins sonnets in this anthology (pp. 114–19) you will recognize the division here between the exposition in the octave (first eight lines, though Wordsworth uses eight and half) and the conclusion in the sestet (last six lines).

l. 4 *boon:* gift.

l. 13 *Proteus:* Greek sea-god. *Triton:* one of a race of minor sea-gods in Greek mythology, with a man's form but the tail of a fish, often depicted as carrying a shell-trumpet.

(A) What 'world' is spoken of in the opening phrase, and is it fair to say that in this 'world' we use most of our time 'getting' (earning) and 'spending' (l. 2)? What do you think the poet means by saying that this 'lays waste our powers'—what powers? In what sense are we no longer part of nature (l. 3), and in what sense have we 'given our hearts away'—to whom or what? With what two great powers of nature are we 'out of tune', and what does this expression mean (ll. 5–8)? How can the winds be 'up-gathered' like 'sleeping flowers' (l. 7)? What change of mood or emphasis occurs in l. 9? Suggest what is meant by 'suckled in a creed outworn' (T. S. Eliot's *Journey of the Magi*, p. 219, has a similar idea). If he was a pagan he would believe in the old gods: why would belief in such gods as these bring him closer into contact with *nature*? Why only 'glimpses' (l. 12) and why '*wreathèd* horn' (l. 14)? Summarize finally why Wordsworth feels that he might have been happier as a pagan.

To a Skylark (p. 25)

l. 1   *ethereal:* heavenly.

l. 3   *aspire:* aim upwards.

(A) Why is the skylark a 'minstrel' and a 'pilgrim' (l. 1)? What sort of cares abound on the earth (l. 2)? Does the poem imply that the skylark *does* despise the earth? In what sense might 'heart and eye' be 'both with thy nest' (l. 4)? Why is the ground 'dewy'—*i.e.*, when especially do skylarks sing? Where does it imply that skylarks sing only in flight? What contrast is shown between nightingale and skylark in ll. 7–8 and which two words bring out this contrast? (Refer to Keats's *Ode to a Nightingale*, p. 67, for the surroundings in which the bird usually sings). Why 'privacy' (l. 8)? Is this word what you would expect for the sky, and how does it fit? The last couplet of the poem gives it a 'moral' and says that the skylark is typical or representative of a certain wisdom: say carefully what this wisdom is, why 'Heaven' and 'Home' are 'kindred points' and bring out the contrast between 'soar' and 'never roam' (ll. 11 and 12).

Nutting (p. 26)

Another poem, written when Wordsworth was in his late twenties, in which he draws on the rich memories of his childhood, as he did through much of his best poetry, and fulfils his own definition of poetry as "emotion recollected in tranquillity".

l. 6   *wallet:* bag, haversack.

l. 7   *nutting-crook:* a crooked stick to pull down the hazel branches.

l. 9   *tricked out:* dressed.

l. 11   *frugal:* economical.

l. 12   *motley accoutrement:* incongruous equipment, trappings.

l. 30   *bower:* here, a place closed in with foliage.

l. 45   *ravage:* devastation, damage.

(A)   Describe the boy's appearance when he left his 'cottage-threshold', and explain why he was dressed thus (ll. 6–13). Which lines suggest that he has difficulty in finding the spot, and that it is seldom visited? What would a 'broken bough' show (l. 17)? What is implied by 'a virgin scene' (l. 21)? How could he be both 'restrained' and 'voluptuous' in his attitude to the 'tempting clusters' (ll. 23–24)? Describe the 'bower' (ll. 30–32) and the stream (ll. 33–34) in your own words. Why were the stones green and how were they disposed (ll. 35–37)? Describe the 'sweet mood' when one's activities are suspended (ll. 39–43). Where does his mood change, and which words and phrases show the violence of this change (ll. 44–48)? Point out three words which show that he feels now that he has harmed the peaceful scene, and where does he express a doubt that he felt it at the time?

In what sense was he also 'rich beyond the wealth of kings' (l. 52)? What advice does he give to the 'dearest Maiden' and why? What exactly does the last phrase of the poem mean? Relate the 'sense of pain' he feels to Hopkins's *Binsey Poplars* (p. 116).

(B)   If you have ever felt that you have damaged something natural (when, for example, bird-nesting, digging up wild plants, or climbing trees) write about the experience and your feelings.

Composed upon Westminster Bridge (p. 28)

This magnificent sonnet shows Wordsworth appreciating and indeed demonstrating the beauty of a great city—though perhaps it is characteristic of his love for solitude that it is set in the early morning, when there is no bustle and noise.

l. 9   *steep:* soak.

(A)   What powerful claim is made by the first line? What contrast is there between 'touching' and 'majesty' in l. 3 and how do you think it is resolved? In what sense are the buildings 'open unto the fields' as well as to the sky? (Remember that this is 1800!) Why would the buildings be particularly 'bright and glittering' (l. 8) at this time, rather than later in the day, and which adjective confirms this?

Why does he say 'in *his* first splendour' about the sun and 'at *his* own sweet will' about the river (ll. 10 and 12)? From what you know of Wordsworth so far, what is remarkable about the implied comparison of ll. 9–11? What does he mean in the last line by 'that mighty heart'? Which words in the poem suggest calmness and motionlessness?

(B)   Write freely in prose or verse about a town or city in the early morning.

'Lucy Poems' (pp. 28–29)

These three poems are taken from a sequence of five lyrics about love, usually known as the 'Lucy poems'. We do not know the identity of Lucy, but it seems probable that the poems are based on a real experience of young love for a girl who died suddenly. They express with great tenderness and sensitivity the sense of loss he felt, and the simplicity of language should not be mistaken for naïvety.

I.   This poem was written after a tour of Germany in the winter of 1799, and shows the isolation and homesickness the poet felt.

(A)   What is meant by ll. 3 and 4? What 'melancholy dream' is past (l. 5) and what decision does he express as a result?

What do you think 'turning her wheel' means (l. 11) and what do the words 'they' and 'thine' refer to (ll. 9, 13 and 15)? Show how the idea of England remembered when abroad is linked to his love for Lucy (verses 3 and 4). Refer back to the extracts from *The Prelude* (p. 22-24) and explain ll. 9 and 10. Why is the 'green field' (l. 15) especially dear to the poet?

II. This poem expresses the isolation and apparent unimportance of Lucy, and the indifference of the world when she died, in contrast to its shattering impact on the young Wordsworth.

l. 2   *the springs of Dove:* the Dove river.

(A) What is the significance of 'untrodden' (l. 1)? Which lines suggest that Lucy was neglected and isolated? In what sense is Lucy like the violet (and where in this selection have you previously met 'a violet by a mossy stone?')? What compliment to her beauty is made in ll. 7–8? Why was it that 'few could know' (l. 9) when Lucy died? What weight can be attached to the word 'difference'?

III. This is by far the greatest poem of this sequence, and deserves the closest study.

(A) Try to explain what the opening line means: consider especially the word 'seal'. What sort of fears are 'human fears' (l. 2)? What is meant by 'the touch of earthly years'? Do we have this feeling about all the people whom we love? What has 'happened' between the two verses? What is the poet facing in its full truth in ll. 5–6? What comfort or compensation is there in the last couplet? (See l. 36 of the second extract from *The Prelude*, p. 24, for 'diurnal'.) How has the girl who 'lived unknown' now become a part of the nature that Wordsworth loved so deeply, and in what sense is she 'Rolled round in earth's diurnal course'?

(B) Write freely about the death, or imagined death, of any person you love.

FURTHER READING

Michael (perhaps the finest of the narrative poems, too long to be printed here); *The Old Cumberland Beggar; Resolution and*

Independence; the remainder of the 'Lucy poems'; *The Prelude* (sample only; a good selection is *From the Prelude*, ed. H. S. Taylor).

Collected Poems (many editions: a one-volume edition is ed. Hutchinson, revised de Sélincourt).

CRITICAL WRITING

R. O. C. Winkler. "Wordsworth's Poetry" (in *Pelican Guide to English Literature*, Vol. 5, "From Blake to Byron").

A. C. Bradley. *Oxford Lectures on Poetry* (use the index).

W. Wordsworth. *Preface to Lyrical Ballads* (gives the poet's basic theories on poetry and its language).

William Blake

WILLIAM BLAKE, poet, engraver, painter, and mystic, was born in 1757, the son of a London draper. He early showed a vivid imagination, and saw visions of angels in the fields. He learned drawing from the age of ten, and was apprenticed to an engraver at fourteen; student at the Royal Academy School 1778–9. He married in 1782, and his first poems, *Poetical Sketches*, appeared in 1783. *Songs of Innocence* followed in 1789, and *Songs of Experience* (1794). He met a group of radicals including Tom Paine and Godwin and wrote some revolutionary poems (*e.g. The French Revolution*, 1791). He spent a period at Felpham under the protection of a friend, but apart from this lived in London, making a poor livelihood from engraving with some help from a small group of understanding friends. He produced an extraordinary series of long poems now called the 'Prophetic Books' based on his visions, and many paintings and engravings, but none of these brought success. Among the long poems are *The Book of Urizen* and *The Song of Los*, which are haunted by the world's evil and the restraints of law and reason on the imagination; later he wrote three epics, one of them called *Jerusalem*, which express a belief in salvation through love and forgiveness. All but his first volume were produced by a special process of illuminated writing, with decorative borders and designs combined with the text. He illustrated the work of other poets in engravings and woodcuts. He died in 1827.

Blake's poetry was met with bewilderment or contempt during most of his life, and the way in which his imagination worked was scarcely understood; even Wordsworth, who liked what he knew of Blake's work, called it "undoubtedly the production of insane genius". His usual method of publication was an invention of his own which he called "illuminated printing"; the poems were engraved in reverse on copper plates with pictorial decorations on each page and subsequently coloured delicately in water-colour; *Songs of Innocence* and *of Experience* were first produced in this way. *The Songs of Innocence* are simple in language and tender in feeling and contrast strongly with the corresponding *Songs of Experience* (there are, for example, two *Holy Thursdays*, two *Chimney Sweepers*, an *Infant Love* and an *Infant Sorrow*, and *The Lamb* contrasts with *The Tiger*). The *Songs of Experience* show the inhumanity and cruelty under the surface of civilization and the spirit and imagination of man struggling against the 'mind-forged manacles' of convention, 'reason', and law. His later 'prophetic books' are well beyond the scope of this anthology, and all we can say here about them is that they contain passages of magnificent poetry; but all his work shows the power of his vision, which for him was reality. He was never interested in fantasy for its own sake; he was aware of a reality beyond what we can perceive through the senses. He once said about his drawings, "Nature has no outlines, but imagination has"; and this applies to the way in which the artist and the poet gives form to a vision of truth beyond that of appearance. Even if we limit our attention to the short and relatively simple lyrical poems represented here, we are aware of an imaginative power under an apparent simplicity and naïvety of form which is unique in English poetry.

On Another's Sorrow

Can I see another's woe,
And not be in sorrow too?
Can I see another's grief,
And not seek for kind relief?   4

Can I see a falling tear,
And not feel my sorrow's share?
Can a father see his child
Weep, nor be with sorrow fill'd?   8

Can a mother sit and hear
An infant groan, an infant fear?
No, no! never can it be!   12
Never, never can it be!

And can He who smiles on all
Hear the wren with sorrows small,
Hear the small bird's grief and care,
Hear the woes that infants bear,   16

And not sit beside the nest,
Pouring pity in their breast;
And not sit the cradle near,
Weeping tear on infant's tear;   20

And not sit both night and day,
Wiping all our tears away?
O, no! never can it be!
Never, never can it be!   24

He doth give His joy to all;
He becomes an infant small;
He becomes a man of woe;
He doth feel the sorrow too.   28

Think not thou canst sigh a sigh,
And thy Maker is not by;
Think not thou canst weep a tear,
And thy Maker is not near.   32

O! He gives to us His joy
That our grief He may destroy;
Till our grief is fled and gone
He doth sit by us and moan.   36

The Divine Image

To Mercy, Pity, Peace, and Love
All pray in their distress;
And to these virtues of delight
Return their thankfulness.   4

For Mercy, Pity, Peace, and Love
Is God, our Father dear,
And Mercy, Pity, Peace, and Love
Is Man, his child and care.   8

For Mercy has a human heart,
Pity a human face,
And Love, the human form divine,
And Peace, the human dress.   12

Then every man, of every clime,
That prays in his distress,
Prays to the human form divine,
Love, Mercy, Pity, Peace.   16

And all must love the human form,
In heathen, Turk, or Jew;
Where Mercy, Love, and Pity dwell
There God is dwelling too.   20

A Divine Image

Cruelty has a human heart,
And Jealousy a human face;
Terror the human form divine,
And Secrecy the human dress.   4

The human dress is forgèd iron,
The human form a fiery forge,
The human face a furnace seal'd,
The human heart its hungry gorge.   8

The Tiger

Tiger! Tiger! burning bright
In the forests of the night,
What immortal hand or eye
Could frame thy fearful symmetry?   4

In what distant deeps or skies
Burnt the fire of thine eyes?
On what wings dare he aspire?
What the hand dare seize the fire? 8

And what shoulder, and what art,
Could twist the sinews of thy heart?
And when thy heart began to beat,
What dread hand? And what dread feet? 12

What the hammer? What the chain?
In what furnace was thy brain?
What the anvil? What dread grasp
Dare its deadly terrors clasp? 16

When the stars threw down their spears,
And water'd heaven with their tears,
Did he smile his work to see?
Did he who made the Lamb make thee? 20

Tiger! Tiger! burning bright
In the forests of the night,
What immortal hand or eye
Dare frame thy fearful symmetry? 24

The Clod and the Pebble

"Love seeketh not itself to please,
Nor for itself hath any care,
But for another gives its ease,
And builds a Heaven in Hell's despair." 4

So sung a little Clod of Clay,
Trodden with the cattle's feet,
But a Pebble of the brook
Warbled out these metres meet: 8

"Love seeketh only Self to please,
To bind another to its delight,
Joys in another's loss of ease,
And builds a Hell in Heaven's despite."   12

Holy Thursday

Is this a holy thing to see
In a rich and fruitful land,
Babes reduc'd to misery,
Fed with cold and usurous hand?   4

Is that trembling cry a song?
Can it be a song of joy?
And so many children poor?
It is a land of poverty!   8

And their sun does never shine,
And their fields are bleak and bare,
And their ways are fill'd with thorns:
It is eternal winter there.   12

For where'er the sun does shine,
And where'er the rain does fall,
Babe can never hunger there,
Nor poverty the mind appall.   16

The Garden of Love

I went to the Garden of Love,
And saw what I never had seen:
A Chapel was built in the midst,
Where I used to play on the green.   4

And the gates of this Chapel were shut,
And "Thou shalt not" writ over the door;
So I turn'd to the Garden of Love
That so many sweet flowers bore;   8

And I saw it was filled with graves,
And tombstones where flowers should be;
And priests in black gowns were walking
    their rounds,
And binding with briars my joys and
    desires.   12

Infant Sorrow

My mother groan'd, my father wept,
Into the dangerous world I leapt;
Helpless, naked, piping loud,
Like a fiend hid in a cloud.   4

Struggling in my father's hands,
Striving against my swaddling-bands,
Bound and weary, I thought best
To sulk upon my mother's breast.   8

He Who Bends . . .

He who bends to himself a Joy
Doth the wingèd life destroy;
But he who kisses the Joy as it flies
Lives in Eternity's sunrise.   4

London

I wander thro' each charter'd street,
Near where the charter'd Thames does flow,
And mark in every face I meet
Marks of weakness, marks of woe.   4

In every cry of every Man,
In every Infant's cry of fear,
In every voice, in every ban,
The mind-forg'd manacles I hear.   8

How the chimney-sweeper's cry
Every black'ning church appalls;
And the hapless soldier's sigh
Runs in blood down palace walls.   12

But most thro' midnight streets I hear
How the youthful harlot's curse
Blasts the new-born infant's tear,
And blights with plagues the marriage hearse. 16

Never Seek to Tell thy Love

Never seek to tell thy love,
Love that never told can be;
For the gentle wind does move
Silently, invisibly.   4

I told my love, I told my love,
I told her all my heart;
Trembling, cold, in ghastly fears,
Ah! she doth depart.   8

Soon as she was gone from me,
A traveller came by,
Silently, invisibly:
He took her with a sigh.   12

from *Auguries of Innocence*

To see a World in a grain of sand,
And a Heaven in a wild flower,
Hold Infinity in the palm of your hand,
And Eternity in an hour.
A robin redbreast in a cage   5
Puts all Heaven in a rage.
A dove-house fill'd with doves and pigeons
Shudders Hell thro' all its regions.
A dog starv'd at his master's gate
Predicts the ruin of the State.   10
A horse misus'd upon the road
Calls to Heaven for human blood.

Each outcry of the hunted hare
A fibre from the brain does tear.
A skylark wounded in the wing,   15
A cherubim does cease to sing.
The game-cock clipt and arm'd for fight
Does the rising sun affright.
Every wolf's and lion's howl
Raises from Hell a human soul.   20
The wild deer, wandering here and there,
Keeps the human soul from care.
The lamb misus'd breeds public strife,
And yet forgives the butcher's knife.
The bat that flits at close of eve   25
Has left the brain that won't believe.
The owl that calls upon the night
Speaks the unbeliever's fright.
He who shall hurt the little wren
Shall never be belov'd by men.   3c
He who the ox to wrath hath mov'd
Shall never be by woman lov'd.
The wanton boy that kills the fly
Shall feel the spider's enmity.
He who torments the chafer's sprite   35
Weaves a bower in endless night.
The caterpillar on the leaf
Repeats to thee thy mother's grief.
Kill not the moth or butterfly,
For the Last Judgement draweth nigh.   40

A Poison Tree

I was angry with my friend:
I told my wrath, my wrath did end.
I was angry with my foe:
I told it not, my wrath did grow.   4

And I water'd it in fears,
Night and morning with my tears;
And I sunnèd it with smiles,
And with soft deceitful wiles.   8

And it grew both day and night,
Till it bore an apple bright;
And my foe beheld it shine,
And he knew that it was mine,   12

And into my garden stole
When the night had veil'd the pole:
In the morning glad I see
My foe outstretch'd beneath the tree.   16

Notes

On Another's Sorrow (p. 41)

This poem is characteristic of the early poems of Blake, and one of the *Songs of Innocence*. Like nearly all of the poems selected here, it has an apparently naïve and simple movement, language, and rhythm, which conceals profound ideas. It insists that sympathy and pity are both human and divine.

(A) Having read the poem through carefully, show how it divides into three sections, and say what the main subjects of these three sections are. What role is played by the 'chorus' ending verses 3 and 6? Why does the poem start with a series of questions, and where are they answered? The poem starts in the first person: does this stand for the poet alone, and where does it change to the third person? What do the father and mother represent in relation to the child (verses 2 and 3)? How is this relationship extended in verse 4? In what sense does Blake think of God 'smiling on all' (l. 13) and why should the wren's sorrows be 'small' (l. 15)? How are the two couplets of verse 4 linked with those of verse 5? What relationship is parallel to that of God's with the wren and the child? Suggest two meanings for ll. 25 and 26. What word might we use now instead of 'And' in ll. 30 and 32? What, then, is the general point of the poem—if God is intimately concerned with our sorrow, in what sense is this inevitable for each of us, and how is the parents' involvement in their children's sorrow a model?

The Divine Image and A Divine Image (p. 42–43)

These poems both contrast and 'cross-fertilize' each other: the first belongs to *Songs of Innocence* and the second to a manuscript (not published in the poet's lifetime) of *Songs of Experience*. When reading them, think of them as belonging to these two aspects of human life, innocence and experience—and (much more difficult) try to see that there is a sense in which they are both true. *The Divine Image* is accompanied in the original engraving by drawings showing God raising fallen man and woman at the foot of the page, and from them rises a tree of the flame of divine love which curls round the text and rises to the top of the page, where angels are guarding two praying figures.

The Divine Image

(A) What relationship is there between the four qualities in l. 1? Are they in rising order of importance? In what sense can they be *identified* with God (l. 5) and with Man (l. 8)? What does verse 3 mean—that animals haven't these qualities, that we get our conception of Mercy from the human heart, etc.? Verse 4 says that man when he 'prays in his distress' prays to the 'human form divine'; how can a 'human form' be 'divine', how does this follow logically from the previous verses, and what reversal might it suggest of the well-known statement that "God created man in his image"? What is the relationship between the two couplets of the last verse, why must all therefore 'love the human form', and what revolutionary suggestion (in terms of conventional religion) is made in the last couplet?

A Divine Image

(A) How do the four qualities of the first verse 'go with' 'Mercy, Pity, Peace, and Love'? Do you think they 'pair up'? Is the poet implying that these qualities are to be found only in human beings, that all humans have them, that side by side with a capacity for Mercy, Pity, etc., we all have in us potential Cruelty, Jealousy, etc.? What is Secrecy doing here, why does it wear 'the human dress', and is Secrecy always evil, or do you think he is using the word in a special sense? If you number the lines of the first verse 1-4, what is the order of terms in ll. 5-8? Why? Is he suggesting that the four evils are equal, or that Cruelty, which begins and ends the poem, is the worst? In what sense is the human dress 'forgèd iron'? (Look at verse 2 of *London*, p. 47; the expression perhaps means something like chains or manacles.) Suggest when the human face is 'a furnace seal'd' by relating it to verse 1; and why 'hungry gorge' (*i.e.*, throat) for the human heart?

The Tiger (p. 43)

Like the previous one, this powerful and formidable poem recognizes that the world includes fierceness and strength as well as gentleness and peace, and faces the challenge of the idea that a gentle and kind Creator could imagine or make such a terrible and yet beautiful creature as the Tiger. Thus it implies that fierceness and gentleness are conflicting but jointly present elements in human psychology as well.

(A) What does 'burning bright' in l. 1 suggest to you; has it perhaps multiple meanings? Suggest a paraphrase for ll. 3 and 4; where does the stress fall on two adjacent words in l. 4, and why? Where is there the suggestion in verse 2 that the Tiger is forged by God in a furnace, and where is this conception picked up later? How does the 'shoulder' come in (l. 9), and in what sense have the 'sinews' (here meaning muscles) to be 'twisted' (l. 10)? Where is the moment of creation in verse 3, and what meaning do you attach to l. 12? How do the 'hand' and 'feet' link with the opening of verse 4? Where is God shown as almost wrestling with the Tiger? Verse 5 is notably difficult but vitally important: the stars are figures like angels, usually carrying spears which symbolize their glitter, who are so appalled by the ferocity of the Tiger that they weep; how do you understand the second two lines and in what sense is this the key idea of the poem? What significant change is there between the first and last verses, and what does this add to the effect of the conclusion?

The Clod and the Pebble (p. 44)

This curiously touching little poem from *Songs of Experience* again hides profundity behind apparent simplicity.

The original illustration shows cattle coming to drink from the brook in which the pebble 'lives'.

l. 8 *metres meet:* suitable lines of verse.

l. 11 *joys in:* enjoys.

l. 12 *in Heaven's despite:* by injuring Heaven.

(A) What kind of love is described in the first verse, and what is the result of such love? Why is it appropriate that this should be the song of the 'Clod of Clay/Trodden with the cattle's feet' (ll. 5–6)? What qualities of a pebble make it suit its own song? Can the pebble's song be described as about love or is it *mere* selfishness? Where is this love shown as selfish, sadistic, harmful, destructive? Do you feel that these aspects of human love exist?

Holy Thursday (p. 45)

The Charity Schools of Blake's time held annual services of commemoration for their children, from 1782 onwards in St Paul's; the services were arranged by the Society of Patrons of these schools. Holy Thursday is Maundy Thursday, when Christ washed the feet of the disciples and when it was traditional to serve the poor and give alms.

At the time this poem was written Blake was closely associated with a group of British revolutionaries, and about ten years later was tried for sedition. The original edition of the poem shows a woman looking at a baby exposed in open country. The mood of the poem is one of strong indignation that children in a wealthy country like Britain should have so wretched a life, and worse, that we should feel smug about such charity.

(A) Why does he start by asking 'Is this a *holy* thing to see?' What picture of the patrons of these schools do you get from l. 4? The children are supposed to be singing: what does Blake hear their song as? What is meant by l. 8, in view of l. 2? What do the three metaphorical lines 9–11 mean in terms of the children's lives? With which line do ll. 13–14 contrast, and what sort of society does Blake wish for in the last three lines?

The Garden of Love (p. 46)

This powerful poem is typical of Blake's attitude to organized religion. He was an intensely religious man, but his religion was a private revelation, and he saw the Church as a repressive force destroying human qualities and the power of love.

(A) Suggest why the child's experience of the Garden of Love was a place where 'I used to play on the green' and in what sense the 'Chapel' has spoiled it. What aspect of organized Christianity is stressed in l. 6, and does this seem fair to you? When did the garden bear 'sweet flowers' (l. 8) in the experience of the narrator? What do the 'graves and tombstones' symbolize (ll. 9–10)? How do the rhymes work in the last two lines? What is the significance of the priests' 'black gowns' and their 'walking their rounds'? What characteristics of 'briars' (l. 12) are implied and what is the effect of 'binding' my 'joys and desires'?

Infant Sorrow (p. 46)

This poem re-creates the experience of birth as a protest by the child, having to face danger and restraint. It might be compared with King Lear's famous lines:

> When we are born, we cry that we are come
> To this great stage of fools.

(A) Why did my mother groan, and for what was my father weeping? Why does Blake see the baby's first experience of the world as 'dangerous' (l. 2)? Is the human child notably helpless at birth? What do you think 'piping' means (see the lines from *King Lear* above), and what does the nurse do if the child *doesn't* cry? What picture do you get from the mysterious l. 4? Where is the father seen as inevitably a tyrant, and is he necessarily meaning to be so? Children were wrapped in 'swaddling-bands' (l. 6) as in the Bible; what does this symbolize? (Compare it also with the last line of the previous poem.) Where is the child reluctantly submissive, and is it so out of love or thwarted rage? Does this poem seem to you to give a new insight into the great moment of birth?

He who Bends . . . (p. 47)

This quatrain embodies a profound truth—that if you try to force experience or demand happiness you will destroy it, whereas if you 'go with' it you will find fulfilment.

London (p. 47)

The illustration for this poem in the original version of *Songs of Experience* shows a crippled beggar led by a child. It draws an appalling picture of the life of London's people, especially of the poor.

ll. 1 *charter'd:* privileged, by right of royal charter; but with
& 2 the contrary implication in l. 2 of 'restricted'.

l. 8 *mind-forg'd manacles:* the chains or restrictions made by the mind of authority—the laws, religion, and customs of the time, which, as we have seen, Blake thinks of as restrictive, and as ultimately responsible for prisons and brothels.

l. 16 *marriage hearse:* the funeral of married love.

(A) What sort of people might one expect in a great and privileged city like London, and what sort of people are in fact seen? Can you see such faces in a modern city? What does 'ban' mean in l. 7, and how does he 'hear' the 'mind-forg'd manacles' (l. 8)? Blake wrote a number of poems about the dreadful conditions of the child chimney-sweepers (see, if you can, the chapter on this subject in E. S. Turner's *The Shocking History of Social Reform*); how does the cruelty he hears in the sweeper's cry ('he cried "Weep, weep,"' according to another poem) 'appall' the Church, and what two senses do you detect in the word 'black'ning' (remember that this is the centre of London)? The soldier here typifies the evil of war; in what sense does his 'sigh' 'run in blood' and what is the connexion with the palace? The third evil is lust; the harlot is a prostitute; how does her existence 'blast' the baby's 'tear', and how does it blight with plagues the 'marriage hearse' (l. 16)?

Never Seek to Tell thy Love (p. 48)

This is a mysterious poem, which implies that the man
in love tries to establish verbally the nature of his love,
but the woman finds this unendurable, and some agent,
perhaps death itself or the destructive force of time, steals
her away. Perhaps the poem means that love should be
lived but not analysed, perhaps that there is a destructive
principle in love, perhaps merely that man should never
'bend to himself a joy'. Many interpretations have been
offered but the symbols are not fully worked out, in spite
of the undeniable power and beauty of the poem.

from *Auguries of Innocence (p. 48)*

This is part of a longer poem, in which Blake writes with
horror about the cruelty of man and prophesies various
evils to those who are cruel to even the smallest and most
insignificant creature. It is worth remembering that
Blake's period was notably callous about animal suffering, and his protest challenges the general indifference;
but the poem is more than this—as the first four lines
suggest, he sees 'a World in a grain of sand' and therefore
cruelty, even to an ant, could shake the fabric of the
universe, being contrary to the natural law which respects
all life equally.

l. 7   The dove-house is presumably used for providing food—
in any case the birds are 'imprisoned', like the robin of
l. 5.

l. 17   *game-cock :* used in cock-fighting; they were equipped with
metal spurs.

ll. 25 A strange couplet; *can* it refer to 'bats in the belfry'?
–26

l. 33   Perhaps a reference to Gloucester's words in *King Lear*:
'As flies to wanton boys are we to the gods;/They kill us
for their sport.'

l. 35   *chafer :* cockchafer, a kind of beetle.

A Poison Tree (p. 49)

Blake first wrote the opening verse as an epigram on its
own, and then expanded it into a kind of fable. It shows
the poet's conviction, which we have already seen in

several poems, that a natural impulse, even of anger, should never be thwarted or it will promote a destructive hate. Modern psychological theories about the harm of certain repressions seem to endorse this; in any case it remains a brilliant image of the growth of suppressed anger, which in the end poisons a relationship.

(A) Why was he able to tell his friend of his anger but not his foe? (Consider your own definition of friendship.) Where does his wrath begin to be a tree? How did he tend it, and what does this mean in psychological terms ('nursing a grievance' is the popular phrase)? What does the apple symbolize, and what other story about an apple is it reminiscent of? Where does he, as it were, tempt his foe? What is his foe's object in stealing 'into my garden', what is meant by 'when the night had veil'd the pole' (l. 14), and what is his fate? Do you find that this poem embodies a truth in your own experience?

FURTHER READING

Poems of Innocence and Experience. Try if you can to see facsimiles of some of the original plates.

Poetical Works of William Blake, ed. J. Sampson (Oxford). Most of Blake's longer poems are well beyond the scope of this anthology, and present very great difficulties, but you might be interested in 'sampling' some of them.

CRITICAL WRITING

D. W. Harding. "William Blake" (a valuable but difficult short essay in the *Pelican Guide to English Literature*, Vol. 5).

J. Bronowski. *A Man Without a Mask.* A detailed treatment of Blake's life and works: only for reference.

John Keats

JOHN KEATS was born in London in 1795, the son of a livery-stable keeper. His parents died in his youth and he was educated in London. He was apprenticed to an apothecary and worked for a time at Guy's Hospital, but soon abandoned this for poetry. His first publication, *Poems*, 1817, was fiercely attacked as a product of the 'Cockney school'. He published *Endymion*, a long narrative poem, in 1818, living on family income; he was deeply affected by the death of his brother Tom: he went to live in Hampstead, and it became evident that he was suffering from consumption; he fell in love with a girl who lived next door called Fanny Brawne and she inspired much of his poetry. He published in 1820 *Lamia, Isabella, The Eve of St Agnes and Other Poems* (including a fragment of *Hyperion* and the great odes); this was well received but too late to comfort him. He went to Italy on doctor's advice with a friend but died in Rome in 1821 and was buried in the cemetery there, where his grave shows only the words "Here lies one whose Name was Writ in Water".

Keats is usually thought of as the most typical representative of romantic poetry: he was utterly dedicated to his work as a poet, and his early death at the age of twenty-six cut off a talent already of extraordinary maturity. His second published poem, *Endymion*, met with ridicule from some critics, one of whom sneered at him as an "apothecary's boy" and advised him to return to his "plasters, pills and ointment boxes". Yet he wrote in a letter of 1818:

> My own domestic criticism has given me pain without comparison beyond what Blackwood or the Quarterly [critical reviews] could possibly inflict.... In *Endymion* I leaped headlong into the sea, and thereby have become better acquainted with the soundings, the

> quicksands, and the rocks, than if I had stayed upon the green shore, and piped a silly pipe, and took tea and comfortable advice.

So he persisted, convinced that he had something to offer ("I think," he wrote, "I shall be among the English Poets after my death"). He had one superb burst of creative work in the spring of 1819, when he produced three of the *Odes*, *Hyperion*, *Lamia*, and *The Eve of St Agnes*, and when the 1820 volume that included these was published it was more favourably reviewed. The richness of his language ('loading every rift with ore' is his own phrase) widely influenced poetry throughout the nineteenth century, but too often it was the weaker Keats who was imitated—a strain of morbidity and understandable self-pity, and in some early work a mawkishness and excessive sweetness. But the mature Keats, who wrote the *Ode to Autumn* and the remarkable revised version of *Hyperion*, is the one we most value now. Here he has a universality which is inimitable—a beauty of language and a sensitive flexibility which are indeed like Shakespeare's. A full grasp of his fineness of spirit can best be obtained by reading some of his letters alongside the poems: they are among the best letters in the language for their generosity, humour, and warmth, and their powers of self-criticism and understanding.

from *Isabella*

XXVII

So the two brothers and their murder'd man
   Rode past fair Florence, to where Arno's stream
Gurgles through straiten'd banks, and still doth
    fan
   Itself with dancing bulrush, and the bream
Keeps head against the freshets. Sick and wan   5
   The brothers' faces in the ford did seem,
Lorenzo's flush with love.—They pass'd the water
Into a forest quiet for the slaughter.

XXVIII

There was Lorenzo slain and buried in,
   There in that forest did his great love cease;   10
Ah! when a soul doth thus its freedom win,
   It aches in loneliness—is ill at peace
As the break-covert blood-hounds of such sin:
   They dipp'd their swords in the water, and did
    tease
Their horses homeward, with convulsèd spur,   15
Each richer by his being a murderer.

from *Lamia*

As men talk in a dream, so Corinth all,
Throughout her palaces imperial,
And all her populous streets and temples lewd,
Mutter'd, like tempest in the distance brew'd,
To the wide-spreaded night above her towers.   5
Men, women, rich and poor, in the cool hours,
Shuffled their sandals o'er the pavement white,
Companion'd or alone; while many a light
Flared, here and there, from wealthy festivals,
And threw their moving shadows on the walls,   10
Or found them cluster'd in the corniced shade
Of some arch'd temple door, or dusky colonnade.

from *The Eve of St Agnes*

(i)

I

St Agnes' Eve—Ah, bitter chill it was!
     The owl, for all his feathers, was a-cold;
The hare limp'd trembling through the frozen
          grass,
     And silent was the flock in woolly fold:
Numb were the Beadsman's fingers, while he told   5
     His rosary, and while his frosted breath,
Like pious incense from a censer old,
     Seem'd taking flight for heaven, without a death,
Past the sweet Virgin's picture, while his prayer he
          saith.

II

His prayer he saith, this patient, holy man;   10
Then takes his lamp, and riseth from his knees,
And back returneth, meagre, barefoot, wan,
Along the chapel aisle by slow degrees:
The sculptur'd dead, on each side, seem to freeze,
Emprison'd in black, purgatorial rails: 15
Knights, ladies, praying in dumb orat'ries,
He passeth by; and his weak spirit fails
To think how they may ache in icy hoods and mails.

III

Northward he turneth through a little door,
And scarce three steps, ere Music's golden tongue   20
Flatter'd to tears this aged man and poor;
But no—already had his deathbell rung;
The joys of all his life were said and sung:
His was harsh penance on St Agnes' Eve:
Another way he went, and soon among   25
Rough ashes sat he for his soul's reprieve,
And all night kept awake, for sinners' sake to grieve. . . .

*   *   *   *

(ii)

XXIII

Out went the taper as she hurried in;
Its little smoke, in pallid moonshine, died:
She clos'd the door, she panted, all akin
To spirits of the air, and visions wide:
No uttered syllable, or, woe betide!   5
But to her heart, her heart was voluble,
Paining with eloquence her balmy side;

As though a tongueless nightingale should swell
Her throat in vain, and die, heart-stifled, in her dell.

XXIV

A casement high and triple-arch'd there was,   10
All garlanded with carven imag'ries
Of fruits, and flowers, and bunches of knot-grass,
And diamonded with panes of quaint device,
Innumerable of stains and splendid dyes,
As are the tiger-moth's deep-damask'd wings;   15
And in the midst, 'mong thousand heraldries,
And twilight saints, and dim emblazonings,
A shielded scutcheon blush'd with blood of queens and
          kings.

XXV

Full on this casement shone the wintry moon,
And threw warm gules on Madeline's fair breast,   20
As down she knelt for heaven's grace and boon;
Rose-bloom fell on her hands, together prest,
And on her silver cross soft amethyst,
And on her hair a glory, like a saint:
She seem'd a splendid angel, newly drest,   25
Save wings, for heaven:—Porphyro grew faint:
She knelt, so pure a thing, so free from mortal taint. . . .

*   *   *   *

(iii)

XL

She hurried at his words, beset with fears,
For there were sleeping dragons all around,
At glaring watch, perhaps, with ready spears—

Down the wide stairs a darkling way they found.—
In all the house was heard no human sound.   5
A chain-droop'd lamp was flickering by each door;
The arras, rich with horseman, hawk, and hound,
Flutter'd in the besieging wind's uproar;
And the long carpets rose along the gusty floor.

XLI

They glide, like phantoms, into the wide hall;   10
Like phantoms, to the iron porch, they glide;
Where lay the Porter, in uneasy sprawl,
With a huge empty flagon by his side:
The wakeful bloodhound rose, and shook his hide,
But his sagacious eye an inmate owns: 15
By one, and one, the bolts full easy slide:—
The chains lie silent on the footworn stones;—
The key turns, and the door upon its hinges groans.

XLII

And they are gone: ay, ages long ago
These lovers fled away into the storm.   20
That night the Baron dreamt of many a woe,
And all his warrior-guests, with shade and form
Of witch, and demon, and large coffin-worm,
Were long be-nightmar'd. Angela the old
Died palsy-twitch'd, with meagre face deform;   25
The Beadsman, after thousand aves told,
For aye unsought for slept among his ashes cold.

Ode to Autumn

I

Season of mists and mellow fruitfulness,
　　Close bosom-friend of the maturing sun;
Conspiring with him how to load and bless
　　With fruit the vines that round the thatch-eaves run;
To bend with apples the moss'd cottage-trees,　　5
　　And fill all fruit with ripeness to the core;
　　　　To swell the gourd, and plump the hazel shells
With a sweet kernel; to set budding more,
　　And still more, later flowers for the bees,
　　Until they think warm days will never cease,　　10
　　　　For Summer has o'erbrimm'd their clammy cells.

2

Who hath not seen thee oft amid thy store?
　　Sometimes whoever seeks abroad may find
Thee sitting careless on a granary floor,
　　Thy hair soft-lifted by the winnowing wind;　　15
Or on a half-reap'd furrow sound asleep,
　　Drows'd with the fume of poppies, while thy hook
　　Spares the next swathe and all its twinèd flowers:
And sometimes like a gleaner thou dost keep
　　Steady thy laden head across a brook;　　20
　　Or by a cider-press, with patient look,
　　　　Thou watchest the last oozings hours by hours.

3

Where are the songs of Spring? Ay, where are they?
　　Think not of them, thou hast thy music too,—

While barrèd clouds bloom the soft-dying day,   25
   And touch the stubble-plains with rosy hue:
Then in a wailful choir the small gnats mourn
   Among the river sallows, borne aloft
     Or sinking as the light wind lives or dies;
And full-grown lambs loud bleat from hilly bourn; 30
   Hedge-crickets sing; and now with treble soft
   The red-breast whistles from a garden-croft;
     And gathering swallows twitter in the skies.

Ode to a Nightingale

1

My heart aches, and a drowsy numbness pains
   My sense, as though of hemlock I had drunk,
Or emptied some dull opiate to the drains
   One minute past, and Lethe-wards had sunk:
'Tis not through envy of thy happy lot,   5
   But being too happy in thine happiness,—
     That thou, light-wingèd Dryad of the trees,
     In some melodious plot
Of beechen green, and shadows numberless,
     Singest of summer in full-throated ease.   10

2

O, for a draught of vintage! that hath been
   Cool'd a long age in the deep-delvèd earth,
Tasting of Flora and the country green,
   Dance, and Provençal song, and sunburnt mirth!
O for a beaker full of the warm South,   15
   Full of the true, the blushful Hippocrene,

With beaded bubbles winking at the brim,
   And purple-stainèd mouth;
That I might drink, and leave the world unseen,
   And with thee fade away into the forest dim: 20

3

Fade far away, dissolve, and quite forget
   What thou among the leaves hast never known,
The weariness, the fever, and the fret
    Here, where men sit and hear each other
      groan;
Where palsy shakes a few, sad, last gray hairs,   25
    Where youth grows pale, and spectre-thin, and
      dies;
      Where but to think is to be full of sorrow
        And leaden-eyed despairs,
    Where beauty cannot keep her lustrous eyes,
      Or new Love pine at them beyond tomorrow. 30

4

Away! Away! for I will fly to thee,
   Not charioted by Bacchus and his pards,
But on the viewless wings of Poesy,
   Through the dull brain perplexes and retards:
Already with thee! tender is the night,   35
    And haply the Queen-Moon is on her throne,
      Cluster'd around by all her starry Fays;
        But here there is no light,
    Save what from heaven is with the breezes
    blown
      Through verdurous glooms and winding mossy
      ways.   40

5

I cannot see what flowers are at my feet,
  Nor what soft incense hangs upon the boughs,
But, in embalmèd darkness, guess each sweet
  Wherewith the seasonable month endows
The grass, the thicket, and the fruit-tree wild;   45
    White hawthorn, and the pastoral eglantine;
      Fast fading violets cover'd up in leaves;
        And mid-May's eldest child,
  The coming musk-rose, full of dewy wine,
    The murmurous haunt of flies on summer
      eaves.   50

6

Darkling I listen; and, for many a time
  I have been half in love with easeful Death,
Call'd him soft names in many a musèd rhyme,
  To take into the air my quiet breath;
Now more than ever seems it rich to die,   55
  To cease upon the midnight with no pain,
    While thou art pouring forth thy soul abroad
      In such an ecstasy!
  Still wouldst thou sing, and I have ears in vain—
    To thy high requiem become a sod.   60

7

Thou wast not born for death, immortal Bird!
  No hungry generations tread thee down;
The voice I hear this passing night was heard
  In ancient days by emperor and clown:
Perhaps the self-same song that found a path   65
  Through the sad heart of Ruth, when, sick for
    home,
    She stood in tears amid the alien corn;

The same that oft-times hath
Charm'd magic casements, opening on the foam
Of perilous seas, in faery lands forlorn.　70

8

Forlorn! the very word is like a bell
To toll me back from thee to my sole self!
Adieu! the fancy cannot cheat so well
As she is fam'd to do, deceiving elf.
Adieu! adieu! thy plaintive anthem fades　75
Past the near meadows, over the still stream,
Up the hill-side; and now 'tis buried deep
In the next valley-glades:
Was it a vision, or a waking dream?
Fled is that music:—Do I wake or sleep?　80

Notes

from *Isabella (p. 61)*

This is a small extract from a long poem which Keats based on a story of Boccaccio (author of a fine collection of Italian stories called *The Decameron*). It is not necessary to know the whole story to understand this short fragment; all we need say here is that Isabella, the only daughter of a mercantile family, has fallen in love with a poor 'clerk' called Lorenzo, and her two evil brothers, wishing her to marry someone of wealth, trick Lorenzo into going on a journey with them, murder him and bury him secretly in a forest. The poem is written in an Italian verse-pattern called *ottava* (eight-lined) *rima*, and you can work out how the rhymes are arranged from this sample.

l. 1   *murder'd:* a strange poetic device called *prolepsis*, in which an adjective is applied to a noun as a kind of prophecy (he is as good as murdered).

l. 2   *Arno:* the great river which flows through Florence.

l. 3   *straiten'd:* narrowed.

ll. 4 *bream:* a fresh-water fish; *freshets:* streams of fresh water.
–5

ll. 12 When the soul (Lorenzo's) wins its freedom by murder
–13 it is as lonely as the murderers themselves.

l. 13 *break-covert blood-hounds:* the murderers are as fierce and ruthless as blood-hounds breaking out from cover, perhaps to track down a murderer; both are compared with the restless soul of the victim.

(A) What is the effect of 'murder'd' in l. 1? With what is the freshness of the river contrasted? What contrast is there between the appearance of the murderers and their victim-to-be, and where exactly do we see their faces? Why is the forest 'quiet' and in what sense 'quiet for the slaughter' (l. 8)? What happens between the end of the first verse and the beginning of the second? How did the brothers conceal their crime? Why were their spurs 'convulsed' and in what sense are we to take the last line?

from *Lamia (p. 62)*

A short extract from another long narrative poem, the subject of which need not be described here, except to say that it is set in the ancient world. It is written throughout in rhyming ('heroic') couplets.

l. 3   *lewd*: ignorant.

(A)   What features in the opening sentence suggest that rumours or news are passing round the city of Corinth? Describe in your own words the 'muttering'. Which line suggests the sound as well as the sight of the citizens' movements? What might the 'wealthy festivals' be, and what sorts of lights do you imagine coming from them? Why were the shadows moving (l. 10)? Suggest or find out the meaning of the two architectural words 'corniced' and 'colonnade'.

from *The Eve of St Agnes (p. 62)*

There are three substantial extracts here from this fine narrative poem, and as it is probably by far the best of the three poems, it is suggested that you read the whole if possible. The title refers to a medieval legend that girls who obeyed certain rituals would dream of their lover on St Agnes' Eve in January. The verse-pattern is a very demanding one called the Spenserian stanza, as it was first used by Spenser in *The Faerie Queene*, and the rhyme scheme, which is elaborately interlocked, is worth studying; a major feature is that the last line of each verse (called the Alexandrine) is longer by two syllables than the other lines.

(i)   The first three stanzas establish an atmosphere of bitter cold and old age, in a great medieval castle.

l. 5   *Beadsman*: person employed to say prayers on behalf of the castle's owner.

l. 6   *rosary*: prayer-beads; to 'tell' them is to pass them through the fingers with a prayer for each.

l. 7   *censer:* vessel in which the sweet-smelling incense is burned
in churches.

l. 16 *oratories:* small chapels.

l. 20 *Music's golden tongue:* a banquet is beginning, and he hears
the accompanying music in the distance.

(A)   What is added to the sense of intense cold by 'for all his
feathers', 'the hare limp'd trembling' (why is it especially
effective for the limping animal to be a *hare*?)? What
picture do you get from l. 4, and what noises might the
sheep usually make? Describe in your own words what is
happening to the Beadsman's breath; where is he kneeling, and why 'without a death' (l. 8)? What picture do
you get from the three adjectives in l. 12? What are 'the
sculptur'd dead', what do you think they are made of,
and what are the 'purgatorial rails' that enclose them
(l. 15)? The figures of kneeling ladies and knights may
be seen on tombs in many cathedrals; why are the
oratories 'dumb' (l. 16)? What sort of clothing are the
figures wearing, and why does the Beadsman's 'weak
spirit fail' at the thought of them? In l. 22 what is the
force of 'But no', and are we to take literally the phrase
'already had his deathbell rung'? (Compare with the
word 'murder'd' in the first line of the extract from
Lamia above (p. 62).) The old man goes to some hidden
part of the castle and does penance for the sins of everyone in the castle, who are dancing and banqueting. What
use does Keats make of the Alexandrine in each of the
first three verses?

(ii)   Madeline, the daughter of the Baron who owns the
castle, has attended the dance, but leaves as soon as she
can, having carried out the necessary rituals, in the hope
of dreaming of her lover. Meanwhile the young man who
loves her, Porphyro, has come secretly to the castle and
managed to gain entrance and hide in her bedchamber,
where he sees her come in.

l. 5   She mustn't speak or the charm will be broken.

l. 12 *knot-grass:* a plant with intricate patterns of stem; here
perhaps part of the stone carvings round the window.

l. 13 *of quaint device:* elaborately ornamented.

l. 15 *deep-damask'd:* velvety red, like certain old roses.

ll. 16 *heraldries, emblazonings, scutcheon:* words describing the coats of arms and heraldic designs of the stained-glass window.

l. 20 *gules:* heraldic word meaning 'red'—it also suggests 'jewels'.

(A) Describe in your own words what happened to the candle (ll. 1–2). Which words in the first verse show Madeline's longing to speak and which the repressing forces preventing her from doing so? How can her heart be 'voluble to her heart' (l. 6), and how could her silence pain her 'with eloquence'? Describe, or even draw, the window; in what ways might the patterns look like the wings of a tiger-moth? How could the 'scutcheon' (shield showing armorial bearings) 'blush with blood of queens and kings' (think of marriages and conquests)? How were the colours in the third verse thrown on Madeline's figure? Where is her cross (l. 23) and what colour is 'amethyst'? What colour might be intended in l. 24; how is she like an angel, and how unlike?

(iii) The last three verses of the poem describe how Porphyro and Madeline, after a night of violent storm, escape from the castle (its owner has a long-standing feud with Porphyro's family and would kill him at sight) under cover of darkness and the fact that guests and guards are all drunk after the banquet.

l. 1 Porphyro has just persuaded Madeline to escape to a home he has ready for her 'over the southern moors'.

l. 4 *darkling:* usually an adverb—'in the dark'.

l. 7 *arras:* tapestry.

l. 15 *sagacious:* wise.

l. 23 *coffin-worm:* the Elizabethans called this the 'conqueror worm' which consumes the bodies of the dead.

l. 24 *Angela:* Madeline's old maid, who knows of her secret.

l. 26 *after thousand aves told:* after repeating a thousand prayers ('Ave Maria').

(A) Suggest who the 'sleeping dragons' might be and why they would be dangerous. What are the subjects pictured on the arras, and what picture do you get from the last two lines of the verse (consider the meaning of 'besieging' in l. 8)? In the second verse what is the effect of the repetition of 'they glide' and 'like phantoms' (ll. 10–11)? What has the porter been doing, and why is the bloodhound in contrast, 'wakeful'? What characteristics of a bloodhound make 'shook his hide' and 'his sagacious eye' appropriate, and what is meant by 'an inmate owns' (l. 15)? What chains are referred to in l. 17? What is the effect, after all the loving detail of the two previous verses, of the opening two lines of the last verse? Suggest why the Baron and his guests had nightmares and why old Angela should die (in terms of the story). What is significant about the poem finishing with the Beadsman, in view of your study of the first three verses of the poem? Suggest, finally, how the poet makes a contrast between the old, poor, and miserable on the one hand, and the happy and young on the other.

(B) Tell the three story-fragments in your own words, adding freely any further details you imagine.

Ode to Autumn (p. 66)

This magnificent ode is justly famous, and is often re-garded as the most perfect of Keats's poems. Its structure is quite complex, but after a couple of readings it will not be difficult to see that the first verse describes the 'posi-tive' side of autumn—the side that looks back to summer and brings it to fruition, while the third verse describes the 'negative' side—a suggestion of chilliness, a series of thin sounds, and the sadness of the approaching winter. The middle verse balances these two with four glimpses of a figure representing both the spirit of autumn and a farm-worker engaged in a series of typical autumnal activities.

l. 7   *gourd*: here, any member of the cucumber family with lush watery fruits—marrows, pumpkins, squashes, etc.

l. 15   *winnowing*: literally, blowing the lighter chaff from the heavier grain.

l. 18   *swathe*: a small ridge of corn or grass lying after being cut by hook or scythe; thus the amount cut by the sweep of the implement.

l. 26   *stubble-plain*: field after the corn is cut.

l. 28   *sallows*: willow-trees.

l. 30   *bourn*: here perhaps, enclosure.

l. 31   *hedge-cricket*: grasshopper.

l. 32 *croft:* enclosed piece of land (compare 'crofter').

(A) Which words and expressions in the first verse suggest fruition and abundance? Are these images of taste and touch as well as sight? Why might the cottage-trees be 'moss'd' (l. 5)? What do the bees think about the season, and why are their cells 'clammy' (ll. 10–11)? Make a list of the verbs which suggest weighing down and filling up with ripeness and sweetness.

In verse 2 suggest another meaning for 'store' except the modern one ('storehouse', hence 'shop'). Make a careful list of the four autumn tasks in the verse; then consider what the four figures have in common and what links them together. Why is 'winnowing' appropriate in l. 15 and what *should* the breeze from the doorway be doing? Why should the 'fume of poppies' be smelled by the reaper, and why should it make him 'drows'd' (l. 17)? In what sense has he 'spared' the next swathe, and what would make the small weeds and flowers twining among the cornstalks especially visible? In ll. 19–20, what is a gleaner, what is 'laden' on his head, in what sense is he 'across a brook' and how does the break between 'keep' and 'steady' imply his stillness? The cider-press squashes apples; what else does 'the *last* oozings' mean? In verse 3 he starts by comparing the many poems and songs of spring with the neglect of autumn; which words or phrases in the rest of the verse pick up 'music' in l. 24, and what have these words in common? Explain in your own words the visual effect of ll. 25–26. What are the gnats doing among the 'river sallows', what is the effect of the wind on them, how are they like a 'choir', and what are they mourning (ll. 27–29)? Why are the swallows 'gathering', how do they contrast with the robin, and what makes the image a sad one?

(B) Write freely in verse or prose about autumn and your attitude to it.

Ode to a Nightingale (p. 67)

This elaborate and beautiful ode needs close and continuous reading before it yields its full meaning. Some writers have emphasized its treatment of the nightingale's song as one leading towards 'the supreme ecstasy of death', others have found in it a contrary movement rejecting death as a luxury, and instead asserting a love for life. It seems that both feelings are present, playing against each other, and the final decision as to which dominates must be for the individual reader. The elaborate verse-form and rhyme-scheme is worth close study, especially the varying effect of the short eighth line in each stanza.

v. 1 The nightingale's song has already begun, and the poet is drugged by its beauty into a state half painful, half delicious.

l. 2 *hemlock:* a poison.

l. 3 *opiate:* a drug easing pain or inducing sleep.

l. 4 *Lethe-wards:* towards Lethe, the river of forgetfulness in Hades.

l. 7 *Dryad:* literally, a wood-nymph; here the nightingale, which nests in woods.

v. 2 The poet longs for a glass of some splendid wine, perfumed and evoking love and happiness and fulfilment; with such a wine he could escape with the nightingale.

l. 13 *Flora:* goddess of flowers.

l. 14 *Provençal:* from the French wine-producing district of Provence.

l. 16 *Hippocrene:* a spring on Mount Helicon, sacred to the Muses, and thus to poetry.

v. 3 He longs to forget the misery of human beings—the anxiety, illness, poverty, old age, and the young dying prematurely (his brother Tom had died recently and he expected to die soon), and beauty cannot survive for long or the love it stimulates.

l. 25 *palsy:* a shaking disease; here the personification of sickness and old age.

l. 26 a perfect one-line description of a death from tuberculosis

l. 29 *lustrous:* bright, brilliant.

v. 4 He rejects wine in favour of poetry, and as he sits in his garden listening to the bird in the gathering darkness he feels that he is joining it.

l. 32 Bacchus is the god of wine; his chariot was drawn by leopards.

l. 33 *viewless:* invisible; *Poesy:* poetry.

ll. 37 The moon is imagined as Queen of the Night with the
−38 stars as her attendants.

ll. 39 As the wind parts the branches a little moonlight is cast
−40 on him from the sky.

l. 40 *verdurous:* green.

v. 5 He is aware of the late spring flowers that surround him
only through their perfume, and imagines them in the
darkness.

l. 42 *incense:* sweet-smelling flowers.

l. 43 *embalmed:* again a suggestion of perfume, like 'sweet'.

l. 44 Which comes into bloom at its appropriate season.

l. 46 *eglantine:* sweet-briar.

l. 47 As the violets fade the leaves grow larger and cover the
blossom.

l. 49 *musk-rose:* various kinds of perfumed rose.

v. 6 He listens in the dark and half-longs for death to take
him; perhaps it would be a fulfilment to die at this
moment of beauty, but then he would no longer hear the
nightingale's song.

l. 51 *Darkling:* in the dark (see also *The Eve of St Agnes*, p. 65).

l. 60 *requiem:* musical setting for a mass sung for the repose of
the soul of the dead; *sod:* mere unfeeling earth.

v. 7 He feels that the bird is, in a sense, immortal—a succes-
sion of nightingales all with the same song; its song has
been heard in ancient days, perhaps was heard by Ruth
in exile, and has often opened magic windows into a
world of romance and myth.

l. 61 Men always compete against one another, and the bird
is immune from this.

l. 64 *clown:* probably peasant.

ll. 65 *Ruth:* the story of Ruth, who exiled herself for love of
−67 Naomi from Moab, and worked in the fields near
Bethlehem, is told in the Biblical *Book of Ruth*.

ll. 68 As the song dies and the enchantment wears off, the
−70 imagination begins to fade, and his vision of vague
figures from romances of the past hearing the bird's song
ends with the word 'forlorn'. *Faery:* magic, mythical.

v. 8 The word 'forlorn' brings him back to his 'sad self'; fancy
cannot for long cheat us, the song fades away and the
poet is left wondering whether he has dreamed it—or
perhaps whether *that* was reality and he is now asleep.

l. 75 *plaintive anthem :* melancholy song.

(A) Suggest how the sounds reinforce the sense in ll. 1–4 and
by contrast in ll. 7–9. Why is 'full-throated' especially
suitable in l. 10? (Compare also stanza XXIII of *The
Eve of St Agnes.*) Where has the wine been kept 'for a long
age' (l. 12); how could it taste of all the things in ll. 13–
14? In what sense could a beaker (vessel) be full of 'the
warm South' (l. 15)? Describe in your own words what
the wine in its glass looks like. What picture of mankind's
life is given in verse 3 (remember that Keats writes this
poem in Hampstead, looking out, perhaps, to the countryside, but with the great heart of London behind him)?
How does the rhythm of ll. 25 and 26 help the meaning?
What is contrasted with 'leaden-eyed' (l. 28)? Describe
what picture you get from ll. 39–40. Which flowers are
dying, and which coming into bloom? Consider how the
sound of l. 50 helps the meaning. Put into your own
words l. 56. What is suggested by the phrase 'emperor
and clown' (l. 64)? Having read the relevant passages
in the Bible, comment on the lines about Ruth (consider
'found a path', and why should so familiar a thing as
corn be 'alien' to her (l. 67)?)

Find words in the first two lines of the last verse that
suggest the sound of a bell. What is happening to the bird
in ll. 75–78, do you think? What is the mood of the last
two lines?

When you have finished the detailed work on this
poem, it is essential, especially with so complex a structure, that you should 'put it together' again, *i.e.*, read
it aloud or at least hear it as a whole.

FURTHER READING

The whole of *The Eve of St Agnes.*

The other 'great' odes: *To a Grecian Urn, To Melancholy, To
Psyche.*

Ode to Fancy.

Sample passages from *Endymion* and *Hyperion.*

Some of the sonnets (especially "On First Looking into Chap-
man's Homer", "To Fanny", "When I have Fears").

Keats's letters are magnificent; there is a good selection in *Selected Letters and Poems of John Keats* (ed. J. H. Walsh).

CRITICAL WRITING

John Middleton Murry. *Keats* (Oxford).

F. R. Leavis in *Revaluation* (Chatto and Windus).

William Walsh. "John Keats" (an essay in *Pelican Guide to English Literature*, Vol. 5).

Alfred Tennyson

ALFRED TENNYSON was born in Lincolnshire, 1809, the son of a clergyman, and educated at grammar school and Trinity College, Cambridge. *Poems Chiefly Lyrical* appeared in 1830, and *Poems* in 1833. Arthur Hallam, his closest friend, died in 1833, and he composed *In Memoriam* during this dark period of his life (not published till 1850). *Poems* (1842) brought him recognition as the greatest poet of his day. He had serious financial troubles and was very ill, until friends persuaded the Government to grant him a pension. In 1850 he became Poet Laureate on the death of Wordsworth, and married Emily Sellwood in the same year. He settled in the Isle of Wight and became extremely popular and widely admired as a poet; among his most successful long poems was *Idylls of the King*. He became a peer in 1884 and died in 1892.

Tennyson's reputation as a poet has fluctuated greatly. In his own time he was almost an institution—a Great Poet admired by Queen Victoria, fashionable and revered. There was a sharp reaction against this estimate in the first half of our century, and we have become aware of many features we now find negative. He often introduced a bogus medievalism (as in much of *Idylls of the King*); he tried to be a deep thinker though his powers were often inadequate (long stretches of *In Memoriam*); he produced many lyrics (some of them very often anthologized) with a surface beauty but little real depth; and in his 'official' voice as Poet Laureate he was often shamelessly complacent and contemptuous of the poor and the foreign. Perhaps he had too much success during his life. But we have become aware of real power in Tennyson: in some of the early poems like *Mariana* (p. 84), though he draws heavily from Keats, he creates a real imaginative atmosphere; he can produce richly meaningful and courageous poems like *Ulysses* (p. 92) and *Tithonus* (p. 94), and there

is a sturdy sympathy and warmth in a dialect poem like
Northern Farmer: Old Style (p. 88). His love of nature took
the form of patiently recording natural effects (he kept
notebooks in which he would write down, for example,
that growing corn in the wind is like italics), and this
makes at its best for great vividness and concreteness (the
'blacken'd moss' on the flowerpots, the waterfall 'like a
downward smoke', the window at dawn which 'slowly
grows a glimmering square'). Above all, perhaps, he was
a devoted craftsman of poetic effect and had an exquisite
ear. This can act negatively in hiding poverty of thought
or feeling, but is at its best a source of great strength. The
often-quoted lines from *Morte d'Arthur* illustrate the way
in which sound and rhythm *enact* the effect of climbing
down a rocky path in armour to a smooth lake:

> Dry clash'd his harness in the icy caves
> And barren chasms, and all to left and right
> The bare black cliff clang'd round him, as he based
> His feet on juts of slippery crag that rang
> Sharp-smitten with the din of armed heels—
> And on a sudden, lo! the level lake
> And the long glories of the winter moon.

The careful relationship of sound, movement, and vocabulary shown here (though this example is perhaps over-
selfconscious) is characteristic, and will be found in many
of the poems which follow.

(I) *The Splendour Falls*

The splendour falls on castle walls
    And snowy summits old in story:
The long light shakes across the lakes,
    And the wild cataract leaps in glory.
Blow, bugle, blow, set the wild echoes flying,
Blow, bugle; answer, echoes, dying, dying,
    dying.   6

O hark, O hear! how thin and clear,
    And thinner, clearer, farther going!
O sweet and far from cliff and scar
    The horns of Elfland faintly blowing!
Blow, let us hear the purple glens replying:
Blow, bugle; answer, echoes, dying, dying,
    dying.   12

O love, they die in yon rich sky,
    They faint on hill or field or river:
Our echoes roll from soul to soul,
    And grow for ever and for ever.
Blow, bugle, blow, set the wild echoes flying,
And answer, echoes, answer, dying, dying,
    dying.   18

(II) *Now Sleeps the Crimson Petal*

Now sleeps the crimson petal, now the white;
Nor waves the cypress in the palace walk;
Nor winks the gold fin in the porphyry font:
The fire-fly wakens: waken thou with me.   4

Now droops the milkwhite peacock like a ghost,
And like a ghost she glimmers on to me.

Now lies the Earth all Danaë to the stars,
And all thy heart lies open unto me.   8

Now slides the silent meteor on, and leaves
A shining furrow, as thy thoughts in me.

Now folds the lily all her sweetness up,
And slips into the bosom of the lake: 12
So fold thyself, my dearest, thou, and slip
Into my bosom and be lost in me.

Mariana

With blackest moss the flower-pots
    Were thickly crusted, one and all:
The rusted nails fell from the knots
    That held the pear to the garden-wall.
The broken sheds look'd sad and strange: 5
    Unlifted was the clinking latch;
    Weeded and worn the ancient thatch
Upon the lonely moated grange.

She only said, "My life is dreary,
   He cometh not," she said;   10
She said, "I am aweary, aweary,
   I would that I were dead!"

Her tears fell with the dews at even;
   Her tears fell ere the dews were dried;
She could not look on the sweet heaven,   15
   Either at morn or eventide.
After the flitting of the bats,
   When thickest dark did trance the sky,
   She drew her casement-curtain by,
And glanced athwart the glooming flats.   20
   She only said, "The night is dreary,
      He cometh not," she said;
   She said, "I am aweary, aweary,
      I would that I were dead!"

Upon the middle of the night,   25
   Waking she heard the night-fowl crow:
The cock sung out an hour ere light:
   From the dark fen the oxen's low
Came to her: without hope of change,
   In sleep she seem'd to walk forlorn,   30
   Till cold winds woke the gray-eyed morn
About the lonely moated grange.
   She only said, "The day is dreary,
      He cometh not," she said;
   She said, "I am aweary, aweary,   35
      I would that I were dead!"

About a stone-cast from the wall
   A sluice with blacken'd waters slept,
And o'er it many, round and small,
   The cluster'd marish-mosses crept.   40

Hard by a poplar shook alway,
   All silver-green with gnarlèd bark:
For leagues no other tree did mark
The level waste, the rounding gray.
     She only said, "My life is dreary,   45
       He cometh not," she said:
     She said, "I am aweary, aweary,
       I would that I were dead!"

And ever when the moon was low,
   And the shrill winds were up and away,   50
In the white curtain, to and fro,
   She saw the gusty shadow sway.
But when the moon was very low,
   And wild winds bound within their cell,
The shadow of the poplar fell   55
Upon her bed, across her brow.
     She only said, "The night is dreary,
       He cometh not," she said:
     She said, "I am aweary, aweary,
       I would that I were dead!"   60

All day within the dreamy house,
   The doors upon their hinges creak'd;
The blue fly sung in the pane; the mouse
   Behind the mouldering wainscot shriek'd,
Or from the crevice peer'd about.   65
     Old faces glimmer'd thro' the doors,
     Old footsteps trod the upper floors,
Old voices called her from without.
     She only said, "My life is dreary,
       He cometh not," she said;   70
     She said, "I am aweary, aweary,
       I would that I were dead!"

The sparrow's chirrup on the roof,
  The slow clock ticking, and the sound
Which to the wooing wind aloof   75
  The poplar made, did all confound
Her sense; but most she loathed the hour
  When the thick-moted sunbeam lay
Athwart the chambers, and the day
  Was sloping toward his western bower.   80
    Then, said she, "I am very dreary,
      He will not come," she said;
    She wept, "I am aweary, aweary,
      O God, that I were dead!"

The Owl

I

When cats run home and light is come,
  And dew is cold upon the ground,
  And the far-off stream is dumb,
  And the whirring sail goes round,
  And the whirring sail goes round;   5
    Alone and warming his five wits,
    The white owl in the belfry sits.

II

When merry milkmaids click the latch,
  And rarely smells the new-mown hay,
  And the cock hath sung beneath the thatch   10
  Twice or thrice his roundelay,
  Twice or thrice his roundelay;
    Alone and warming his five wits,
    The white owl in the belfry sits.

Northern Farmer : Old Style

I

Wheer 'asta beän saw long and meä liggin' 'ere aloän?
Noorse? thoort nowt o' a noorse: whoy, Doctor's abeän an'
    agoän:
Says that I moänt 'a naw moor yaäle: but I beänt a fool:
Git ma my yaäle, for I beänt a-gooin' to breäk my rule.

II

Doctors, they knaws nowt, for a says what's nawways true:
Naw soort o' koind o' use to saäy the things that a do.
I've 'ed my point o' yaäle ivry noight sin' I beän 'ere,
An' I've 'ed my quart ivry market-noight for foorty year.

III

Parson's a beän loikewoise, an' a sittin' 'ere o' my bed.
"The amoighty's a taäkin o' you to 'issén, my friend," a
    said,
An' a towd ma my sins, an's toithe were due, an' I gied it in
    hond;
I done my duty by un, as I 'a done by the lond.

IV

Larn'd a ma' beä. I reckons I 'annot sa mooch to larn.
But a cost oop, thot a did, 'boot Bessy Marris's barn.
Thof a knaws I hallus voäted wi' Squoire an' choorch an'
    staäte,
An' i' the woost o' toimes I wur niver agin the raäte.

V

An' I hallus comed to 's choorch afoor moy Sally wur
    deäd,
An' 'eerd un a bummin' awaäy loike a buzzard-clock ower
    my yeäd,
An' I niver knaw'd whot a meän'd but I thowt a 'ad
    summ⁞ to saäy,
An I thowt a said whot a owt to 'a said an' I comed
    awaäy.

VI

Bessy Marris's barn! tha knaws she laäid it to meä.
Mowt 'a beän, mayhap, for she wur a bad un, sheä.
'Siver, I kep un, I kep un, my lass, tha mun understond;
I done my duty by un as I 'a done by the lond.

VII

But Parson a comes an' a goos, an' a says it eäsy an' freeä
"The amoighty's a taäkin' o' you to 'issén, my friend,"
    says 'eä.
I weänt saäy men be loiars, thof summun said it in
    'aäste:
But a reäds wonn sarmin a weeäk, an' I 'a stubb'd Thorn-
    aby waäste.

VIII

D'ya moind the waäste, my lass? naw, naw, tha was not
    born then;
Theer wur a boggle in it, I often 'eerd un mysen;
Moäst loike a butter-bump, for I 'eerd un aboot an' aboot,
But I stubb'd un oop wi' the lot, an' raäved an rembled un
    oot.

IX

Keäper's it wur; fo' they fun un theer a-laäid on 'is faäce
Doon i' the woild 'enemies afoor I comed to the plaäce.
Noäks or Thimbleby—toner 'ed shot un as deäd as a naäil.
Noäks wur 'ang'd for it oop at 'soize—but git ma my yaäle.

X

Dubbut looäk at the waäste: theer warn't not feäd for a
    cow:
Nowt at all but bracken an' fuzz, an' looäk at it now—
Warnt worth nowt a haäcre, an' now theer's lots o' feäd,
Fourscore yows upon it an' some on it doon in seäd.

XI

Nobbut a bit on it's left, an' I meän'd to 'a stubb'd it at
    fall,
Done it ta-year I meän'd, an' runn'd plow thruff it an' all,
If godamoighty an' parson 'ud nobbut let me aloän,
Meä, wi' haäte oonderd haäcre o' Squoire's, an' lond o'
    my oän.

XII

Do godamoighty knaw what a's doing a-taäkin' o'meä?
I beänt wonn as saws 'ere a beän an' yonder a peä;
An Squoire 'ull be sa mad an' all—a' dear a' dear!
And I 'a monaged for Squoire come Michaelmas thirty
    year.

XIII

A mowt 'a taäken Joänes, as 'ant a 'aäpoth o' sense,
Or a mowt 'a taäken Robins—a niver mended a fence:
But godamoighty a moost taäke meä an' taäke ma now
Wi 'auf the cows to cauve an' Thornaby holms to plow!

XIV

Looäk 'ow quoloty smoiles when they sees ma a passin' by,
Says to thessén naw doot "what a mon a beä sewer-ly!"
For they knaws what I beän to Squoire sin fust a comed to
      the 'All;
I done my duty by Squoire an' I done my duty by all.

XV

Squoire's in Lunnon, an' summun I reckons 'ull 'a to
      wroite,
For who's to howd the lond ater meä thot muddles ma
      quoit;
Sartin-sewer I beä, thot a weänt niver give it to Joänes,
Noither a moänt to Robins—a niver rembles the stoäns.

XVI

But summun 'ull come ater meä mayhap wi' 'is kittle o'
      steäm
Huzzin' an' maäzin' the blessed feälds wi' the Divil's oän
      teäm.
Gin I mun doy I mun doy, an' loife they says is swect,
But gin I mun doy I mun doy, for I couldn abear to see it.

XVII

What atta stannin' theer for, an' doesn bring ma the
      yaäle?
Doctor's a 'tottler, lass, an a 's hallus i' the owd taäle;
I weänt breäk rules for Doctor, a knaws naw moor nor a
      floy;
Git ma my yaäle I tell tha, an' gin I mun doy I mun doy.

Ulysses

It little profits that an idle king,
By this still hearth, among these barren crags,
Match'd with an aged wife, I mete and dole
Unequal laws unto a savage race,
That hoard, and sleep, and feed, and know not
    me.   5
I cannot rest from travel: I will drink
Life to the lees: all times I have enjoy'd
Greatly, have suffer'd greatly, both with those
That loved me, and alone; on shore, and when
Thro' scudding drifts the rainy Hyades   10
Vext the dim sea: I am become a name;
For always roaming with a hungry heart
Much have I seen and known; cities of men
And manners, climates, councils, governments,
Myself not least, but honour'd of them all;   15
And drunk delight of battle with my peers,
Far on the ringing plains of windy Troy.
I am a part of all that I have met;
Yet all experience is an arch wherethro'
Gleams that untravell'd world, whose margin
    fades   20
For ever and for ever when I move.
How dull it is to pause, to make an end,
To rust unburnish'd, not to shine in use!
As tho' to breathe were life. Life piled on life
Were all too little, and of one to me   25
Little remains: but every hour is saved
From that eternal silence, something more,
A bringer of new things; and vile it were
For some three suns to store and hoard myself,

And this grey spirit yearning in desire   30
To follow knowledge, like a sinking star,
Beyond the utmost bound of human thought.

    This is my son, mine own Telemachus,
To whom I leave the sceptre and the isle—
Well-loved of me, discerning to fulfil   35
This labour, by slow prudence to make mild
A rugged people, and thro’ soft degrees
Subdue them to the useful and the good.
Most blameless is he, centred in the sphere
Of common duties, decent not to fail   40
In offices of tenderness, and pay
Meet adoration to my household gods,
When I am gone. He works his work, I mine.

    There lies the port: the vessel puffs her sail:
There gloom the dark broad seas. My mariners, 45
Souls that have toil’d, and wrought, and thought
   with me—
That ever with a frolic welcome took
The thunder and the sunshine, and opposed
Free hearts, free foreheads—you and I are old;
Old age hath yet his honour and his toil;   50
Death closes all: but something ere the end,
Some work of noble note, may yet be done,
Not unbecoming men that strove with Gods.
The lights begin to twinkle from the rocks:
The long day wanes: the slow moon climbs: the
   deep   55
Moans round with many voices. Come, my
   friends,
’Tis not too late to seek a newer world.
Push off, and sitting well in order smite
The sounding furrows; for my purpose holds
To sail beyond the sunset, and the baths   60
Of all the western stars, until I die.

It may be that the gulfs will wash us down:
It may be we shall touch the Happy Isles,
And see the great Achilles, whom we knew.
Tho' much is taken, much abides; and tho'   65
We are not now that strength which in old days
Moved earth and heaven; that which we are,
    we are;
One equal temper of heroic hearts,
Made weak by time and fate, but strong in will
To strive, to seek, to find, and not to yield.   70

Tithonus

The woods decay, the woods decay and fall,
The vapours weep their burthen to the ground,
Man comes and tills the field and lies beneath,
And after many a summer dies the swan.
Me only cruel immortality   5
Consumes: I wither slowly in thine arms,
Here at the quiet limit of the world,
A white-hair'd shadow roaming like a dream
The ever silent spaces of the East,
Far-folded mists, and gleaming halls of morn.   10

Alas! for this grey shadow, once a man—
So glorious in his beauty and thy choice,
Who madest him thy chosen, that he seem'd
To his great heart none other than a God!
I ask'd thee, "Give me immortality".   15
Then didst thou grant mine asking with a smile,
Like wealthy men who care not how they give.
But thy strong Hours indignant work'd their wills,

And beat me down and marr'd and wasted me,
And tho' they could not end me, left me maim'd 20
To dwell in presence of immortal youth,
Immortal age beside immortal youth,
And all I was, in ashes. Can thy love,
Thy beauty, make amends, tho' even now,
Close over us, the silver star, thy guide, 25
Shines in those tremulous eyes that fill with tears
To hear me? Let me go: take back thy gift:
Why should a man desire in any way
To vary from the kindly race of men,
Or pass beyond the goal of ordinance 30
Where all should pause, as is most meet for all?

A soft air fans the cloud apart; there comes
A glimpse of that dark world where I was born.
Once more the old mysterious glimmer steals
From thy pure brows, and from thy shoulders pure, 35
And bosom beating with a heart renew'd.
Thy cheek begins to redden thro' the gloom,
Thy sweet eyes brighten slowly close to mine,
Ere yet they blind the stars, and the wild team
Which love thee, yearning for thy yoke, arise, 40
And shake the darkness from their loosen'd manes,
And beat the twilight into flakes of fire.
Lo! ever thus thou growest beautiful
In silence, then before thine answer given
Departest, and thy tears are on my cheek. 45

Why wilt thou ever scare me with thy tears,
And make me tremble lest a saying learnt
In days far-off, on that dark earth, be true?
"The Gods themselves cannot recall their gifts."

Ay me! ay me! with what another heart 50
In days far-off, and with what other eyes
I used to watch—if I be he that watch'd—
The lucid outline forming round thee; saw
The dim curls kindle into sunny rings;
Changed with thy mystic change, and felt my blood 55
Glow with the glow that slowly crimson'd all
Thy presence and thy portals, while I lay,
Mouth, forehead, eyelids, growing dewy-warm
With kisses balmier than half-opening buds
Of April, and could hear the lips that kiss'd 60
Whispering I knew not what of wild and sweet,
Like that strange song I heard Apollo sing,
While Ilion like a mist rose into towers.

Yet hold me not for ever in thine East:
How can my nature longer mix with thine? 65
Coldly thy rosy shadows bathe me, cold
Are all thy lights, and cold my wrinkled feet
Upon thy glimmering thresholds, when the steam
Floats up from those dim fields about the homes
Of happy men that have the power to die, 70
And grassy barrows of the happier dead.
Release me, and restore me to the ground;
Thou seest all things, thou wilt see my grave:
Thou wilt renew thy beauty morn by morn;
I earth in earth forget these empty courts, 75
And thee returning on thy silver wheels.

from *In Memoriam*

VII

Dark house, by which once more I stand
    Here in the long unlovely street,
    Doors, where my heart was used to beat
So quickly, waiting for a hand,   4

A hand that can be clasp'd no more—
    Behold me, for I cannot sleep,
    And like a guilty thing I creep
At earliest morning to the door.   8

He is not here; but far away
    The noise of life begins again,
    And ghastly thro' the drizzling rain
On the bald street breaks the blank day.   12

CXIV

Now fades the last long streak of snow,
    Now burgeons every maze of quick
    About the flowering squares, and thick
By ashen roots the violets blow.   4

Now rings the woodland loud and long,
    The distance takes a lovelier hue,
    And drown'd in yonder living blue
The lark becomes a sightless song.   8

Now dance the lights on lawn and lea,
    The flocks are whiter down the vale,
    And milkier every milky sail
On winding stream or distant sea;   12

Where now the seamew pipes, or dives
    In yonder greening gleam, and fly
    The happy birds, that change their sky
To build and brood; that live their lives   16

From land to land; and in my breast
    Spring wakens too; and my regret
    Becomes an April violet,
And buds and blossoms like the rest.   20

Notes

Two Songs from 'The Princess' (p. 83)

The Princess is a long discursive poem first published in
1847 and subtitled 'A Medley', which became very
popular and ran into seventeen editions in twenty years.
The six 'songs' were added in 1853, and these can be
read independently of the rest of the poem. They illustrate, perhaps chiefly, Tennyson's mastery of sound; and
even those who don't respond to the tone of much of his
poetry concede that he has a fine ear.

(I)   *The Splendour Falls (p. 83)*

The castle walls and the bugles evoke a vaguely medieval
landscape, but it is as a study and 'enactment' of sound-
echoes that the poem stands.

l. 4   *cataract:* waterfall.

l. 9   *scar:* steep craggy part of mountain-side.

(A)   What is 'the splendour' in l. 1, where is the idea repeated
in the first verse, and what is meant by calling the
mountain-tops 'old in story' (l. 2)? What visual effect is
described in l. 3, and how and why does the rhythm of
l. 4 contrast with it? Consider the last two lines of each
verse, and show in detail how they describe and also
'enact' the effect of echoes of the bugle-notes. What is
meant by 'the horns of Elfland' (l. 10), how does it fit the
echoes being described, and what is appropriate about
the words 'thin', 'clear', 'far', 'sweet', 'faintly' (ll. 7–9)?
Why the change from 'thin and clear' to 'thinner,
clearer, farther' (ll. 7 and 8)? Why are the glens 'purple'
and in what sense do they 'reply' (l. 11)? In verse 3, why
is the sky 'rich' (refer back to the opening) and what is
'they' (ll. 13 and 14)? What word does 'faint' (l. 14)
pick up, and what does it mean here? What generaliza-
tion beyond the particular sound-effect is touched on in
ll. 15–16? Show where there are internal rhymes within

the lines, and why this is appropriate for a poem on this subject.

NOTE. Benjamin Britten has composed a remarkable setting of this song for tenor voice, horn, and strings in a work called *Serenade*, which you should hear on record if possible: it brings out the echoes very well, and the horn acts as the 'bugle' of the poem.

(B) Write freely in verse or prose about echoes.

(II) *Now Sleeps the Crimson Petal (p. 84)*

Again the setting is medieval, and the poem catches the warm nights of summer in a palace garden; it is, of course, a love poem, but tied very closely to the mood of the scene.

l. 3 *porphyry font:* here, a pool made of a hard crystalline stone.

l. 4 *firefly:* a winged insect giving off phosphorescent light.

l. 7 *Danaë:* a maiden in Greek mythology who was confined by her father in a brazen tower but visited by Jupiter, who was in love with her, in the form of a shower of gold, and so gave birth to Perseus.

(A) Crimson and white were dominant colours of Victorian roses; in what sense do they 'sleep' (l. 1)? Why doesn't the cypress-tree 'wave' (l. 2)? What would have a 'gold fin' in the 'font', what is appropriate about the word 'winks', and why isn't it winking now (l. 3)? How does the firefly contrast with the rest of the verse? White peacocks are rare and admired, and would fit such a setting; why is 'droops' (l. 5) at first sight an odd word to use for a peacock, and how is it suitable here? Suggest what coloured dress 'she' is wearing (l. 5). Explain l. 7 with reference to the note on Danaë above; how does l. 8 go with it? Why would the meteor be specially noticeable, and what is meant by 'slides' and 'furrow' (ll. 9 and 10)? Again, how does this fit the love theme? What happens to water-lilies at dusk (ll. 11–12) and how is this related by the poet to the love theme? Notice that this poem has no rhymes, but do you detect any 'ghost-rhymes', *i.e.*, faint suggestions of rhyme? Do they play any part in the atmosphere of the poem?

Mariana (p. 84)

This is one of an early group of poems with girls' names, and by far the best. It is an evocation of the girl's psychological state in an old and lonely house, and the mood and its surroundings are brilliantly related. Mariana is a character in Shakespeare's *Measure for Measure*, who was jilted by Angelo, and symbolizes hopeless but faithful love; she is described as 'Mariana of the moated grange' in the play.

l. 8 *moated:* surrounded with a deep wide ditch of water; *grange:* farmhouse with outbuildings.

l. 20 *athwart:* across; *flats:* low-lying land.

l. 40 *marish:* marshy.

l. 64 *wainscot:* wooden panelling.

(A) What have the three images in ll. 1–5 in common? What is suggested by l. 6 and which sound might Mariana want to hear? How are her tears related to the dew in ll. 13–16? What period of day is defined in l. 17, and how was the sky 'tranced' in l. 18? Why are the flats 'gloomy' as well as dim or dark (l. 20)—why does a flat landscape suggest melancholy? What is the significance of the three sounds in verse 3, and which words in ll. 29–32 further suggest sadness and isolation? What exactly do ll. 37–40 describe, and what is added by the words 'sluice', 'blacken'd', 'slept', 'crept'? What does the monotony of the poplar-trees contribute (ll. 41–43) and the words 'waste' and 'rounding grey'? (Why 'rounding'?) How do the poplars come again in the next verse, and what is implied by their shadow falling 'upon her bed, across her brow' (l. 56)? What sounds does she hear in the next verse? Suggest another word for 'blue fly'; what do it and the mice contribute to the atmosphere? What are the 'old faces', 'old footsteps', and 'old voices'—are they actually sounding through the old house, or only in her imagination? How do the sounds in the last verse emphasize her isolation, and why did she 'loathe' the evenings most (ll. 77–80)? Finally, consider two general questions on the poem: how the 'chorus' of each verse differs and for what reasons; and how the physical conditions of the house and its surroundings colour the mental and emotional condition of Mariana, and represent her despair.

The Owl (p. 87)

In contrast to *Mariana*, this is a light and lively lyric, enlivened by an energetic rhythm.

l. 11   *roundelay:* originally any short simple song with a chorus.
(A)   When do 'cats run home' (l. 1)? What is the 'whirring sail' and what is the effect of repeating this line? What is meant by the owl 'warming his five wits' and what is he doing in the belfry (ll. 6 and 7)? Relate the first line of the second verse to a contrasting image in *Mariana*; if there it suggests solitude and hopelessness, what does it suggest here? Again, what effect is made by the repetition of ll. 11 and 12? The whole poem might be considered in relation to Edward Thomas's *Cock-crow* (p. 174).

Northern Farmer: Old Style (p. 88)

An old farmer lies ill in bed, and this is a poem expressing his ruminations about life, his achievements, his sense of values, and his thoughts of death. It has great vigour and a ripe humour (not excluding pathos) in contrast with what some readers have considered a tendency to melancholy and passivity in Tennyson. North Country readers probably won't need a glossary but one is provided here for the less obvious words.

v. 1   *liggin':* lying; *noorse:* nurse; *yaäle:* ale.
v. 3   *toithe:* tithe (originally a tenth part of annual proceeds of land, etc., paid to support church and clergy); *gied it in hond:* put it in hand.
v. 4   *Larn'd:* learnèd; *a cost oop:* he brought up; *thof:* though.
v. 5   *bummin':* wandering on, perhaps; *buzzard-clock:* cockchafer.
v. 6   *laäid it to meä:* blamed it on me; *'siver:* howsoever.
v. 7   *stubb'd:* cleared a patch of land by stubbing up trees, bushes, etc.; *waäste:* patch of waste land.
v. 8   *moind:* remember; *boggle:* phantom, goblin; *butter-bump:* bittern (marsh-bird with curious booming note); *raäved an rembled:* carried off and removed (?).

v. 9   *Keäper's it wur:* it was a gamekeeper's (ghost); *'enemies:* anemones; *toner:* one or the other; *at 'soize:* at the assizes.

v. 10   *Dubbut:* do but (*i.e.,* 'only'); *fuzz:* furze, gorse; *yows:* ewes.

v. 11   *Nobbut:* only ('no but'); *ta-year:* this year; *thruff:* through.

v. 15   *holms:* usually flat ground by a river.

v. 14   *quoloty:* the 'gentry'; *what a mon a beä sewer-ly:* what a (fine) man he is indeed!

v. 15   *thot muddles ma quoit:* that confuses me utterly; *rembles:* removes; *sartin-sewer:* certain sure.

v. 16   *kittle o' steäm:* steam kettle, *i.e.,* farm machinery run by steam; *huzzin' an' mäazin':* spoiling and cutting up (?).

v. 17   *'tottler:* teetotaller; *hallus i' the owd taäle:* always telling the same tale; *floy:* fly.

(A)   What request or instruction to the nurse begins, 'punctuates', and ends the poem? What is his 'rule' (verses I and II)? What picture of the parson emerges in verse III—especially 'he told me my sins'? We don't know about 'Bessy Morris's barn' (verses IV and VI), but can you make a suggestion? What are the old farmer's politics, do you think (verse IV)? When did he stop going to church, what kind of pulpit did the parson preach from, and what kind of sermons did he deliver (verse V)? What contrast does the farmer express between his work and that of the parson (verse VII), and which seems to him more useful? What joke is concealed in verse VIII (the bittern is a very shy bird keeping to the hidden parts of overgrown marshes)? What local tragedy and superstition is described in verse IX? How is his pride in his work expressed in verse X? Where does he show that he feels there is a conspiracy between the parson and 'godamoighty'? What opinion has he of the other local farmers? What might the gentry's smile mean apart from the interpretation he offers (verse XIV)? Where does he show anxiety for the fate of the land he has farmed, and where does he show that he fears and despises new kinds of agricultural machine, and how does this half-resign him to death? What 'note' does the poem end on?

(B) Try to read this poem aloud or at least hear it: each 'umlaut' (dots over a vowel) indicates that the two vowels are pronounced separately. Then try writing in verse or prose a monologue by an old man in any dialect you know.

Ulysses (p. 92)

There is a general agreement, even among those who find much of Tennyson's poetry lifeless or morbid, that this poem and the next, *Tithonus*, are among his finest achievements. One way of looking at them is as dramatic monologues. *Ulysses* was written, like *In Memoriam* (extracts from which come next in this selection), soon after the death of his close friend Arthur Hallam, and shows 'his resolution to overcome the mood of despair'. Ulysses is the great hero whose long journey back from the Trojan wars to his own kingdom is the subject of Homer's *Odyssey*. Here he is an old man, looking back over his travels.

l. 3   *mete and dole:* allot and deal out.

l. 7   *lees:* drains.

l. 10   *Hyades:* group of stars near the Pleiades, associated with rain and bad weather.

l. 33   *Telemachus:* the son and heir of Ulysses.

l. 53   Not unsuitable for men who strove with gods.

l. 64   *Achilles:* Greek hero, who killed the Trojan leader Hector.

l. 68   *temper:* disposition.

(A) In what sense does Ulysses feel himself 'idle' (l. 1) in spite of the activities listed? How do 'still heath', 'barren crags', 'savage race' contrast with the things he remembers (ll. 2–4), and what picture are we given of his subjects (l. 5)? Summarize what he remembers of his travels (l. 9–14); what is meant by 'I am become a name' (l. 11)? What picture do you get from l. 17? Try to paraphrase the important but difficult idea in ll. 19–21: how does 'the margin fade' when 'I move'? Explain ll. 22–24 and relate it to a modern phrase like 'settling down' or 'retiring'. What is he ridiculing in 'as tho' to breathe were life' (l. 24)? Where does he show that he knows he has not long to live, why won't he 'store and hoard' himself (l. 29) and what will he rather do (ll. 30–33)? In what terms does he analyse his son, and what is the force, and the limitations, implied in 'blameless', 'decent', 'meet' (ll. 33–43)? Which phrase shows how difficult he knows he is for his son? In the paragraph beginning on l. 44, what picture do we get of the excitements and adventure of travel, and where is there a note of hope contrasting with the sadness and age (ll. 44–56)? Put in your own words 'sitting well in order smite/The sounding furrows' (ll. 58–59). Is this journey to be a factual one, or one of the imagination and intellect? On what note does the aged Ulysses end, and to what is he determined 'not to yield'?

Tithonus (p. 94)

Tithonus was a handsome youth who was carried off by the goddess of the dawn, Aurora; he begged her for the gift of immortality, which she granted, but forgot to ask for the vigour of youth to remain with him, so grew old and decrepit, till he begged Aurora to release him. Aurora is traditionally represented as veiled, drawn in a rose-coloured chariot by white horses.

l. 2   *burthen:* burden.
l. 25   *star:* the morning star.
l. 30   *ordinance:* what is laid down (in this case the ordinary span of life).
l. 62   *Apollo:* the god of music.
l. 63   *Ilion:* a name for Troy.
l. 71   *barrows:* burial mounds.
(A)   The first four lines are justly famous: what is Tithonus envying here about the natural world? Suggest why the dawn-goddess lives 'at the quiet limit of the world' (l. 7) and in 'the East' (l. 9); point out other expressions describing this place. What made Tithonus ask for immortality, how did 'thy strong Hours' (why 'thy'?) defeat this wish, and why did he then have 'To dwell in presence of immortal youth' (l. 22)? Why is the silver star 'thy guide' and in whose eyes does it shine? What stress falls on 'man' and 'men' (ll. 28 and 29) and what 'ordinance' is 'most meet (fitting) for all' (ll. 30–31)?

Why does Aurora 'glimmer' (l. 34), and how is her heart, unlike his, 'renewed' (l. 36)? In what sense does Aurora's beauty 'blind the stars' (l. 39) and why is her 'wild team' 'yearning for the yoke' (ll. 39–40)? What natural effect is described in ll. 41–42? In what sense does she *grow* beautiful and why does she weep (ll. 43–45)? Why is the earth 'dark' to Tithonus (l. 48), and why does he fear the 'saying' of l. 49? What period of his life is Tithonus describing in ll. 50–63, and where does he express his doubts that it was really he? What *else* is described in this passage in addition to his love affairs with Aurora? (Consider 'sunny rings', 'mystic change', 'glow', 'crimson'd', etc.) The last section of the poem suggests that he can no longer respond to the dawn as well as no longer be her lover; why does he speak of 'happy men that can die' and 'happier dead' (ll. 70–71)? What ground does he want to be restored to (l. 72)? Explain fully the last couplet. How does Tithonus's attitude contrast with that of Ulysses?

from *In Memoriam (p. 97)*

This selection ends with two short sections from the long poem *In Memoriam* which Tennyson wrote in memory of Arthur Hallam (see note on *Ulysses* above). It is in the main a reflective and philosophical poem, of great beauty and power in places though not now often admired as a whole.

VII Notice the verse pattern (called the *In Memoriam* stanza) with eight syllables to the line and the outside and inside pairs of lines rhyming. This section evokes with unusual power the sense of loss that he experiences in a town setting.

(A) Why is the house 'dark' and who do you think lived here (l. 1)? What sort of town street do you picture in l. 2? How is the sense of loss echoed by the weather, what does the 'drizzling rain' symbolize and what double meaning do you get from 'bald street' and 'blank day'? What is there special about the rhythm of the last line (compare it with l. 4), and how do the stresses increase the sense of desolation?

CXIV This section contrasts vividly with the tragic quality of the previous one.

l. 2   *burgeons:* bursts into bud; *quick:* hawthorn.

l. 4   *blow:* come into bloom.

l. 13   *seamew:* seagull.

(A)   Where might the 'last long streak of snow' be, and what time of year is being described? What 'rings' in the woodland (l. 5), and what 'lovelier hues' are seen in the distance (l. 6)? How is the lark 'drown'd in yonder living blue' and how does it become a 'sightless song'? What colour is stressed in the third verse, and which words and phrases here and in the next verse suggest vigour and movement? How does the last verse relate the landscape to the poet's feelings, and how can his 'regret' 'bud and blossom'? How do the last eight lines contrast with Hopkins's sonnet *Thou art indeed just, Lord* (p. 119)?

FURTHER READING

A Selection from Tennyson's Poems (ed. W. H. Auden).
Collected Poems (there are many editions).

CRITICAL WRITING

R. Mayhead. "The Poetry of Tennyson" (in *Pelican Guide to English Literature*, Vol. 6, "From Dickens to Hardy").

Valerie Pitt. *Tennyson Laureate*. A careful analysis which attempts to reinstate the poet after the partial failure of his reputation.

Gerard Manley Hopkins

GERARD MANLEY HOPKINS was born at Stratford, Essex (now part of Greater London), in 1844, and educated at Highgate School and Balliol College, Oxford. He joined the Roman Catholic Church in 1866, and became a Jesuit in 1868. He was ordained in 1871 and worked as a priest and administrator in various towns including London and Glasgow. He taught classics at the Catholic Stonyhurst College, and was appointed Professor of Greek at University College, Dublin in 1884. He died in 1889 from typhoid fever. His poems remained unpublished during his lifetime, but Robert Bridges, who acted as his literary executor, published a few in anthologies and finally edited and published the collected poems in 1918; a second edition appeared in 1930 and was immensely influential during the 'thirties and since.

Hopkins is in many ways the most remarkable poet of the Victorian period, and I felt he should be represented here in spite of the considerable difficulties his poetry presents at the outset. Like Blake, he was misunderstood or ignored by all but a tiny circle of friends during his lifetime, and Robert Bridges failed to publish more than a handful of his poems till 1918; even then he patronized the poet in his introduction, which admitted that he had great qualities, but also attacked him for 'oddity and obscurity'. We now recognize him as a poet of extraordinary originality, and his rather small body of work includes some of the most profound poems in the language. The 'naked shock' which, as he himself expressed it, his poetry gives at a first reading comes partly from his originality of vocabulary: in the first poem in this selection, 'horseback brown', 'twindles', 'wiry heathpacks', 'flitches of fern', 'the bead-bonny ash', the beautiful modulation form 'wet and wild-ness' to 'weeds and wilderness'—and this is, for Hopkins, a notably simple and straightforward poem. Secondly, perhaps, the shock arises from the newness of his rhythms: his theory of sprung rhythm is dealt with in the Penguin edition, and all we can say here is that he believed that the number of stressed syllables in a line was what determined its pattern, and that any number of unstressed syllables could be used, according to the need of the subject. Thus he can write:

> But we dream we are rooted in earth—Dust!
> Flesh falls within sight of us, we, though our flower the same
> Wave with the meadow, forget that there must
> The so'ur scy'the cr'inge, and the ble'ar sha're co'me.

The last line has two groups of three stressed syllables side by side, which exactly give the scythe cutting down the flowers with the grass, and (according to Catholic doctrine) the tragic fate of man echoing it.

Thirdly there is Hopkins's complex doctrine of 'instress' and 'inscape', derived partly from medieval philosophers, in which the distinctive design or patterning of anything echoes its reason for existence and its uniqueness. Fourthly, there is in his finest poetry a tremendous tension resulting from the clash between the unyielding doctrines he so devotedly believed and his awareness of the beauty of the world. Lastly—and this has become a list of reasons why this poet is worth reading—his imagery is strong and energetic and utterly original. In *The Wreck of the 'Deutschland'* there is a violent storm at sea:

> Wiry and white-fiery and whirlwind-swivellèd snow
> Spins to the widow-making unchilding unfathering deeps.

In a completely different vein he describes the city of Oxford:

> Towery city and branchy between towers;
> Cuckoo-echoing, bell-swarmèd, lark-charmèd, rook-racked, river-rounded.

He writes of an orchard in May:

> When drop-of-blood-and-foam-dapple
> Bloom lights the orchard-apple

> And thicket and thorp are merry
> With silver-surfèd cherry.

He writes of a falcon in *The Windhover*:

> I caught this morning morning's minion, king-
>   dom of daylight's dauphin, dapple-dawn-drawn
>   Falcon, in his riding
> Of the rolling level underneath him steady air, and
>   striding
> High there, how he rung upon the rein of a wimpling
>   wing
> In his ecstasy!

These few fragments may encourage you to look further into Hopkins's poetry, and to find him perhaps the most *original* poet in this anthology, and worth a great deal of trouble to understand.

This darksome burn, horseback brown,
His rollrock highroad roaring down,
In coop and in comb the fleece of his foam
Flutes and low to the lake falls home.   4

A windpuff-bonnet of fawn-froth
Turns and twindles over the broth
Of a pool so pitchblack, fell-frowning,
It rounds and rounds Despair to drowning.   8

Degged with dew, dappled with dew
Are the groins of the braes that the brook treads
        through,
Wiry heathpacks, flitches of fern,
And the beadbonny ash that sits over the burn.   12

What would the world be, once bereft
Of wet and wildness? Let them be left,
O let them be left, wildness and wet;
Long live the weeds and the wilderness yet.   16

Heaven-Haven

A nun takes the veil

I have desired to go
    Where springs not fail,
To fields where flies no sharp and sided hail
    And a few lilies blow.   4

And I have asked to be
Where no storms come,
Where the green swell is in the havens dumb,
And out of the swing of the sea.   8

Felix Randall

Felix Randal, the farrier, O he is dead then? my duty all
ended,
Who have watched his mould of man, big-boned and
hardy-handsome
Pining, pining, till time when reason rambled in it and some
Fatal four disorders, fleshed there, all contended?   4

Sickness broke him. Impatient he cursed at first, but
mended
Being anointed and all; though a heavenlier heart began
some
Months earlier, since I had our sweet reprieve and ransom
Tendered to him. Ah well, God rest him all road ever he
offended!   8

This seeing the sick endears them to us, us too it endears.
My tongue had taught thee comfort, touch had quenched
thy tears,
Thy tears that touched my heart, child, Felix, poor Felix
Randal;

How far from then forethought of, all thy more boisterous
years,   12
When thou at the random grim forge, powerful amidst
peers,
Didst fettle for the great grey drayhorse his bright and
battering sandal!

Spring and Fall

to a young child

Margaret, are you grieving
Over Goldengrove unleaving?
Leaves, like the things of man, you
With your fresh thoughts care for, can you?   4
Ah! as the heart grows older
It will come to such sights colder
By and by, nor spare a sigh
Though worlds of wanwood leafmeal lie;   8
And yet you will weep and know why.
Now no matter, child, the name:
Sorrow's springs are the same.
Nor mouth had, no nor mind, expressed   12
What heart heard of, ghost guessed:
It is the blight man was born for,
It is Margaret you mourn for.

Spring

Nothing is so beautiful as spring—
    When weeds, in wheels, shoot long and lovely and lush;
    Thrush's eggs look little low heavens, and thrush
Through the echoing timber does so rinse and wring   4
The ear, it strikes like lightnings to hear him sing;
    The glassy peartree leaves and blooms, they brush
    The descending blue; that blue is all in a rush
With richness; the racing lambs too have fair their fling.   8

What is all this juice and all this joy?
   A strain of the earth's sweet being in the beginning
In Eden garden.—Have, get, before it cloy,
   Before it cloud, Christ, lord, and sour with sinning,   12
Innocent mind and Mayday in girl and boy,
   Most, O maid's child, thy choice and worthy the winning.

Pied Beauty

Glory be to God for dappled things—
   For skies of couple-colour as a brinded cow;
      For rose-moles all in stipple upon trout that swim;
   Fresh-firecoal chestnut-falls; finches' wings;   4
   Landscape plotted and pieced—fold, fallow, and plough;
      And all trades, their gear and tackle and trim.

All things counter, original, spare, strange;
   Whatever is fickle, freckled (who knows how?)   8
      With swift, slow; sweet, sour; adazzle, dim;
He fathers-forth whose beauty is past change:
         Praise him.

Binsey Poplars
felled 1879

   My aspens dear, whose airy cages quelled,
   Quelled or quenched in leaves the leaping sun,
   All felled, felled, are all felled;
     Of a fresh and following folded rank   4
       Not spared, not one
        That dandled a sandalled
      Shadow that swam or sank

On meadow and river and wind-wandering
  weed-winding bank.   8

O if we but knew what we do
  When we delve or hew—
Hack and rack the growing green!
    Since country is so tender   12
To touch, her being so slender,
That, like this sleek and seeing ball
But a prick will make no eye at all,
Where we, even where we mean   16
    To mend her we end her,
  When we hew or delve:
After-comers cannot guess the beauty been.
Ten or twelve, only ten or twelve   20
Strokes of havoc unselve
    The sweet especial scene,
Rural scene, a rural scene,
Sweet especial rural scene.   24

The Starlight Night

Look at the stars! look, look up at the skies!
  O look at all the fire-folk sitting in the air!
  The bright boroughs, the circle-citadels there!
Down in dim woods the diamond delves! the elves'-eyes!
The grey lawns cold where gold, where quickgold lies!
  Wind-beat whitebeam! airy abeles set on a flare!
  Flake-doves sent floating forth at a farmyard scare!—
Ah well! it is all a purchase, all is a prize.   8

Buy then! bid then!—What?—Prayer, patience, alms,
  vows.

Look, look: a May-mess, like on orchard boughs!
  Look! March-bloom, like on mealed-with-yellow
  sallows!
These are indeed the barn; withindoors house   12
The shocks. This piece-bright paling shuts the spouse
  Christ home, Christ and his mother and all his hallows.

In the Valley of the Elwy

I remember a house where all were good
  To me, God knows, deserving no such thing:
  Comforting smell breathed at very entering,
Fetched fresh, as I suppose, off some sweet wood.   4
That cordial air made those kind people a hood
  All over, as a bevy of eggs the mothering wing
  Will, or mild nights the new morsels of spring:
Why, it seemed of course; seemed of right it should. 8

Lovely the woods, waters, meadows, combes, vales,
All the air things wear that build this world of Wales;
  Only the inmate does not correspond:
God, lover of souls, swaying considerate scales,   12
Complete thy creature dear O where it fails,
  Being mighty a master, being a father and fond.

My Own Heart . . .

My own heart let me have more pity on; let
Me live to my sad self hereafter kind,
Charitable; not live this tormented mind
With this tormented mind tormenting yet.   4

I cast for comfort I can no more get
By groping round my comfortless, than blind
Eyes in their dark can day or thirst can find
Thirst's all-in-all in all a world of wet.   8

Soul, self; come, poor Jackself, I do advise
You, jaded, let be; call off thoughts awhile
Elsewhere; leave comfort root-room; let joy size
At God knows when to God know what; whose   12
  smile
's not wrung, see you; unforeseen times rather—as skies
Betweenpie mountains—lights a lovely mile.

Thou art indeed just, Lord . . .

Thou art indeed just, Lord, if I contend
With thee; but, sir, so what I plead is just.
Why do sinners' ways prosper? and why must
Disappointment all I endeavour end?   4
Wert thou my enemy, O thou my friend,
How wouldst thou worse, I wonder, than thou dost
Defeat, thwart me? Oh, the sots and thralls of lust
Do in spare hours more thrive than I that spend,   8
Sir, life upon thy cause. See, banks and brakes
Now, leavèd how thick! lacèd they are again
With fretty chervil, look, and fresh wind shakes
Them; birds build—but not I build; no, but strain, 12
Time's eunuch, and not breed one work that wakes.
Mine, O thou lord of life, send my roots rain.

Notes

Inversnaid (p. 113)

This poem presents a landscape in the first three verses, and a reflection about it in the last. It is a good poem to start a study of Hopkins, because it is fairly straightforward but illustrates many of his individual uses of words, images, and rhythms. I have made fuller notes on this than on some of the following poems.

l. 1   *burn:* small stream (a Scots word): it is dark in colour and brown from the peat.

l. 2   The mountain stream roars down its bed ('highroad'), rocking the stones in its path.

l. 3   *coop:* hollow or enclosed place; *comb:* water 'combing' over stones, etc.

l. 4   Notice how the verb 'flutes' comes at the beginning of the line, suggesting a kind of echo as the music of the water accompanies a little waterfall.

ll. 5–   Where the waterfall meets the lake there is a disk of froth
6   like a Scots bonnet blown by the wind, making a small whirlpool; *twindles:* a coined word: perhaps twists and dwindles?

l. 7   *fell:* fierce(ly).

l. 9   *Degged:* sprinkled (a dialect word).

l. 10   *groins:* here the edge of the river's path.

l. 11   *flitches:* ragged brown tufts (of bracken).

l. 12   The mountain ash with red berries.

l. 13   *bereft:* deprived of, robbed of.

(A)   Point out some examples of alliteration (words beginning with the same letter or sound) and say how you think they add to the effect. Explain why you think the poet writes 'fleece of his foam', 'fell-frowning', 'wiry heathpacks' (heath is heather—how 'wiry' and why 'packs'?). How is 'beadbonny' appropriate (in what ways are the berries like beads and how does 'bonny' fit into *this* poem?); how does the ash 'sit over' the stream? Explain in your own words the last verse; what repetitions and what echoes of sound do you detect? Is the thought of the last verse still relevant today (National Trust, *etc.*)?

(B) Write in prose or verse about a *wild* landscape you know, trying to give precision and detail in the way Hopkins does. (This exercise may be felt to be too like the one based on Graves's poem "Rocky Acres", p. 258, in which case omit it.)

Heaven-Haven (p. 113)

A delicate poem expressing the wish of a nun to escape from the perils of ordinary life.

l. 2 Where the spring of water never fails.

l. 3 *sided:* sharp-edged.

(A) Look up 'haven' if you don't know it; then explain in your own words the last two lines of the poem and its title, using the sub-title to help you. What do you consider 'hail', 'storms', and 'the swing of the sea' to be metaphors for? Which words and phrases refer to the nun's hopes for her future life? How do the two verses relate—*i.e.*, what correspondences do you find in their pattern?

Felix Randal (p. 114)

This poem is a sonnet—one of Hopkins's favourite forms —but it has an unusually long line and a subtle rhythm. Hopkins was at this time a parish priest, responsible for visiting the sick.

l. 1 *farrier:* blacksmith.

l. 2 *mould of man:* physical frame; *hardy-handsome:* handsome in his physical strength.

l. 6 *a heavenlier heart:* signs of penance for his sins.

l. 7 *reprieve and ransom:* communion.

l. 8 *tendered:* given, handed; *all road ever:* in whatever way (a north-country dialect phrase).

l. 12 How remote then seemed the years of his energetic life.

l. 13 *random:* built with irregularly-sized stones; *powerful amidst peers:* strong among his equals.

l. 14 *fettle:* make ready (dialect: we still say 'in good fettle', in good condition).

(A)   Explain in your own words ll. 3 and 4 ('fleshed' means built into his body). Give some examples of alliteration and sound echoes from the poem. At what stage of the blacksmith's illness does the poet think of him as a 'child', and why? Explain the last line (remember his trade); what is a 'drayhorse', and what effect is given by the rhythm?

(B)   Write a short piece in prose or verse about the death of a worker in some heavy or demanding trade.

Spring and Fall (p. 115)

A deceptively simple-looking poem, but embodying a profound idea. A child stands alone in a wood sadly watching the leaves fall. The poet says that as she grows up she will not have the same intense feelings for mere leaves; yet she will weep, but for her own state. Whatever we call it, all sorrow springs from one source which we cannot express but only understand intuitively. All men are born blighted by the Fall (according to Catholic doctrine), and all sorrow comes from this recognition; perhaps for people who don't accept this stern doctrine, it can mean that we weep for the transience of our own lives, for which the falling of the leaves is a metaphor. The title uses 'fall' for autumn, as the Americans commonly do.

l. 8   This beautiful line suggests an autumnal wood from which all the summer colours have gone ('wanwood') and the leaves lie 'leafmeal' (rather like 'piecemeal') on the ground.

l. 13   *ghost:* spirit (as in 'Holy Ghost').

(A)   Suggest what 'Goldengrove' means. In what sense are Margaret's thoughts 'fresh' (l. 4)? Put into your own words ll. 5–8, and ll. 12–13. If you take the word 'blight' as meaning the Fall of man, how does the title relate to it? If we were immortal would we feel sadness at the passing of summer? (This is a very difficult question.)

Spring (p. 115)

Another sonnet, in which the lush growth of spring is vividly described in the octave, (*i.e.*, first eight lines), and

the sestet (the last six lines) relates spring to the innocence of the Garden of Eden and of children before they
are 'soured with sinning'. The richness of the poem is
largely a matter of subtle rhythms and sound echoes.

l. 2 *wheels:* a surprising word here; perhaps it refers to the
spiral form of many wild plants before they throw up
their flowering stems ('shoot').

l. 3 Thrush's eggs are a pure shade of blue.

l. 6 *glassy:* shining, glossy; the blossom is, of course, pure
white; *brush:* this is the effect when they are seen against
a blue sky.

l. 8 'To have one's fling' is a common expression.

l. 10 *strain:* note, melody.

ll. 11 This is addressed to Christ; the poet begs Him to win the
-14 innocent minds of children.

(A) Explain 'look little low heavens', and the lines about the
thrush's song (ll. 3–5) in your own words. What picture
do you get of the lambs? Why 'juice' in l. 9? In what ways
does the poet see spring as like Eden? What do you understand by 'cloy' (l. 11) and 'cloud' (l. 12)? What does he
mean by 'Mayday' (l. 13)? Who is the 'maid's child',
and why is this expression fitting here? Give some examples of sound echoes, including alliteration, assonance
(*e.g.,* weeds/wheels, rinse/wring).

Pied Beauty (p. 116)

Hopkins called this poem a 'curtal' (*i.e.,* curtailed)
sonnet, and the proportion of the two sections (six lines
and four and a half) corresponds to the eight and six of
the normal sonnet. It is a song of praise for everything
in nature that is 'pied'—bicoloured, streaked, patched.

l. 2 *brinded:* a form of 'brindled', brown streaked with another
colour, *e.g.,* white.

l. 3 Trout have pink spots on their backs, especially the so-
called 'rainbow trout'.

l. 4 Perhaps a reference to the bright lacquered colours of a
new-fallen chestnut, as fresh and bright as a glowing
'firecoal'; *finches' wings:* in many species these are
barred with contrasting colours.

l. 5 The contrasts of pasture, fallow, and ploughland

interlocking and pieced together, especially when seen from a distance or on a hill.

l. 7   *counter:* contrasting—l. 9 is a series of 'counter' adjectives.

l. 8   *fickle:* here, quickly changing in colour or form.

ll. 9– God's beauty is permanent, not transitory, though He
10   makes the complex beauty of the world described in the poem; the praise for all this beauty is due to God.

(A)   Make a list of the words in the poem which are similar in meaning to 'pied' (particoloured). What picture does l. 6 conjure up for you? Give some examples in nature which would fit the pairs of adjectives in l. 9.

(B)   Suggest some other natural things which are dappled or pied.

Binsey Poplars (p. 116)

Binsey is a village near Oxford, and this poem was written after the cutting down of a fine row of aspens (a variety of poplar with a delicate structure of tiny twigs, noted for its trembling in the lightest wind).

l. 1   *quelled:* defeated, cooled down with their leaves and branches ('airy cages').

l. 4   *folded rank:* this suggests a row or avenue of trees growing by a river and following its curves.

l. 6   *dandled:* caused to shake (to dandle is to jog or dance a child on one's knees); *sandalled:* cut into shapes like the upper part of a sandal.

l. 8   *wind-wandering weed-winding:* the river bank wanders apparently as casually as the wind, and winds through the weeds which cover its banks.

l. 10 *delve or hew:* dig up or hack down.

l. 11 *rack:* stretch, injure (literally, torture).

ll. 12 The countryside is tender to the touch, easily injured,
–13 because her existence is so delicate a thing ('her being so slender').

ll. 16 Even where we try to improve on wild nature we ruin it
–17 (compare *Inversnaid*, p. 113).

l. 19 Those who come after the country has been spoiled cannot guess how lovely it was ('the beauty been').

ll. 22 every country scene is unique ('especial').
–24

(A)   What is the effect of the repetitions and the rhythm in l. 3? Put ll. 9–11 in your own words. What do you understand by 'this sleek and seeing ball' (see the following line), and why is this comparison appropriate to a visual scene? What is the main purpose of the first verse, and what of the second? Put into your own words ll. 20 and 21. Why the repetitions in ll. 22–24? What is the relevance of this poem to the present day? (Go back again to *Inversnaid* for a related idea).

(B)   Write in prose or verse about a scene you know which has been harmed or ruined.

The Starlight Night (p. 117)

This is another sonnet, similar in pattern to *Spring* (p. 115), and like that poem, the octave is mainly descriptive and the sestet draws a religious conclusion.

The poet stares entranced at the night sky, and declares that all this beauty can only be fully enjoyed if we pay God back for it by prayer and devotion; it finishes with the beautifully-expressed idea, common in childhood, that God is up in the heavens, as it were behind the stars.

l. 2   *fire-folk:* many legends refer to the stars as people or gods.

l. 3   As one stares more and more at the sky, one begins to see a kind of landscape, with towns and citadels.

l. 4   Continuing this idea, he imagines diamond-mines glittering in woods, and the eyes of the elves traditionally associated with them.

l. 5   Patches of grey 'mist' (as in the Milky Way) with twinkling yellowish stars at intervals.

l. 6   A whitebeam on a windy day shows the nearly white underside of its leaves in a flickering pattern (this is a characteristic Hopkins touch, related to *Pied Beauty*); *abele:* the white poplar with cut leaves and white undersides exposed when blown by the wind and, as it were, set alight.

ll. 8– We have to pay for such beauty by devotion to God, and
9   the beauty is the prize. 'What?' means 'With what?'

ll. 10 We are taken back to the beauty in case we doubt

−11 whether the cost of the 'purchase' is too high, and reminded again of the glories of the night sky.

l. 10 *mess:* medley, rich confusion.

l. 11 *mealed-with-yellow:* a typical Hopkins word: the blooms
of certain varieties of willow (commonly called 'palm')
are a downy grey dusted ('mealed') with bright yellow
pollen.

l. 12 *the barn:* the outside of a granary, which 'houses' within
its doors the 'shocks' (sheaves of corn).

ll. 13 *piece-bright paling:* the stars are like a bright fence hiding
−14 the 'spouse Christ' who is home (in heaven) with his
mother and all the Saints ('hallows'—compare All
Hallows Day—All Saints' Day).

(A) What is the purpose of the repeated word 'look', and why
are there so many exclamation-marks? Explain carefully
what picture is given by l. 7 (a dovecote or pigeon-house
would be a common feature of farmyards in the past).
What metaphors, from nature, from farming, and from
mythology, are used to give a picture of the night sky
with its stars? Summarize what such a natural scene of
beauty meant for Hopkins.

(B) Write a descriptive passage in prose or verse about a
starry sky at night.

In the Valley of the Elwy (p. 118)

This sonnet is a delicate picture of kind people in a
beautiful landscape (though in fact Hopkins was thinking
of a Kentish family, the Watsons, who had been kind to
him); in the sestet he says that the Welsh people are not
so good as they should be in such natural beauty, and
begs God to make them so.

l. 4 The smell of woodsmoke?

l. 9 *combes:* valleys.

l. 11 Only the person who dwells in the 'lovely' landscape 'does
not correspond'.

l. 12 Weighing and balancing all things.

l. 14 God is both all-powerful ('mighty a master') and all-
merciful ('a father and fond').

(A) Explain carefully what is meant by a 'hood' in l. 5, and
what two other things it is compared to. Suggest meanings

for 'cordial' (l. 5), 'bevy' (l. 6). Point out some examples of alliteration and sound echoes. Say whether you think this poem as successful as *The Starlight Night*, giving your reasons.

My Own Heart . . . (p. 118)

This very powerful sonnet and the following one belong to a group written towards the end of the poet's life, and sometimes referred to as 'the terrible sonnets'. Here he is, as it were, advising himself to make less stern demands on himself, to give comfort room for growth ('root-room'), to accept that pleasure and beauty will come not by an act of will, but when God wishes it.

ll. 5 –8   I cast around for a comfort which I can no more get by groping round my comfortless world than a blind man can see day or a thirsty mariner quench his thirst though surrounded by water.

l. 9   *Jackself:* his ordinary workaday self (compare 'Jack Tar' for an ordinary sailor, jack-knife).

l. 10   *let be:* stop being jaded.

l. 11   *size:* grow or diminish according to circumstances (a verb).

ll. 11 –12   *whose smile's not wrung:* pleasure or happiness doesn't come from being forced ('wrung') but rather in unforeseen circumstances.

l. 14   *betweenpie:* an extraordinary word, apparently meaning that the skies between dark mountains may be brightly dappled (see *Pied Beauty*) and light up casually and accidentally a 'lovely mile'.

(A)   What is the effect of the repetitions in ll. 3 and 4? Do you consider them successful poetically? Where do you find inversions of the usual order of words, and what is their effect? Express in your own words l. 11 (from 'let joy size') to the end of the poem. Do you find the language strained, and if so, where? Is there some excuse for this in such a poem?

Thou art indeed just, Lord . . . (p. 119)

A most touching poem, one of the latest that Hopkins wrote, expressing his almost total despair at his failure and sense of impotence in the face of evil; it is saved by the faint hope that even now he may be able to grow if Gód will 'send my roots rain'.

ll. 1– A very close transcription of the opening of Chapter 12
4 of Jeremiah in the Old Testament, which you should look up.

l. 7 *sots*: drunkards; *thralls*: slaves.

l. 9 *brakes*: thickets.

l. 11 *chervil*: a herb rather like cow-parsley appearing early in spring and with beautifully cut and ruffled ('fretty') foliage.

(A) Explain ll. 5–7. What is the purpose of the lines about the spring plants and the birds, and with what do they contrast? Why does he call himself 'Time's eunuch', and how does this relate to 'breed' (l. 13)? Why is the last line fitting to what has gone before, and what does it mean?

FURTHER READING

Selection of Poems and Prose, ed. W. H. Gardner (Penguin); a very full selection.

Notebooks and Papers, ed. H. House (Oxford). Sample only: Hopkins's journals show some of the precise observation of nature in his poems.

CRITICAL WRITING

F. N. Iles. "Gerard Manley Hopkins" (an essay in *Pelican Guide to English Literature*, Vol. 5).

John Pick. *G. M. Hopkins, Priest and Poet* (Oxford). A good short analysis of his life and poetry.

W. H. Gardner. *Gerard Manley Hopkins: a Study* (long and difficult: only for reference).

F. R. Leavis. *New Bearings in English Poetry* (Chatto and Windus). Use the index for reference to Hopkins.

Thomas Hardy

THOMAS HARDY was born in Dorset in 1840, the son of a stonemason, and passed his childhood among still vigorous village traditions, which affected his imagination and outlook throughout his life. He was educated locally with some private tuition in languages. He was trained as an ecclesiastical architect, worked on church restorations and won architectural prizes. He wrote verse as a young man, and then mainly worked as a novelist from 1871–97. His last novel, *Jude the Obscure*, offended orthodox opinion, and he ended his career as a novelist and returned to his first love, poetry. From then till his death he wrote entirely in verse, including a huge epic drama, *The Dynasts*. He married first Emma Gifford in 1874; she died in 1912 and he married Florence Dugdale in 1914. He was awarded the Order of Merit, but remained as a person simple and generous until his death in 1928.

Hardy is remarkable—probably unique apart from D. H. Lawrence and possibly Robert Graves—in being both a leading novelist and a leading poet. He was very close to country life and country people, and spent most of his adult life in or near Dorchester; one way of looking at his work is as a chronicle of the rapid changes taking place in the life of the country throughout the wide span of his life. His language, highly wrought though it is, always has the firmness and simplicity of rural speech somewhere in the background. Most of his poems are lyrics—that is, the direct embodiment of a personal feeling—but he wrote in several other modes; for example, he wrote many narrative poems, often in rural settings, many of which now seem melodramatic, though some still have real power. He saw man as the victim of destiny, not its master—a victim of chance and the remorselessness of time; and some of the titles of his volumes of verse reflect this belief—*Time's Laughing-stocks, Life's Little Ironies, Satires of Circumstance.*

This sense of an 'Ironic Will' governing the universe is apparent in some of the poems that follow (for example *The Darkling Thrush* and *To an Unborn Pauper Child*, pp. 134 and 137).

Hardy's total output of verse is large—the collected poems run to 800 pages—and a good deal of it is 'occasional' verse. The bulk of it is highly individual in tone and style, and it is possible for an experienced reader to identify almost any short passage as being Hardy's. Perhaps its overwhelming quality is its honesty—an honesty which sometimes causes clumsiness, cragginess, awkwardness, but precludes entirely the elegant smoothness which was common in Victorian poetry, and so often concealed insincerity, or at least lack of real concern, in the poet. This honesty produces a strange tang in the writing, which grows on one with experience; he describes the newly-unfurled leaves of the beech:

> . . . the May month flaps its glad green leaves like wings
> Delicate-filmed as new-spun silk.

(Only Hardy, perhaps, could have used 'flaps' and 'glad' in this way.)

A stretch of ploughland in February:

> While the fallow ploughland turned up nigh
> In raw rolls, clammy and clogging lie—

'Raw rolls' (and the rest of the line) is not pretty, but it gives exactly the sticky consistency of a clayey soil in the month of 'February fill-dyke'; it is as if the rhythm itself is sticky to express our physical sensations

> Too cloggy for feet to pass.

At dawn by the sea:

> The waked birds preen and the seals flop lazily.

Tennyson and most of the Victorians would have avoided so commonplace and prosaic a word as 'flop'; yet it seems exactly the word for the movement, and the sound, of seals on a wet sandbank.

Hardy's greatest achievement is now considered to be in his elegiac poetry, particularly in a group of poems he wrote in 1912–13 in which he calls up memories of his early married life. These show a fortitude and sensitivity in the face of loss which is all the more impressive because it is set against the cruelty of time, and because he shows no touch of self-pity. These poems show an exquisite sense of place combined with a profound understanding of his own experiences, and a courageous and stoical facing of inevitable loss; among the elegiac poems in this selection are *The Voice* (p. 136), and *During Wind and Rain* (p. 142). Right to the end, though 'frail' and 'faltering forward', and though revered as one of the greatest writers of his time, he remains a man of utter simplicity and modesty, as his own elegy shows; he hopes to be remembered as one who sympathized with hedgehogs, had an eye for the nightjar landing on 'the wind-swept upland thorn'—as one who 'used to notice such things'.

An August Midnight

I

A shaded lamp and a waving blind,
And the beat of a clock from a distant floor:
On this scene enter—winged, horned, and spined—
A longlegs, a moth, and a dumbledore;   4
While 'mid my page there idly stands
A sleepy fly, that rubs its hands ...

II

Thus meet we five, in this still place,
At this point of time, at this point in space.   8
— My guests besmear my new-penned line,
Or bang at the lamp and fall supine.
'God's humblest, they!' I muse. Yet why?
They know Earth-secrets that know not I.   12

Weathers

I

This is the weather the cuckoo likes,
    And so do I;
When showers betumble the chestnut spikes,
    And nestlings fly:
And the little brown nightingale bills his best,

And they sit outside at 'The Travellers' Rest',
And maids come forth sprig-muslin drest,
And citizens dream of the south and west,   8
    And so do I.

II

This is the weather the shepherd shuns,
    And so do I;
When beeches drip in browns and duns,   12
    And thresh, and ply;
And hill-hid tides throb, throe on throe,
And meadow rivulets overflow,
And drops on gate-bars hang in a row,   16
And rooks in families homeward go,
    And so do I.

The Darkling Thrush

I leant upon a coppice gate
    When Frost was spectre-gray,
And Winter's dregs made desolate
    The weakening eye of day.   4
The tangle bine-stems scored the sky
    Like strings of broken lyres,
And all mankind that haunted nigh
    Had sought their household fires.   8

The land's sharp features seemed to be
    The Century's corpse outleant,
His crypt the cloudy canopy,
    The wind his death-lament.   12

The ancient pulse of germ and birth
    Was shrunken hard and dry,
And every spirit upon earth
    Seemed fervourless as I.   16

At once a voice arose among
    The bleak twigs overhead
In a full-hearted evensong
    Of joy illimited;   20
An aged thrush, frail, gaunt, and small,
    In blast-beruffled plume,
Had chosen thus to fling his soul
    Upon the growing gloom.   24

So little cause for carollings
    Of such ecstatic sound
Was written on terrestrial things
    Afar or nigh around,   28
That I could think there trembled through
    His happy good-night air
Some blessed Hope, whereof he knew
    And I was unaware.   32

The Self-Unseeing

Here is the ancient floor,
Footworn and hollowed and thin,
Here was the former door
Where the dead feet walked in.   4

She sat here in her chair,
Smiling into the fire;
He who played stood there,
Bowing it higher and higher.   8

Childlike, I danced in a dream;
Blessings emblazoned that day;
Everything glowed with a gleam;
Yet we were looking away!   12

The Voice

Woman much missed, how you call to me, call to me,
Saying that now you are not as you were
When you had changed from the one who was all to me,
But as at first, when our day was fair.   4

Can it be you that I hear? Let me view you, then,
Standing as when I drew near to the town
Where you would wait for me: yes, as I knew you then,
Even to the original air-blue gown!   8

Or is it only the breeze, in its listlessness
Travelling across the wet mead to me here,
You being ever dissolved to wan wistlessness,
Heard no more again far or near?   12

Thus I; faltering forward,
Leaves around me falling,
Wind oozing thin through the thorn from norward,
And the woman calling.   16

To an Unborn Pauper Child

I

Breathe not, hid Heart: cease silently,
And though thy birth-hour beckons thee,
    Sleep the long sleep:
    The Doomsters heap
Travails and teens around us here,
And Time-wraiths turn our songsingings to fear.

II

Hark, how the peoples surge and sigh,
And laughters fail, and greetings die:
    Hopes dwindle; yea,
    Faiths waste away,
Affections and enthusiasms numb;
Thou canst not mend these things if thou dost come.

III

Had I the ear of wombèd souls
Ere their terrestrial chart unrolls,
    And thou wert free
    To cease, or be,
Then would I tell thee all I know,
And put it to thee: Wilt thou take Life so?

IV

Vain vow! No hint of mine may hence
To theeward fly: to thy locked sense
    Explain none can
    Life's pending plan:

Thou wilt thy ignorant entry make
Though skies spout fire and blood and nations quake.

V

Fain would I, dear, find some shut plot
Of earth's wide wold for thee, where not
One tear, one qualm,
Should break the calm.
But I am weak as thou and bare;
No man can change the common lot to rare.

VI

Must come and bide. And such are we—
Unreasoning, sanguine, visionary—
That I can hope
Health, love, friends, scope
In full for thee; can dream thou wilt find
Joys seldom yet attained by humankind!

Neutral Tones

We stood by a pond that winter day,
And the sun was white, as though chidden of God,
And a few leaves lay on the starving sod;
— They had fallen from an ash, and were gray. 4

Your eyes on me were as eyes that rove
Over tedious riddles of years ago;
And some words played between us to and fro
On which lost the more by our love. 8

The smile on your mouth was the deadest thing
Alive enough to have strength to die;
And a grin of bitterness swept thereby
  Like an ominous bird a-wing . . .   12

Since then, keen lessons that love deceives,
And wrings with wrong, have shaped to me
Your face, and the God-curst sun, and a tree,
  And a pond edged with grayish leaves.   16

We Sat at the Window

We sat at the window looking out,
And the rain came down like silken strings
That Swithin's day. Each gutter and spout
Babbled unchecked in the busy way   4
  Of witless things:
Nothing to read, nothing to see
Seemed in that room for her and me
  On Swithin's day.   8

We were irked by the scene, by our own selves; yes,
For I did not know, nor did she infer
How much there was to read and guess
By her in me, and to see and crown   12
  By me in her.
Wasted were two souls in their prime,
And great was the waste, that July time
  When the rain came down.   16

At Middle-Field Gate in February

The bars are thick with drops that show
   As they gather themselves from the fog
Like silver buttons ranged in a row,
And as evenly spaced as if measured, although
   They fall at the feeblest jog.   5

They load the leafless hedge hard by,
   And the blades of last year's grass,
While the fallow ploughland turned up nigh
In raw rolls, clammy and clogging lie—
   Too clogging for feet to pass.   10

How dry it was on a far-back day
   When straws hung the hedge and around,
When amid the sheaves in amorous play
In curtained bonnets and light array
   Bloomed a bevy now underground!   15

Molly Gone

No more summer for Molly and me;
   There is snow on the tree,
And the blackbirds plump large as rooks are, almost,
   And the water is hard
Where they used to dip bills at the dawn ere her figure was
   lost
   To these coasts, now my prison close-barred.

No more planting by Molly and me
    Where the beds used to be
Of sweet-william; no training the clambering rose
    By the framework of fir
Now bowering the pathway, whereon it swings gaily and
blows
    As if calling commendment from her.   12

No more jauntings by Molly and me
    To the town by the sea,
Or along over Whitesheet to Wynyard's green Gap,
    Catching Montacute Crest
To the right against Sedgmoor, and Corton-Hill's far-
distant cap,
    And Pilsdon and Lewsdon to west.   18

No more singing by Molly to me
    In the evenings when she
Was in mood and in voice, and the candles were lit,
    And past the porch-quoin
The rays would spring out on the laurels; and dumbledores
hit
    On the pane, as if wishing to join.   24

Where, then, is Molly, who's no more with me?
    — As I stand on this lea,
Thinking thus, there's a many-flamed star in the air,
    That tosses a sign
That her glance is regarding its face from her home, so
that there
    Her eyes may have meetings with mine.   30

During Wind and Rain

They sing their dearest songs—
He, she, all of them—yea,
Treble and tenor and bass,
    And one to play;
With the candles mooning each face . . .   5
    Ah, no; the years O!
How the sick leaves reel down in throngs!

They clear the creeping moss—
Elders and juniors—aye,
Making the pathways neat   10
    And the garden gay;
And they build a shady seat . . .
    Ah, no; the years, the years;
See, the white storm-birds wing across!

They are blithely breakfasting all—   15
Men and maidens—yea,
Under the summer tree,
    With a glimpse of the bay,
While pet fowl come to the knee . . .
    Ah, no; the years O!   20
And the rotten rose is ript from the wall.

They change to a high new house,
He, she, all of them—aye,
Clocks and carpets and chairs
    On the lawn all day,   25
And brightest things that are theirs . . .
    Ah, no; the years, the years;
Down their carved names the rain-drop ploughs.

The Walk

You did not walk with me
Of late to the hill-top tree
    By the gated ways,
    As in earlier days;
    You were weak and lame,
    So you never came,
And I went alone, and I did not mind,
Not thinking of you as left behind.

I walked up there today
Just in the former way;
    Surveyed around
    The familiar ground
    By myself again:
    What difference, then?
Only that underlying sense
Of the look of a room on returning thence.

The Five Students

The sparrow dips in his wheel-rut bath,
    The sun grows passionate-eyed,
And boils the dew to smoke by the paddock-path;
    As strenuously we stride,—
Five of us; dark He, fair He, dark She, fair She, I,
    All beating by.   6

The air is shaken, the high-road hot,
    Shadowless swoons the day,

The greens are sobered and cattle at rest; but not
    We on our urgent way, —
Four of us; fair She, dark She, fair He, I, are there,
    But one—elsewhere.   12

    Autumn moulds the hard fruit mellow,
      And forward still we press
Through moors, briar-meshed plantations, clay-pits
    yellow,
      As in the spring hours—yes,
Three of us; fair He, fair She, I, as heretofore,
    But—fallen one more.   18

    The leaf drops: earthworms draw it in
      At night-time noiselessly,
The fingers of birch and beech are skeleton-thin,
      And yet on the beat are we, —
Two of us; fair She, I. But no more left to go
    The track we know.   24

    Icicles tag the church-aisle leads,
      The flag-rope gibbers hoarse,
The home bound foot-folk wrap their snow-flaked heads,
      Yet I still stalk the course —
One of us . . . Dark and fair He, dark and fair She, gone:
    The rest—anon.   30

Afterwards

When the Present has latched its postern behind my
    tremulous stay,
  And the May month flaps its glad green leaves like wings,
Delicate-filmed as new-spun silk, will the neighbours say,
  "He was a man who used to notice such things"?   4

If it be in the dusk when, like an eyelid's soundless blink,
  The dewfall-hawk comes crossing the shades to alight
Upon the wind-warped upland thorn, a gazer might
      think,
    "To him this must have been a familiar sight."   8

If I pass during some nocturnal blackness, mothy and
      warm,
  When the hedgehog travels furtively over the lawn,
One may say, "He strove that such innocent creatures
      should come to no harm,
    But he could do little for them; and now he is gone." 12

If, when hearing that I have been stilled at last, they
      stand at the door,
  Watching the full-starred heavens that winter sees,
Will this thought rise on those who will meet my face no
      more,
    "He was one who had an eye for such mysteries"?   16

And will any say when my bell of quittance is heard in
      the gloom,
  And a crossing breeze cuts a pause in its outrollings,
Till they rise again, as they were a new bell's boom,
    "He hears it not now, but used to notice such things"? 20

Notes

An August Midnight (p. 133)

l. 4   *dumbledore:* dialect word for a cockchafer, a clumsy flying beetle.

(A)   Consider in detail what the poet is doing and where. Who are 'we five', and what are the implications of this phrase? What do the last two lines mean?

(B)   Write a poem or short story in the first person, in which you meet some animals or insects alone in a quiet place at night.

Weathers (p. 133)

l. 3   The horse chestnut (conker tree) which has spikes of blossom like candelabra, which sometimes cover the ground below after a shower.

l. 7   *sprig-muslin:* cotton material for summer dresses printed over with small sprigs of blossom

l. 13   *thresh and ply:* beat and move restlessly against the wind.

l. 14   Perhaps a reference to the sea, audible but not visible, or perhaps to underground streams.

(A)   Suggest a month which would best suit verse I, and another for verse II. What features link the two verses, and what features offer a contrast? Why do citizens 'dream of the south and west'? Contrast the last two lines of verse I with those of verse II, and say what different sensations they express.

(B)   Write a corresponding poem of two verses in which summer and winter (rather than spring and autumn) are contrasted; use Hardy's 'burden-lines', or, better, invent your own.

The Darkling Thrush (p. 134)

It is necessary to know that Hardy wrote this poem at the turn of the nineteenth century (see verse 2).

l. 5   *bine-stems:* dead stems of a climbing plant, perhaps bindweed (bell-bine).

l. 11   *crypt:* burial-place; *canopy:* covering, *e.g.,* of a bed.

l. 27   *terrestrial:* earthly.

(A)   What features of the landscape promote the poet's gloom, and which lines stress his solitude? What significance do you attach to the description of the thrush (ll. 21–22)? Express in your own words the meaning of the last verse. In what ways does the theme of this poem link with *An August Midnight?*

The Self-Unseeing (p. 135)

(A)   In what sense did 'the *dead* feet' walk in? Who might 'she' and 'he' be? What does the poet mean by the last line? What does the title mean?

(B)   Write a poem or short story in which you remember a childhood occasion when everything was perfect and yet you did not recognize it at the time.

The Voice (p. 136)

Hardy here writes as an old man, remembering the happy days of his first marriage ('when our day was fair').

l. 8   This line describes a vivid memory of a dress his wife wore and its colour.

l. 9   *listlessness:* weariness, without energy or vigour.

l. 11   *wistlessness:* state of being unknown, forgotten.

(A)   In which lines does the poet express the belief that he hears his wife, and wants to see her? In what circumstances? Where does he doubt that it can be her voice? What is the effect of the shorter lines in verse 4? What meaning do you attach to the landscape in this last verse?

To an Unborn Pauper Child (p. 137)

A note to Hardy's poem says: '"She must go to the Union-house to have her baby": Casterbridge Petty Sessions.' The children of paupers would often have to be born into the dreadful bleakness of a workhouse (see *Far from the Madding Crowd*, where Fanny Robin's child is born in 'the Union'—Chapters 40–43).

v. 1   The poet advises the unborn child not to be born; *Doomsters*: the fates or destinies; *travails and teens*: worries and troubles; *Time-wraiths*: phantom powers of time.

v. 2   He sees life as inherently hopeless; the child cannot cure these evils.

v. 3   If he could speak to the unborn before the chart of their earthly life begins he would ask them whether such a life is worth living.

v. 4   But he cannot do so, and the child will be born whatever disasters may lie ahead.

v. 5   He wishes he could find some safe place for the child, but knows he can't. *Fain would I*: I wish that I could; *wold*: open country.

v. 6   We must all be born and endure life, and he wishes for the impossible—complete fulfilment.

(A)   Which lines show that Hardy sees human hopes as doomed to failure? Which line seems prophetic of modern war? Where does he show a personal affection for the unborn child, where does he feel helpless, and where is there a hint of hope? How does this poem relate to *The Darkling Thrush*?

Neutral Tones (p. 138)

l. 2   *chidden of God*: rebuked by God.

v. 4   Every time he learns again that love brings wrong, he recalls again the exact spot in which he quarrelled with his wife. l. 14. *have shaped*: have brought back to my mind.

(A)   What features of the landscape are memorable to the poet, and why are they repeated? How do these features relate to the title, and how are they appropriate?

(B)   Write a poem or short story in which a lovers' quarrel takes place in a landscape appropriate to it.

We Sat at the Window (p. 139)

Again the poet looks back to the early years of his first marriage, and again with a sense of great loss.

l. 3   Swithin's Day: there is a legend that if it rains on St

Swithin's Day (July 15th) it will rain every day for forty days.

l. 5   *witless:* things lacking in knowledge or understanding.
l. 9   *irked:* irritated.
(A)   What does the poet now think they should have done on that day? Is there any significance in its being St Swithin's Day in relation to their behaviour? What exactly was the 'waste'?
(B)   Write a poem or short story in which two people fail to make contact or see the opportunities of even unpromising circumstances.

At Middle-Field Gate in February (p. 140)

l. 10   A description of heavy wet soil newly ploughed.
(A)   Where else in this selection does Hardy remind you of the first verse of this poem? What contrast in the weathers and scene is there between verses 2 and 3? Put the last three lines in your own words.

Molly Gone (p. 140)

Once again Hardy remembers vividly a past friendship or love affair; Molly might be his sister, or his wife.
ll. 4–6   The birds cannot now sip from the ice-covered water as they did before Molly vanished ('ere her figure was lost') from these parts, where I am now, as it were, imprisoned.
l. 12   As if seeking her praise.
v. 3   The place-names are all in Dorset or the West Country.
l. 22   *porch-quoin:* the corner of the porch, where the shiny leaves of the laurel outside would 'pick up' the candle-light.
l. 23   *dumbledores:* see notes on *An August Midnight.*
v. 5   He fancies that she is looking at the same star that he is, though she is long dead.
(A)   How are the subjects of verses 2, 3, and 4 contrasted? Describe in your own words the three contrasting kinds of activity.
(B)   Write a poem or short composition describing activities of three contrasted kinds with a friend, real or imaginary, whom you have lost contact with.

During Wind and Rain (p. 142)

In this poem, Hardy recalls the family life of many years ago, contrasting his memories with the present truths of the last line of each verse.

ll. 1– A Victorian family group singing round the piano.
5

ll. 17 A distant view of the sea from the garden breakfast-table.
–18

l. 19 *pet fowl:* wild birds, half-tame, coming for crumbs.

l. 21 A dead climbing rose is torn from the wall, by the wind or human agency.

ll. 21 The excitement of moving house.
–25

(A) Suggest what is meant by 'dearest' and 'mooning' in verse 1, 'blithely' in verse 3 and 'brightest' in verse 4. The whole poem is in the present tense: what distinction would you draw between the tense of (for example) 'sing' and 'reel' in verse one? What have the last lines of the four verses in common, and how do they contrast with the rest of the verses? Explain in your own words the last line of the poem.

(B) Write a story or poem in which an old man sits by his study window and remembers the remote past when he was a young married man.

The Walk (p. 143)

An apparently slight but subtle poem of memory; he was alone on his walk in the past, and is only conscious of her absence from the room and therefore, in a sense, from his walk, when he returns.

The Five Students (p. 143)

This poem is close in feeling to *Molly Gone*.

l. 15 *briar-meshed:* tangled with briars or wild roses.

l. 25 *leads:* the eaves, made of lead, are hung with icicles.

l. 26 *The flag-rope gibbers hoarse:* perhaps the rope holding the flag on its staff groans in the wind.

(A) How do the five verses relate? What do you take to be the season of each verse, and why is this appropriate? In which verse are there five *students?* Is there any contrast in the verbs or phrases describing their movements? What does the last line mean?

Afterwards (p. 144)

This makes a fitting ending to this group of poems, as Hardy anticipates, but not at all gloomily, his own death.

l. 1   *latched its postern:* shut its small door; the idea is that the poet's 'tremulous stay' is his life, and that the 'Present' will at length shut him out.

l. 3   A description which would well fit the silky unfolding leaves of the beech.

l. 6   *dewfall-hawk:* perhaps a barn-owl, or a nightjar.

l. 7   *wind-warped:* permanently twisted and misshapen by the wind.

l. 17   *bell of quittance:* passing-bell, indicating that he has died.

l. 18   The wind cuts across the sound of the bell and momentarily stops it.

(A)   Explain 'tremulous stay', 'delicate-filmed', 'like an eyelid's soundless blink', 'mothy', 'furtively'. What signs of modesty and unobtrusiveness do you see here? How does he show detachment and calm about his own death? What would he most like to be remembered for? Show how he displays a special interest in transitory, delicate, or fleeting things. How does the poem show that he "used to notice such things" and why is this refrain used for the first *and* last verse?

(B)   Write an epitaph in prose or verse for yourself or someone you know, showing what you or he would like to be remembered for.

FURTHER READING

(1) *Poetry.*
Selected Poems of Thomas Hardy, ed. Furbank (Longman): an attractive fairly short selection.
Collected Poems (Macmillan).
(2) *Novels* (a selection).
Far from the Madding Crowd.

The Mayor of Casterbridge.
The Return of the Native.
Tess of the d'Urbervilles.
The Woodlanders.

CRITICAL WRITING

Introduction to the Furbank selection, above.
Douglas Brown. *Thomas Hardy* (Macmillan).

Wilfred Owen

WILFRED OWEN was born in Oswestry, Shropshire, in 1893, and educated at the Birkenhead Institute, Liverpool, and at London University. He early had ambitions to be a poet, and wrote a good deal of youthful verse. After a severe illness in 1913 he went to France for health reasons, and became a tutor at Bordeaux, where he remained till 1915. He joined the Artists' Rifles in that year and later the Manchester Regiment. He fell ill after a long experience of trench warfare, and was sent to a military hospital near Edinburgh, where he met the poet Siegfried Sassoon, who had a great influence on him and encouraged him to write directly about the war. Plans were made to publish some of his poems. He was redrafted to France, awarded the M.C., but was killed on November 4th, 1918, a week before the armistice. A very few poems appeared in periodicals during his lifetime; Siegfried Sassoon collected and published them in 1920.

Examples of Owen's pre-war poetry can be studied in Edward Blunden's memoir of 1931; it began as rather lush and imitative verse very much in the manner of Keats, whom he deeply admired. The radical change in his art came when he met Sassoon, already an established 'war poet', who had no illusions about the war and wrote powerful satirical poems against it as well as *Memoirs of an Infantry Officer* (which, together with Blunden's *Undertones of War*, is among the finest first-hand accounts of the First World War in English). Owen had earlier experimented with various new technical devices, especially with 'half-rhymes' (see, for example, *Strange Meeting*, p. 160) and was now able in one magnificent burst of poetry to make his protest at the savagery of war from the bitterest personal experience of life in the trenches (see his letters from the front). His range in this short time is wide: he can write bitter satire (*Inspection*, for example, p. 159, or *The*

Dead-Beat, p. 157, touching and delicate elegiac poetry (*The Send-Off*, p. 155, and *Anthem for Doomed Youth*, p. 158), and perhaps at his strongest, poems which speak directly to humanity and put the anguish of the individual soldier in a truly universal frame (*Strange Meeting*, p. 160, *Futility*, p. 161).

Edmund Blunden writes that Owen till the last moment was preparing himself for "a volume of poems, to strike at the conscience of England in regard to the continuance of the war", and among Owen's papers was found a hastily written draft preface to the volume he was planning, in which he writes: "This book is not about heroes. English Poetry is not yet fit to speak of them. Nor is it about deeds, or lands, nor anything about glory, honour, might, majesty, dominion, or power, except War. Above all I am not concerned with Poetry. My subject is War, and the pity of War. The Poetry is in the pity. Yet these elegies are to this generation in no sense consolatory. They may be to the next. All a poet can do today is warn. That is why the true Poets must be truthful." These jottings—they were no more—express with a touching and yet powerful authority Owen's sense of his duty and his sense of his own rôle; it is a thousand miles away from the soft dreaminess of his Keatsian verses of so few years before. Here is a poet utterly dedicated to a task beyond all thoughts of himself or indeed of poetry for its own sake; "Above all I am not concerned with Poetry" is an extraordinary statement for so dedicated a poet to make, and by a paradox it is in the act of forgetting about art and poetry that he wrote his most successful poems; driven by an experience which he shared with millions of his fellow-soldiers, he became a kind of spokesman for them all, and thus used poetry in the most powerful way that it can be used: "The Poetry is in the pity."

The Send-Off

Down the close, darkening lanes they sang their way
To the siding-shed,
And lined the train with faces grimly gay.

Their breasts were stuck all white with wreath and spray
As men's are, dead.   5

Dull porters watched them, and a casual tramp
Stood staring hard,
Sorry to miss them from the upland camp.
Then, unmoved, signals nodded, and a lamp
Winked to the guard.   10

So secretly, like wrongs hushed-up, they went.
They were not ours:
We never heard to which front these were sent.

Nor there if they yet mock what women meant
Who gave them flowers.   15

Shall they return to beatings of great bells
In wild train-loads?
A few, a few, too few for drums and yells,
May creep back, silent, to village wells
Up half-known roads.   20

Dulce et Decorum Est

Bent double, like old beggars under sacks,
Knock-kneed, coughing like hags, we cursed through
   sludge,
Till on the haunting flares we turned our backs,
And towards our distant rest began to trudge.
Men marched asleep. Many had lost their boots, 5
But limped on, blood-shod. All went lame, all blind;
Drunk with fatigue; deaf even to the hoots
Of gas-shells dropping softly behind.

Gas! Gas! Quick, boys!—An ecstasy of fumbling,
Fitting the clumsy helmets just in time, 10
But someone still was yelling out and stumbling
And floundering like a man in fire or lime.—
Dim through the misty panes and thick green light,
As under a green sea, I saw him drowning.

In all my dreams before my helpless sight 15
He plunges at me, guttering, choking, drowning.

If in some smothering dreams, you too could pace
Behind the wagon that we flung him in,
And watch the white eyes writhing in his face,
His hanging face, like a devil's sick of sin; 20
If you could hear, at every jolt, the blood
Come gargling from the froth-corrupted lungs,
Bitter as the cud
Of vile, incurable sores on innocent tongues,—
My friend, you would not tell with such high zest 25
To children ardent for some desperate glory,
The old Lie: *Dulce et decorum est
Pro patria mori.*

The Dead-Beat

He dropped,—more sullenly than wearily,
Lay stupid like a cod, heavy like meat,
And none of us could kick him to his feet;
Just blinked at my revolver, blearily;
—Didn't appear to know a war was on,   5
Or see the blasted trench at which he stared.
"I'll do 'em in," he whined. "If this hand's spared,
I'll murder them, I will."

                   A low voice said,
"It's Blighty, p'raps, he sees; his pluck's all gone,   10
Dreaming of the valiant, that aren't dead:
Bold uncles, smiling ministerially;
Maybe his brave young wife, getting her fun
In some new home, improved materially.
It's not these stiffs have crazed him; nor the Hun."   15

We sent him down at last, out of the way.
Unwounded;—stout lad, too, before that strafe.
Malingering? Stretcher-bearers winked, "Not half!"
Next day I heard the Doc.'s well-whiskied laugh:
"That scum you sent last night soon died. Hooray!"   20

Mental Cases

Who are these? Why sit they here in twilight?
Wherefore rock they, purgatorial shadows,
Drooping tongues from jaws that slob their relish,
Baring teeth that leer like skulls' teeth wicked?

Stroke on stroke of pain,—but what slow panic   5
Gouged these chasms round their fretted sockets?
Ever from their hair and through their hands' palms
Misery swelters. Surely we have perished
Sleeping, and walk hell; but who these hellish?

—These are men whose minds the Dead have ravished.   10
Memory fingers in their hair of murders,
Multitudinous murders they once witnessed.
Wading sloughs of flesh these helpless wander,
Treading blood from lungs that had loved laughter.
Always they must see these things and hear them,   15
Batter of guns and shatter of flying muscles,
Carnage incomparable, and human squander,
Rucked too thick for these men's extrication.

Therefore still their eyeballs shrink tormented
Back into their brains, because on their sense   20
Sunlight seems a blood-smear; night comes blood-black;
Dawn breaks open like a wound that bleeds afresh.
—Thus their heads wear this hilarious, hideous,
Awful falseness of set-smiling corpses.
—Thus their hands are plucking at each other;   25
Picking at the rope-knouts of their scourging;
Snatching after us who smote them, brother,
Pawing us who dealt them war and madness.

Anthem for Doomed Youth

What passing-bells for these who die as cattle?
　　Only the monstrous anger of the guns.
　　Only the stuttering rifles' rapid rattle
Can patter out their hasty orisons.   4

No mockeries for them from prayers or bells,
   Nor any voice of mourning save the choirs,—
The shrill, demented choirs of wailing shells;
   And bugles calling for them from sad shires.   8

What candles may be held to speed them all?
   Not in the hands of boys, but in their eyes
Shall shine the holy glimmers of goodbyes.
   The pallor of girls' brows shall be their pall; 12
Their flowers the tenderness of silent minds,
And each slow dusk a drawing-down of blinds.

Inspection

"You! What d'you mean by this?" I rapped.
"You dare come on parade like this?"
"Please, sir, it's "—"'Old yer mouth," the sergeant snapped.
"I take 'is name, sir?"—"Please, and then dismiss."   4

Some days 'confined to camp' he got
For being 'dirty on parade'.
He told me afterwards, the damned spot
Was blood, his own. "Well, blood is dirt," I said.   8

"Blood's dirt," he laughed, looking away
Far off to where his wound had bled
And almost merged for ever into clay.
"The world is washing out its stains," he said.   12
"It doesn't like our cheeks so red.
Young blood's its great objection.
But when we're duly white-washed, being dead,
The race will bear Field-Marshal God's inspection."   16

Strange Meeting

It seemed that out of battle I escaped
Down some profound dull tunnel, long since scooped
Through granites which titanic wars had groined.
Yet also there encumbered sleepers groaned,
Too fast in thought or death to be bestirred.   5
Then, as I probed them, one sprang up, and stared
With piteous recognition in fixed eyes,
Lifting distressful hands as if to bless.
And by his smile, I knew that sullen hall,
By his dead smile I knew we stood in Hell.   10
With a thousand pains that vision's face was grained;
Yet no blood reached there from the upper ground,
And no guns thumped, or down the flues made moan.
"Strange friend," I said, "here is no cause to mourn."
"None," said the other, "save the undone years,   15
The hopelessness. Whatever hope is yours,
Was my life also; I went hunting wild
After the wildest beauty in the world,
Which lies not calm in eyes, or braided hair,
But mocks the steady running of the hour,   20
And if it grieves, grieves richlier than here.
For by my glee might many men have laughed,
And of my weeping something had been left,
Which must die now. I mean the truth untold,
The pity of war, the pity war distilled.   25
Now men will go content with what we spoiled.
Or, discontent, boil bloody, and be spilled.
They will be swift with swiftness of the tigress,
None will break ranks, though nations trek from progress.
Courage was mine, and I had mystery,   30
Wisdom was mine, and I had mastery;

To miss the march of this retreating world
Into vain citadels that are not walled.
Then when much blood had clogged their chariot-wheels
I would go up and wash them from sweet wells,   35
Even with truths that lie too deep for taint.
I would have poured my spirit without stint
But not through wounds; not on the cess of war.
Foreheads of men have bled where no wounds were.
I am the enemy you killed, my friend.   40
I knew you in this dark; for so you frowned
Yesterday through me as you jabbed and killed.
I parried; but my hands were loath and cold.
Let us sleep now. . . ."

Futility

Move him into the sun—
Gently its touch awoke him once,
At home, whispering of fields unsown.
Always it woke him, even in France,
Until this morning and this snow.   5
If anything might rouse him now
The kind old sun will know.

Think how it wakes the seeds,—
Woke, once, the clays of a cold star.
Are limbs, so dear-achieved, are sides,   10
Full-nerved—still warm—too hard to stir?
Was it for this the clay grew tall?
— O what made fatuous sunbeams toil
To break earth's sleep at all?

Notes

The Send-Off (p. 155)

The poem describes soldiers who after training in camp, leave by train for the front, and are 'sent off' by the women of the district.

(A) Explain ll. 4 and 5, by linking them with another line in the poem. What is the significance of the departing soldiers wearing 'wreaths'? How could their faces be 'grimly gay'? What indications are there of acceptance and indifference from the local people and the inanimate objects witnessing their departure? Does anyone seem to care, and if so, why? Comment on 'nodded' and 'winked' (ll. 9 and 10). Why was their departure secret, and how was it 'like wrongs hushed-up'? Will their final return be glorious, and if not, why not? Compare the return with the departure. Why 'half-known roads' (l. 20)?

Dulce et Decorum Est (p. 156)

This bitter and powerful poem tells of exhausted troops returning to billets and subjected to a gas attack. The gas is probably phosgene or chlorine, and its victims 'drown', as it were, in the fluid of their own lungs (ll. 13–15). The title and the last lines are from the Odes of Horace, a Latin poet, and may be translated: 'It is a sweet and seemly thing to die for one's country.'

l. 25 *My friend:* anyone who still accepts the truth of Horace's line; perhaps here a schoolmaster who teaches children to believe such sentiments.

(A) Why are the soldiers 'like old beggars under sacks'? Which line mentions the appalling mud of the battlefield, and which lines describe their fatigue and their loss of the senses? Explain 'blood-shod' (l. 6), 'ecstasy of fumbling' (l. 9). What are the 'helmets' (l. 10) and what are they like? Give carefully in your own words the meaning of ll. 13 and 14, explaining 'misty panes' and 'green light'. The last verse is one long sentence: explain its meaning briefly and the effect of its being one long sentence. In what sense is the 'old Lie' *old*, and how has the poet shown it to be a lie? What is the general impact of such a poem on a new reader?

The Dead-Beat (*p. 157*)

The title refers to someone who is utterly exhausted—in this case even more morally than physically—and the cruel incomprehension of some of his comrades.

l. 10 *Blighty:* England (First World War slang).

l. 15 *stiffs:* corpses.

l. 17 *strafe:* bombardment.

(A) Explain the following words and expressions: 'stupid like a cod' (l. 2), 'ministerially' (l. 12), 'malingering' (l. 18), 'well-whiskied laugh' (l. 19), 'scum' (l. 20). Owen was an officer; why did the 'dead-beat' blink at his revolver? Who do you think are meant by 'them' in l. 8 (see verse 2)? What is the content of each of the three verses? What opinion have the stretcher-bearers and the doctor of the 'dead-beat', and what do you take to be the poet's opinion?

Mental Cases (*p. 157*)

This sombre and terrifying poem draws an unforgettable picture of those soldiers who (like the 'dead-beat', had he lived) have suffered complete mental breakdown as a result of the horrors of trench warfare.

l. 2 *purgatorial:* here, of hell (see ll. 8 and 9).

l. 6 What slow terror of mind hollowed the flesh round their eye-sockets; *fretted:* ridged, or eaten away.

v. 2 They are haunted for ever by the deaths they have witnessed.

l. 17 *squander:* waste.

l. 18 *rucked:* perhaps piled up or heaped.

l. 22 The normal and comforting features of sun and darkness are both stained with blood in their imaginations.

l. 24 The smile of madness.

ll. 25 They pick meaninglessly at one another—but the poet
–28 sees a meaning.

l. 26 *knouts:* whips (a Russian word) used in the past to punish wrongdoers; here the terrible sights and experiences they have lived through.

(A) Who is addressed as 'brother' in l. 27 and in what sense did *we* 'deal them war and madness'?

Anthem for Doomed Youth (p. 158)

This poem is in sonnet form and offers an anthem or song of praise for a whole generation of young men doomed to die in battle.

l. 1 *passing-bell:* bell rung when someone dies (or 'passes on').

l. 4 *orisons:* prayers, especially for the dead.

l. 9 *speed:* send them on their way.

l. 12 *pallor:* paleness; *pall:* the cloth spread over a coffin (the line is a kind of poetic pun).

l. 14 It was, and still sometimes is, the custom to draw down the blinds of a house as a mark of respect for someone's death.

(A) In what way does the *sound* of ll. 2 and 3 contrast, and fit the subject? In what sense could the shells be called 'choirs'? The bugles in l. 8 might be those which blew in English camps when the young men were recruited on a county basis ('sad shires'). Explain ll. 10–11, remembering that in peacetime candles might be held by choirboys at a funeral. In the last line how could 'each slow dusk' be a 'drawing-down of blinds', and who then would be the mourner? What is the general effect of this poem in comparison, say, with *Mental Cases* or *Dulce et Decorum Est*?

Inspection (p. 159)

A bitterly satirical poem in which a soldier is punished for parading with blood on his uniform, and is imagined making an ironic defence.

l. 7 *damned spot:* a reference to Shakespeare's *Macbeth*, where Lady Macbeth, haunted by the murders in which she has been involved, imagines while sleep-walking that she can't free her hands of blood and cries 'Out, damned spot!'

(A) Examine the nature of the dialogue in the first verse, and comment on its skill. In the last verse why does the soldier laugh at the statement 'blood's dirt'? In what sense does he 'look far off to where his wound had bled'? He imagines an inspection of dead soldiers; by whom, and why 'Field-Marshal'? What double meaning do you detect in 'white-washed' (l. 15)? What irony is there in the last five lines?

Strange Meeting (p. 160)

This famous poem is a powerful vision of the meaning of war. The narrator dreams of meeting, after death, a man who shares his love of life and his horror of war, and reveals at the end who he is. A notable feature is the half-rhymes throughout (escaped/scooped, friend/frowned; mystery/mastery). You might like to experiment with this device, which is much less restrictive than ordinary rhyme; here its effect is probably one of sadness.

(A) Describe in your own words the place of meeting (ll.1–10); which lines suggest that it is cut off from the war 'above'? What beauty did the 'strange friend' seek beyond that of physical beauty or love? How does he see the dangers of the future? What truth does he long to tell about the war? He would give all his energy to cleanse the world of war but not to fight in war; where does he say this? In which lines does he reveal his identity and the cause of his death? What is meant by the last half-line? What general idea does the poem seem to you to suggest? (Attend particularly to l. 40.)

Futility (p. 161)

A short and intensely moving poem about a dead farm-worker—who symbolizes all the men killed in the war.

l. 9　The sun once brought life itself to the previously dead earth.

l. 11　*stir*: persuade to move, bring back to life.

l. 12　Was the whole process of evolution, from protoplasm to man himself, designed to end with this pointless death?

(A) Explain ll. 2 and 3. Why did the farm-worker wake early 'even in France' and why not on 'this morning'? What hope is expressed in ll. 6 and 7? What is the connexion between l. 8 and something in the first verse? In what sense are the man's limbs 'dear-achieved' (l. 10)? Explain the last two lines, especially 'fatuous'. Then consider the whole poem in relation to its title.

(B) Write a short story or poem about someone who died young, and the effect of his death on the people who knew him.

FURTHER READING

Collected Poems, ed. C. Day Lewis, including E. Blunden's introduction (Chatto and Windus).

CRITICAL WRITING

D. J. Enright. "The Literature of the First World War" (in *Pelican Guide to English Literature*, Vol. 7, "The Modern Age").

D. S. R. Welland. *Wilfred Owen: A Critical Study* (Chatto and Windus).

Harold Owen. *Journey from Obscurity* (Oxford). Mainly biographical.

Brian Gardner (ed.). *Up the Line to Death* (Methuen). An anthology of First World War poetry with an essay on Owen.

Edward Thomas

EDWARD THOMAS was born in Lambeth, London, in 1878, of Welsh parents; his father was a civil servant. He was educated at St Paul's School, Hammersmith, and Lincoln College, Oxford. In 1899 he married Helen Noble, and they lived in great poverty while he tried to make a living at writing, mainly about the English countryside, *e.g.* *The Woodland Life* (1897), *The South Country* (1909), and works of criticism, including full-length studies of poets and prose-writers and also reviews of new poetry. He reviewed a volume of poems by Robert Frost (see the selection in this anthology, pp. 277–87), who encouraged him to attempt poetry; he began to write poetry in 1912, and was killed in action at Arras in April 1917.

Edward Thomas was determined as a very young man to be a writer, and he persisted in spite of continual anxiety and frustration. Though he was born and bred as a Londoner, he very early grew to love the countryside which lay beyond the suburb he lived in, and spent long periods walking, mainly in the South and West of England, not on the main roads but on bridle paths and ancient tracks, and finding always "a rare beauty in commonplace things". These two factors—an early deep love for the country and the firm intention to write in spite of many offers of better-paid work—remained with him throughout his relatively short life. "Everything in his emotional and intellectual being pressed for life in the country and the freedom of the artist," as Helen Thomas wrote, "and every material consideration was against it." His meeting with Robert Frost was a remarkable turning-point in his life: when the American poet urged him to write verse he said, "I couldn't write a poem to save my life." Yet in the next few years he produced a body of verse which includes some of the most original poems of the period. He is often thought of as a nature poet, and he has indeed marvellous powers of observation of nature, perception, and fidelity to detail. As a friend wrote: "To walk with Edward Thomas in any countryside was to see, hear, smell, and know it with fresh senses. He was as alert to what was happening in and on the earth and the air above it as an animal in the grass or a bird on a tree." But the interest of his best work goes beyond the limiting definition of 'nature poetry': for him nature is never an escape, but a means by which he grapples with his own 'nature'. Nature is the starting-point from which he explores himself, and by implication, mankind in general—particularly, perhaps, the moods and complex reactions promoted by natural beauty and the flux of the seasons.

The great majority who now live in urban surroundings may think of Edward Thomas as dated, since his world is so largely a rural one; but a closer look and further thought will show that the poems deal with enduring aspects of human experience, and in grappling with the nature of man, reveal what F. R. Leavis has called "a distinctively modern sensibility". Their quietness and reticence show his lifelong dislike of rhetoric and gush, and after his long practice in the writing of prose he developed a highly individual and subtle but easy and natural manner, close to the rhythms of ordinary speech. He is often melancholy, though never, I think, morbid, and his characteristic mood is a self-questioning one, probing and giving shape to the more elusive kinds of human experience. The balance and poise of his best poems is not easily achieved, because of his scrupulous sensibility and fine perception, and his early death, like Owen's, was a tragic loss to English poetry.

Tall Nettles

Tall nettles cover up, as they have done
These many springs, the rusty harrow, the plough
Long worn out, and the roller made of stone:
Only the elm butt tops the nettles now.

This corner of the farmyard I like most:
As well as any bloom upon a flower
I like the dust on the nettles, never lost
Except to prove the sweetness of a shower.

Adlestrop

Yes. I remember Adlestrop—
The name, because one afternoon
Of heat the express-train drew up there
Unwontedly. It was late June.   4

The steam hissed. Someone cleared his throat.
No one left and no one came
On the bare platform. What I saw
Was Adlestrop—only the name   8

And willows, willow-herb, and grass,
And meadowsweet, and haycocks dry,
No whit less still and lonely fair
Than the high cloudlets in the sky.   12

And for that minute a blackbird sang
Close by, and round him, mistier,
Farther and farther, all the birds
Of Oxfordshire and Gloucestershire.   16

The Manor Farm

The rock-like mud unfroze a little and rills
Ran and sparkled down each side of the road
Under the catkins wagging in the hedge,
But earth would have her sleep out, spite of the sun;
Nor did I value that thin gilding beam   5
More than a pretty February thing
Till I came down to the old Manor Farm,
And church and yew-tree opposite, in age
Its equals and in size. The church and yew
And farmhouse slept in a Sunday silentness.   10
The air raised not a straw. The steep farm roof,
With tiles duskily glowing, entertained
The mid-day sun; and up and down the roof
White pigeons nestled. There was no sound but one.
Three cart-horses were looking over a gate   15
Drowsily through their forelocks, swishing their tails
Against a fly, a solitary fly.

The Winter's cheek flushed as if he had drained
Spring, Summer, and Autumn at a draught
And smiled quietly. But 'twas not Winter —   20
Rather a season of bliss unchangeable
Awakened from farm and church where it had lain
Safe under tile and thatch for ages since
This England, Old already, was called Merry.

Thaw

Over the land freckled with snow half-thawed
The speculating rooks at their nests cawed
And saw from the elm-tops, delicate as flower of grass,
What we below could not see, Winter pass.

As the Team's Head-brass

As the team's head-brass flashed out on the turn
The lovers disappeared into the wood.
I sat among the boughs of the fallen elm
That strewed the angle of the fallow, and
Watched the plough narrowing a yellow square   5
Of charlock. Every time the horses turned
Instead of treading me down, the ploughman leaned
Upon the handles to say or ask a word,
About the weather, next about the war.
Scraping the share he faced towards the wood,   10
And screwed along the furrow till the brass flashed
Once more.
          The blizzard felled the elm whose crest
I sat in, by a woodpecker's round hole,
The ploughman said. "When will they take it away?" 15
"When the war's over." So the talk began —
One minute and an interval of ten,
A minute more and the same interval.
"Have you been out?" "No." "And don't want to,
          perhaps?"
"If I could only come back again, I should.   20

I could spare an arm. I shouldn't want to lose
A leg. If I should lose my head, why, so,
I should want nothing more. . . . Have many gone
From here?" "Yes." "Many lost?" "Yes, a good few.
Only two teams work on the farm this year.   25
One of my mates is dead. The second day
In France they killed him. It was back in March,
The very night of the blizzard, too. Now if
He had stayed here we should have moved the tree."
"And I should not have sat here. Everything   30
Would have been different. For it would have been
Another world." 'Ay, and a better, though
If we could see all all might seem good." Then
The lovers came out of the wood again:
The horses started and for the last time   35
I watched the clods crumble and topple over
After the ploughshare and the stumbling team.

In Memoriam (Easter 1915)

The flowers left thick at nightfall in the wood
This Eastertide call into mind the men,
Now far from home, who, with their sweethearts, should
Have gathered them and will do never again.

Fifty Faggots

There they stand, on their ends, the fifty faggots
That once were underwood of hazel and ash
In Jenny Pinks's Copse. Now, by the hedge
Close packed, they make a thicket fancy alone

Can creep through with the mouse and wren. Next   5
  Spring
A blackbird or a robin will nest there,
Accustomed to them, thinking they will remain
Whatever is for ever to a bird:
This Spring it is too late; the swift has come.
'Twas a hot day for carrying them up: 10
Better they will never warm me, though they must
Light several Winters' fires. Before they are done
The war will have ended, many other things
Have ended, maybe, that I can no more
Foresee or more control than robin and wren.   15

The Long Small Room

The long small room that showed willows in the west
Narrowed up to the end the fireplace filled,
Although not wide. I liked it. No one guessed
What need or accident made them so build.

Only the moon, the mouse, and the sparrow peeped
In from the ivy round the casement thick.
Of all they saw and heard there they shall keep
The tale for the old ivy and older brick.

When I look back I am like moon, sparrow, and mouse
That witnessed what they could never understand
Or alter or prevent in the dark house.
One thing remains the same—this my right hand

Crawling crab-like over the clean white page,
Resting awhile each morning on the pillow,
Then once more starting to crawl on towards age.
The hundred last leaves stream upon the willow.

Cock-crow

Out of the wood of thoughts that grows by night
To be cut down by the sharp axe of light,—
Out of the night, two cocks together crow,
Cleaving the darkness with a silver blow;   4
And bright before my eyes twin trumpeters stand,
Heralds of splendour, one at either hand,
Each facing each as in a coat of arms:
The milkers lace their boots up at the farms.   8

Digging

Today I think
Only with scents,—scents dead leaves yield,
And bracken, and wild carrot's seed,
And the square mustard field;   4

Odours that rise
When the spade wounds the root of tree,
Rose, currant, raspberry, or goutweed,
Rhubarb or celery;   8

The smoke's smell, too,
Flowing from where a bonfire burns
The dead, the waste, the dangerous,
And all to sweetness turns.   12

It is enough
To smell, to crumble the dark earth,
While the robin sings over again
Sad songs of Autumn mirth.   16

Sowing

It was a perfect day
For sowing; just
As sweet and dry was the ground
As tobacco-dust.   4

I tasted deep the hour
Between the far
Owl's chuckling first soft cry
And the first star.   8

A long stretched hour it was;
Nothing undone
Remained; the early seeds
All safely sown.   12

And now, hark at the rain,
Windless and light,
Half a kiss, half a tear,
Saying good-night.   16

Swedes

They have taken the gable from the roof of clay
On the long swede pile. They have let in the sun
To the white and gold and purple of curled fronds
Unsunned. It is a sight more tender-gorgeous
At the wood-corner where Winter moans and drips   5
Than when, in the Valley of the Tombs of Kings,
A boy crawls down into a Pharaoh's tomb

And, first of Christian men, beholds the mummy,
God and monkey, chariot and throne and vase,
Blue pottery, alabaster, and gold.   10

But dreamless long-dead Amen-hotep lies.
This is a dream of Winter, sweet as Spring.

Aspens

All day and night, save winter, every weather,
Above the inn, the smithy, and the shop,
The aspens at the cross-roads talk together
Of rain, until their last leaves fall from the top.   4

Out of the blacksmith's cavern comes the ringing
Of hammer, shoe, and anvil; out of the inn
The clink, the hum, the roar, the random singing—
The sounds that for these fifty years have been.   8

The whisper of the aspens is not drowned,
And over lightless pane and footless road,
Empty as sky, with every other sound
Not ceasing, calls their ghosts from their abode,   12

A silent smith, a silent inn, nor fails
In the bare moonlight or the thick-furred gloom,
In tempest or the night of nightingales,
To turn the cross-roads to a ghostly room.   16

And it would be the same were no house near.
Over all sorts of weather, men, and times,
Aspens must shake their leaves and men may hear
But need not listen, more than to my rhymes.   20

Whatever wind blows, while they and I have leaves
We cannot other than an aspen be
That ceaselessly, unreasonably grieves,
Or so men think who like a different tree.   24

Notes

Tall Nettles (p. 169)

(A) Suggest why the nettles are so tall, and why only in 'this corner' (why didn't they cut them down?). What is a 'butt' and how does it 'top' the nettles? Where do you detect a pun in the second verse? Why should dust be common there, and why should it cling especially to nettles? Explain carefully the meaning of the last two lines.

(B) Write a short poem or paragraph on the attraction you find in something neglected or overlooked.

Adlestrop (p. 169)

This small poem describes a small railway station and the countryside around with great subtlety and fidelity.

l. 4   *unwontedly*: unexpectedly.

l. 10 *haycocks*: heaps of hay raked together and drying in the sun.

l. 9   *willow-herb*: a purple-flowered wild plant.

l. 10 *meadowsweet*: a moisture-loving plant with sweet-smelling whitish flowers.

l. 11 *no whit*: not in the least.

(A) Why the stress on the name (ll. 2 and 8)? Why didn't the train usually stop there? Suggest why it stopped on this occasion. How many sentences are there in the first two verses, and how many in the last two? Why the difference? What is the point of the two sounds in l. 5? Why did no one leave or come 'on the bare platform'? How do you think the poet's eye travelled over the scene described from l. 8 to l. 12? What two things are compared in the third verse, and in what three respects? Show by further comparison how these two things are alike. What does he mean by 'mistier' (l. 14), and what is it that draws his attention to 'all the birds'? Say as exactly as possible where Adlestrop is from the evidence of the poem. Finally, show how the poem reveals the essence of the landscape of 'the English shires'.

(B) Write in verse or prose about a small railway station you know, whether still open or now closed. Can you see any connexion with Graves's *Here Live your Life Out!* (p. 261)?

The Manor Farm (p. 170)

This poem has a dual subject: it is mainly a delicate description of one of those calm days in February when spring seems to have come, but he is also thinking of the farm and church as embodying the traditions of country life, as the title suggests.

l. 1   *rills:* small streams.
l. 3   *catkins:* probably hazel—the long yellow male blossoms.
ll. 23   The life embodied in the two buildings belongs to the
–24   remote past—when England, already 'old', was called 'Merry England'—right back, in fact, to medieval times.

(A) Describe as closely as you can what 'rock-like mud' would look like in a farm lane. Which line suggests that nature was too wise to awaken so early in the year? What time of day do you think is being described (see l. 10)? Where is the stillness suggested, and what responds to the warmth? Why only one fly (l. 17)? Explain ll. 18–20 ('The Winter's cheek . . . smiled quietly').

Thaw (p. 171)

This tiny and delicate poem catches the moment when the rooks (which nest early in March) become aware, before we can be, of the passing of winter. As in *The Manor Farm*, this poem evokes a notably English scene and attitude to the seasons.

l. 3   *delicate as flower of grass:* the fine structure of twigs at the top of the elm; perhaps also a reference to the very early, though insignificant, blossom of elm.

(A) Comment on the word 'freckled' and say what picture it brings to mind. In what sense are the rooks 'speculating'? Why can the rooks see the passing of winter?

As the Team's Head-brass (p. 171)

This is a more complex poem than the preceding ones. It describes an apparently casual dialogue with a plough-man. The lovers who meet in the wood seem to provide a symbol of permanence, as does the ploughman's work, and both are set against the impact of the war on life and especially on the life of the country.

l. 1   *head-brass:* the horses (probably a pair) wear brass orna-ments ('horse-brasses') hanging from the leather thongs of their harness, on forehead or neck.

l. 6   *charlock:* a yellow-flowered weed.

l. 10   *share:* ploughshare.

(A)   Say in your own words where the poet is exactly, why his conversation with the ploughman takes place at intervals of ten minutes (ll. 15–17); then explain the first line of the poem carefully, and say where there is another reference to it. What is 'it' in l. 15, and where is this referred to again? Identify the two speakers in the dialogue that begins on l. 19, and show who makes each remark. Is there a special reason why the speaker could 'spare an arm' but couldn't bear to 'lose a leg'; what is his attitude to being killed? What is the connexion be-tween the blizzard and the war? What does the speaker mean by ll. 30–31? What do you think is the mood of the poem's conclusion?

(B)   Write a dialogue between two civilians about the impact of war on their lives; or write a casual dialogue between a passer-by and a countryman.

In Memoriam (Easter 1915) (p. 172)

One of Thomas's few direct poems about the war, though he is often haunted by it, as in the last poem and *Fifty Faggots*. It needs no comment, but might be compared with Owen's *The Send-Off* (p. 155).

Fifty Faggots (p. 172)

A gentle thoughtful poem about the bundles of sticks cut from a wood for burning in a wood fire.

(A)   Why are the faggots placed 'on their ends' (l. 1)? What is added by the place name in l. 3? Explain ll. 4–5 ('they make a thicket . . . mouse or wren') and l. 8. What does the arrival of the swift mean (see R. Graves's reference to the 'aerobatic swift' in *Flying Crooked* (p. 256), and for what is it then 'too late'? Explain the meaning of 'Better they will never warm me' (l. 11). Comment on the iast four iines of the poem; what might he be thinking of in writing 'many other things/Have ended, maybe', and was he right?

The Long Small Room (p. *173*)

The poet remembers an oddly shaped room; he cannot identify the fascination it held for him; it is only a memory, and his work as a poet alone links him with the memory.

(A) Describe the room in your own words; do we know why it was such a shape? What three things looked into the room, and how do they differ? To what do they report what they saw and heard? How does the poet compare with them? The house, or its memory, has changed; what remains the same? What is his right hand doing as it crawls 'crab-wise'? Why 'crab-wise'? In what sense is it 'crawling towards age'? What is the connexion between the last two lines, and what connects them with the poem's opening?

Cock-crow (p. *174*)

(A) Explain in your own words the meaning of the first two lines, especially 'the wood of thoughts'. Then suggest how this metaphor (wood, axe) is followed on in l. 4. What does 'cock-crow' usually symbolize? Why 'silver' (l. 4)? In what way do the two cocks remind him of a coat of arms, and in what sense are they 'heralds of splendour'? What does the last line mean, and how do the 'milkers' connect with the cock's crow? Do you consider this last line rather a 'let-down'? If not, say why not—*i.e.* defend the effect of the last line, or give reasons for thinking it out of place.

(B)   Write in verse or prose about dawn in any surroundings,
       rural or urban, which you know well.

Digging (p. 174)

This and the following poem relate to gardening, and
anyone who has ever dug or sown seeds will understand
them without much explanation.

l. 3   *wild carrot' seed:* a white-flowered 'umbrella-headed'
       weed, with strongly smelling seeds.
l. 4   *mustard:* a yellow field-crop, with a delicious scent.
l. 7   *goutweed:* ground elder, a vicious and persistent weed,
       with a strong foetid smell when bruised.

(A)   Which smells are borne on the wind, and which come
       directly from the poet's activity? Try to describe the
       smell of dead leaves (l. 2), celery (l. 8), the bonfire
       (l. 10); why is it so difficult to do so? Explain carefully
       ll. 11 and 12. In what sense is it 'enough' to 'smell, to
       crumble the dark earth'? When do robins come closest
       to men, and in what sense is the robin's song a fitting
       ending? How can its song be both 'sad' and 'of Autumn
       mirth'?

(B)   Write a poem or short composition about smells in your
       own house or garden.

Sowing (p. 175)

(A)   What time of the year, and what time of the day, is
       described here? In what sense is the day 'perfect for
       sowing'? Which line corresponds with l. 5? Where does
       he show a sense of satisfaction and achievement? Why is
       it important that the soil is 'dry' and that later it rains?
       What advantage is there in the rain being 'windless and
       light', and in what sense is it 'half a kiss, half a tear'?
       Where do you picture the poet as being in the last verse?

(B)   Write about any garden activity that you remember with
       pleasure.

Swedes (p. 175)

This poem needs a little explanation for some urban
students. Swedes (like potatoes and other root crops) are

often stored in a 'clamp', *i.e.* in a long roof-shaped heap, laid on and covered with straw, with earth beaten down on each side of the ridge to let the rain run off. When they are wanted—probably for cattle-food—the farm-workers open it up, and some of the roots will have grown a little in the dark, but instead of being green the leaves will be 'white and gold and purple', delicate and fragile like forced rhubarb or grass and weeds under a large stone left lying on the lawn. This sudden exposure of bright and delicate colour is compared with the open-ing of Egyptian tombs which took place in the early part of this century, exposing to the light long-hidden treasures.

l. 7   *Pharaoh*: king of ancient Egypt.

l. 11   *Amen-hotep*: a famous Egyptian Pharaoh, responsible for magnificent buildings and tombs.

(A)   Explain all three words in 'curled fronds unsunned'. Discuss the word 'tender-gorgeous' and how it applies to the swede fronds and the tomb-treasures. Why should Winter 'moan and drip' at the 'wood-corner' (l. 5)? Why does a *boy* first go down into the tomb, and in what sense is he the first of *Christian* men to see it? Where are the colours of l. 10 echoed, and what is the point of the echo? The last two lines are quite difficult; the long-dead Pharaoh lies dreamless—what, in contrast, does the poet say about the swede pile?

(B)   This poem, like *Tall Nettles*, shows the poet's great sensitivity to beauty in unexpected places. If you didn't answer (B) on p. 178, write now about beauty in a place or setting usually considered ugly, squalid, or common-place.

Aspens (p. 176)

Aspens are a variety of poplar, noted for their very delicate branch and twig structure, which makes the whole tree tremble and whisper in the slightest breeze. The middle verses are slightly difficult and need several readings; the poem finishes by comparing the continual whisper of the aspens with the poet's voice, who cannot but write poems even if people will not read them.

(A)

v. 1 In what sense do the aspens 'talk of rain' and what silences them?

v. 2 Explain 'cavern', and suggest what might cause the sounds of 'the clink', 'the hum' and 'the roar' in the inn.

v. 3 Explain 'lightless pane' and 'footless road'. What time of day is suggested? (ll. 11–12 means 'though every other sound ceases, the aspens' whisper goes on.')

v. 4 Suggest in your own words the four kinds of weather described; how do the aspens 'turn the cross-roads to a ghostly room'?

v. 5 Distinguish between 'hear' and 'listen' in this verse. Which lines from previous verses are referred to by 'all sorts of weather, men, and times'?

v. 6 How do the expressions 'Whatever wind blows' and 'while I have leaves' refer to the poet? Who are 'we'? What is meant by the last line?

(B) As a change from writing your own poems and stories or descriptions, say in some detail whether you belong to the class of people 'who like a different tree' and whether you find from this selection that Edward Thomas 'ceaselessly, unreasonably grieves'. Do you find that you prefer not to 'listen' to his 'leaves'?

FURTHER READING

Poems of Edward Thomas, selected by R. S. Thomas (Faber Paperback).

Collected Poems, with a foreword by Walter de la Mare (Faber).

Helen Thomas. *As It Was* and *World without End* (Faber).
    Two books by Edward's widow about their life together.

The Prose of Edward Thomas, ed. R. Gant (Falcon Press).

CRITICAL WRITING

H. Coombes. *Edward Thomas* (Chatto and Windus).

F. R. Leavis. *New Bearings in English Poetry* (Chatto and Windus). Use the index.

D. H. Lawrence

D. H. LAWRENCE, novelist, poet, and critic, was born in 1885 at Eastwood, Nottinghamshire, the fourth child and third son of a coal-miner. He went to the local elementary school and won a scholarship to the High School and another to University College, Nottingham. He taught in Croydon at an elementary school (see the first two poems in this selection), but after publishing his first novel, *The White Peacock* (1911), he became a whole-time writer. He eloped with Frieda Weekley, a German national, to Italy, in 1912, and married her after her divorce in 1914. *Sons and Lovers* appeared in 1913, a largely autobiographical novel, and *The Rainbow* (1915) followed but was banned for obscenity. He lived in England, mainly in Cornwall, during the First World War, but left as soon as possible for a series of wanderings in France, Italy, America, Australia, and Mexico. *Women in Love*, a sequel to *The Rainbow*, appeared in 1921, and his other novels included *Kangaroo* (1923), *The Plumed Serpent* (1926), and *Lady Chatterley's Lover* (1928, but banned in England till 1960). He wrote a large number of short stories and tales (*e.g. England, My England* (1922) and *The Woman Who Rode Away* (1928)), a number of travel books (*e.g. Twilight in Italy* (1916), *Mornings in Mexico* (1927)), a great deal of critical writing (collected in *Phoenix* (1936)), philosophical works (*e.g. Fantasia of the Unconscious*), and essays (there are various editions). His complete poems appeared in a collected edition in 1957, and his letters in 1932. He died of tuberculosis in Vence, a village near Nice, in 1930.

D. H. Lawrence is in some ways the most extraordinary writer represented in this book, and perhaps the greatest English writer (though not the greatest poet) of the century. His range of activities in writing is remarkable, and his finest novels (*Sons and Lovers*, *The Rainbow*, *Women in Love*) are unexcelled by any novelist of the century; apart from this he has achieved major distinction and originality in half a dozen different literary forms. Of his work apart from poetry, perhaps a sampling of the travel books and some of the short stories and letters would cast most light back on the poems. His first published work was in fact a group of poems published in 1910 in *The English Review*. His early poems, usually rhyming and fairly conventional in form, are intensely personal in content; in them he fights out, as it were, his fundamental psychological problems—particularly his deep relationship with his mother and the conflict this set up with his love for other women (the crisis worked out so splendidly in *Sons and Lovers*, and embodied so clearly in its title). His early life with the woman he later married is pictured with devastating vividness in a sequence called *Look, We Have Come Through!* Soon, however, he moved into wider and less personal themes, as he did in fiction and his other writing: he was horrified and disgusted by what he believed to be the falseness of modern society; somewhat like Blake in this respect, he saw man weighted down with 'mind-forg'd manacles'—conventions, deadening respectabilities, hatred, pretences, snobbery, materialism, possessiveness—and set against these a vision of 'man alive', proud of his individuality, his sex, his passions, his emotional life. It is fair to add that he was capable of writing hysterically under the influence of violent feeling, and that his growing illness affected some of his writing badly towards the end of his life.

Lawrence soon abandoned most of the conventions of traditional poetry and devised for himself a free flowing verse, spontaneous, powerful, and expressing (and playing directly on) the emotions, yet always reflecting the play of a flexible and profound intelligence. He had always a vivid awareness of and insight into the physical world, the world of *things*, and this produced the intensity of his vision of forms of life—from mosquitos to tortoises, from flowers to fish, from birds to trees (see the collection called *Birds, Beasts and Flowers* from which have been taken *Mosquito*, p. 191, and *Baby Tortoise*, p. 194). He wrote violently satirical poems, many of them short 'dashed-off' single thoughts or outbursts, in *Nettles* and *Pansies*, some of which are reprinted here and referred to in the notes.

The key word to describe Lawrence's poetry is perhaps *intensity*. Aldous Huxley, a close friend at one stage, writes in an introduction to Lawrence's letters:

> I think almost everyone who knew him well must have felt that Lawrence was this . . . a being, somehow, of another order, more sensitive, more highly conscious, more capable of feeling than even the most gifted of common men. . . . For, being himself of a different order, he inhabited a different universe from that of common men—a brighter and intenser world, of which while he spoke he would make you free. He looked at things with the eyes, so it seemed, of a man who had been at the brink of death and to whom, as he emerges from darkness, the world reveals itself as unfathomably beautiful and mysterious. . . . He seemed to know, by personal experience, what it was like to be a tree or a daisy or a breaking wave or even the mysterious moon itself.

In his short life (he died at 45) Lawrence not only lived intensely, but wrote, in prose and verse, with a passion that can free his readers from the scales over their eyes, the varnish of habit and dullness, and enable the visible world around us and our own identity to fuse into unity.

Last Lesson of the Afternoon

When will the bell ring, and end this weariness?
How long have they tugged the leash, and strained apart
My pack of unruly hounds! I cannot start
Them again on a quarry of knowledge they hate to hunt,
I can haul them and urge them no more.   5

No longer now can I endure the brunt
Of the books that lie out on the desks; a full threescore
Of several insults of blotted pages, and scrawl
Of slovenly work that they have offered me.
I am sick, and what on earth is the good of it all?   10
What good to them or me, I cannot see!

                    So, shall I take
My last dear fuel of life to heap on my soul
And kindle my will to a flame that shall consume
Their dross of indifference; and take the toll   15
Of their insults in punishment?—I will not!—

I will not waste my soul and my strength for this.
What do I care for all that they do amiss!
What is the point of this teaching of mine, and of this
Learning of theirs? It all goes down the same abyss.   20

What does it matter to me, if they can write
A description of a dog, or if they can't?
What is the point? To us both, it is all my aunt!
And yet I'm supposed to care, with all my might.

I do not, and will not; they won't and they don't; and
    that's all!   25
I shall keep my strength for myself; they can keep theirs
    as well.
Why should we beat our heads against the wall
Of each other? I shall sit and wait for the bell.

The Best of School

The blinds are drawn because of the sun,
And the boys and the room in a colourless gloom
Of underwater float: bright ripples run
Across the walls as the blinds are blown
To let the sunlight in; and I,   5
As I sit on the shores of the class, alone,
Watch the boys in their summer blouses
As they write, their round heads busily bowed:
And one after another rouses
His face to look at me,   10
To ponder very quietly,
As seeing, he does not see.

And then he turns again, with a little, glad
Thrill of his work he turns again from me,
Having found what he wanted, having got what was to be
    had.   15

And very sweet it is, while the sunlight waves
In the ripening morning, to sit alone with the class
And feel the stream of awakening ripple and pass
From me to the boys, whose brightening souls it laves
For this little hour.   20

This morning, sweet it is
To feel the lads' looks light on me,
Then back in a swift, bright flutter to work:
Each one darting away with his
Discovery, like birds that steal and flee.   25

Touch after touch I feel on me
As their eyes glance at me for the grain
Of rigour they taste delightedly.

As tendrils reach out yearningly,
Slowly rotate till they touch the tree   30
That they cleave unto, and up which they climb
Up to their lives—so they to me.

I feel them cling and cleave to me
As vines going eagerly up; they twine
My life with other leaves, my time   35
Is hidden in theirs, their thrills are mine.

Mosquito

When did you start your tricks,
Monsieur?

What do you stand on such high legs for?
Why this length of shredded shank,
You exaltation?   5

Is it so that you shall lift your centre of gravity upwards
And weigh no more than air as you alight upon me,
Stand upon me weightless, you phantom?

I heard a woman call you the Winged Victory
In sluggish Venice.   10
You turn your head towards your tail, and smile.

How can you put so much devilry
Into that translucent phantom shred
Of a frail corpus?

Queer, with your thin wings and your streaming legs, 15
How you sail like a heron, or a dull clot of air,
A nothingness.

Yet what an aura surrounds you;
Your evil little aura, prowling, and casting numbness on
        my mind.
That is your trick, your bit of filthy magic: 20
Invisibility, and the anaesthetic power
To deaden my attention in your direction.

But I know your game now, streaky sorcerer.
Queer, how you stalk and prowl the air
In circles and evasions, enveloping me,   25
Ghoul on wings,
Winged Victory.

Settle, and stand on long thin shanks
Eyeing me sideways, and cunningly conscious that I am
        aware,
You speck.   30

I hate the way you lurch off sideways into the air
Having read my thoughts against you.

Come then, let us play at unawares,
And see who wins in this sly game of bluff.
Man or mosquito.   35

You don't know that I exist, and I don't know that you
     exist.
Now then!

It is your trump,
It is your hateful little trump,
You pointed fiend,   40
Which shakes my sudden blood to hatred of you:
It is your small, high, hateful bugle in my ear.

Why do you do it?
Surely it is bad policy.
They say you can't help it.   45

If that is so, then I believe a little in Providence protecting
     the innocent.
But it sounds so amazingly like a slogan,
A yell of triumph as you snatch my scalp.

Blood, red blood
Super-magical   50
Forbidden liquor.

I behold you stand
For a second enspasmed in oblivion,
Obscenely ecstasied
Sucking live blood,   55
My blood.

Such silence, such suspended transport,
Such gorging,
Such obscenity of trespass.

You stagger   60
As well as you may.
Only your accursed hairy frailty,
Your own imponderable weightlessness
Saves you, wafts you away on the very draught my anger
     makes in its snatching.

Away with a paean of derision,
You winged blood-drop.   65

Can I not overtake you?
Are you one too many for me,
Winged Victory?
Am I not mosquito enough to out-mosquito you?   70

Queer what a big stain my sucked blood makes
Beside the infinitesimal faint smear of you!
Queer, what a dim dark smudge you have disappeared
     into!

Baby Tortoise

You know what it is to be born alone,
Baby tortoise!

The first day to heave your feet little by little from the
     shell,
Not yet awake,
And remain lapsed on earth,   5
Not quite alive.

A tiny, fragile, half-animate bean.

To open your tiny beak-mouth, that looks as if it would
    never open,
Like some iron door;
To lift the upper hawk-beak from the lower base   10
And reach your skinny little neck
And take your first bite at some dim bit of herbage,
Alone, small insect,
Tiny bright-eye,
Slow one.   15

To take your first solitary bite
And move on your slow, solitary hunt.
Your bright, dark little eye,
Your eye of a dark disturbed night,
Under its slow lid, tiny baby tortoise,   20
So indomitable.

No one ever heard you complain.

You draw your head forward, slowly, from your little
    wimple,
And set forward, slow-dragging, on your four-pinned toes,
Rowing slowly forward.   25
Whither away, small bird?
Rather like a baby working its limbs,
Except that you make slow, ageless progress
And a baby makes none.

The touch of sun excites you,   30
And the long ages, and the lingering chill
Make you pause to yawn,

Opening your impervious mouth,
Suddenly beak-shaped, and very wide, like some suddenly
    gaping pincers;
Soft red tongue, and hard thin gums,   35
Then close the wedge of your little mountain front,
Your face, baby tortoise.

Do you wonder at the world, as slowly you turn your head
    in its wimple
And look with laconic, black eyes?
Or is sleep coming over you again,   40
The non-life?

You are so hard to wake.

Are you able to wonder?
Or is it just your indomitable will and pride of the first life
Looking round
And slowly pitching itself against the inertia   45
Which had seemed invincible?

The vast inanimate,
And the fine brilliance of your so tiny eye,
Challenger.   50

Nay, tiny shell-bird,
What a huge vast inanimate it is, that you must row against,
What an incalculable inertia.

Challenger,
Little Ulysses, fore-runner,   55
No bigger than my thumb-nail,
Buon viaggio.

All animate creation on your shoulder,
Set forth, little Titan, under your battle-shield.

The ponderous, preponderate,   60
Inanimate universe;
And you are slowly moving, pioneer, you alone.

How vivid your travelling seems now, in the troubled
      sunshine,
Stoic, Ulyssean atom;
Suddenly hasty, reckless, on high toes.   65

Voiceless little bird,
Resting your head half out of your wimple
In the slow dignity of your eternal pause.
Alone, with no sense of being alone,
And hence six times more solitary;   70
Fulfilled of the slow passion of pitching through immemorial
      ages
Your little round house in the midst of chaos.

Over the garden earth,
Small bird,
Over the edge of all things.   75

Traveller,
With your tail tucked a little on one side
Like a gentleman in a long-skirted coat.

All life carried on your shoulder,
Invincible fore-runner.   80

Bavarian Gentians

Not every man has gentians in his house
in soft September, at slow, sad Michaelmas.

Bavarian gentians, big and dark, only dark
darkening the day-time, torch-like with the smoking
    blueness of Pluto's gloom,
ribbed and torch-like, with their blaze of darkness spread
    blue   5
down flattening into points, flattened under the sweep of
    white day
torch-flower of the blue-smoking darkness, Pluto's dark-
    blue daze,
black lamps from the halls of Dis, burning dark blue,
giving off darkness, blue darkness, as Demeter's pale
    lamps give off light,
lead me then, lead me the way.   10

Reach me a gentian, give me a torch!
let me guide myself with the blue, forked torch of this
    flower
down the darker and darker stairs, where blue is darkened
    on blueness
even where Persephone goes, just now, from the frosted
    September
to the sightless realm where darkness is awake upon the
    dark   15
and Persephone herself is but a voice
or a darkness invisible enfolded in the deeper dark
of the arms Plutonic, and pierced with the passion of dense
    gloom,
among the splendour of torches of darkness, shedding
    darkness on the lost bride and her groom.

The Oxford Voice

When you hear it languishing
and hooing and cooing and sidling through the front teeth,
    the oxford voice
    or worse still
    the would-be oxford voice   5
you don't even laugh any more, you can't.

For every blooming bird is an oxford cuckoo nowadays,
you can't sit on a bus nor in the tube
but it breathes gently and languishingly in the back of
    your neck.

And oh, so seductively superior, so seductively   10
    self-effacingly
    deprecatingly
    superior. —
We wouldn't insist on it for a moment
    but we are   15
    we are
    you admit we are
    superior. —

Let us be Men —

For God's sake, let us be men
not monkeys minding machines
or sitting with our tails curled
while the machine amuses us, the radio or film or
    gramophone.

Monkeys with a bland grin on our faces. —

Good Husbands make Unhappy Wives —

Good husbands make unhappy wives
so do bad husbands, just as often;
but the unhappiness of a wife with a good husband
is much more devastating
than the unhappiness of a wife with a bad hus-
    band.

The Mosquito Knows —

The mosquito knows full well, small as he is
he's a beast of prey.
But after all
he only takes his bellyful,
he doesn't put my blood in the bank.

Many Mansions

When a bird flips his tail in getting his balance on a tree
he feels much gayer than if somebody had left him a fortune
or than if he'd just built himself a nest with a bathroom —
Why can't people be gay like that?

Riches

When I wish I was rich, then I know I am ill.
Because, to tell the truth, I have enough as I am.
So when I catch myself thinking: Ah, if I was rich. . . !
I say to myself: Hello! I'm not well. My vitality is low. —

To Women, as far as I'm Concerned

The feelings I don't have I don't have.
The feelings I don't have, I won't say I have.
The feelings you say you have, you don't have.
The feelings you would like us both to have, we neither
      of us have.
The feelings people ought to have, they never have.
If people say they've got feelings, you may be pretty sure
      they haven't got them.
So if you want either of us to feel anything at all
you'd better abandon all idea of feelings altogether.

Paltry-looking People

And think how the nightingale, who is so shy,
makes of himself a belfry of throbbing sound!
While people mince mean words through their teeth.

And think how wild animals trot with splendour
till man destroys them!   5
how vividly they make their assertion of life!

But how paltry, mingy and dingy and squalid people look
in their rag garments scuttling through the streets,
or sitting stuck like automata in automobiles!

Notes

Last Lesson of the Afternoon (p. 189)

This poem was first published in 1912 in a sequence called *The Schoolmaster*. Lawrence had been teaching at a school in Croydon until 1911. It expresses a mood of bitter desperation at the thanklessness of the teacher's work.

(A) What connexion is there between the beginning and ending of the poem? What is a 'quarry' (l. 4) and what other words and expressions connect with it? How big might classes be in those days? What is a 'brunt' (l. 6)? What do you think the poet means by 'my last dear fuel of life' (l. 13) and how does it contrast with 'dross' (l. 15)? What is the teacher contemplating doing in ll. 15–16? Which verse most strongly expresses his sense of futility? Which phrase shows that he shares his pupils' indifference to their work? Suggest a modern phrase for 'it is all my aunt' (l. 23). Explain l. 25 ('do not and will not' *what*?). When does he show a recognition that both sides, teacher and pupils, are failing to communicate?

The Best of School (p. 190)

This is very much a companion poem to the first, in setting and subject-matter, but contrasts with it strongly in attitude; here Lawrence is finding teaching creative and purposeful.

(A) Describe in your own words the effect of the light in the classroom (ll. 1–5). Explain 'shores' (l. 6). What is meant by l. 12 (how can you see and yet not see?)? What *was* to be had (l. 15)? In the third verse (ll. 16–20) what relationship do you see between the 'sunlight' and the 'stream of awakening' (comment carefully on 'waves', 'stream', 'ripple', 'laves'). Which earlier phrase corresponds to 'a swift bright flutter' (l. 23), and what does this mean? Suggest a meaning for 'the grain/of rigour' (ll. 27–28). How is the image of birds sustained in the passage ll. 21–28? Which two images suggest that the poet here feels that he is playing an important rôle for the pupils? What do you think they are doing? When does he identify himself with them, and how does this identification differ from that in *Last Lesson of the Afternoon*?

(B) Having studied both these poems, write in prose or verse about a good and a bad lesson, and show how *you* would distinguish between them. What kinds of activity or atmosphere bring you into 'rapport' with your teachers? Is it you or they, or both, who establish this?

Mosquito (p. 191)

This poem is from a collection called *Birds, Beasts and Flowers*, most of which the poet wrote in Italy (remember that mosquitos are important and dangerous in malarial areas). Lawrence wrote rhyming poems mainly at the beginning of his career, but much more characteristic of his mature work is this kind of free verse.

l. 5   *exaltation:* literally, a raising or lifting up; also rapturous emotion.

l. 9   *Winged Victory:* a famous Greek statue.

l. 18   *aura:* a subtle emanation or atmosphere coming from a person or creature.

l. 25   *ghoul:* literally, a spirit preying on corpses.

ll. 53 *enspasmed, ecstasied:* probably coinages from 'spasm' and
–54   'ecstasy', both meaning 'in a state of utter bliss'.

l. 65   *paean:* song of praise for deliverance.

(A) Early in the poem two aspects of the mosquito are stressed—its physical smallness and the way it suggests evil; point out expressions in the first seven 'verses' which describe each of these. Why are there so many questions in the first part of the poem, as the mosquito obviously can't answer? Why does he call it 'monsieur' (l. 2)? What picture do you get from 'shredded shank' (l. 4), and how does this fit with 'exaltation' (see note above)? Why did the woman call the mosquito 'the Winged

Victory' (l. 9), why is Venice 'sluggish', and why might
it be a place for mosquitos? What picture do you get
from l. 11? Where in the poem does the mosquito first
fly? Which word in the next verse contradicts 'a nothingness' (l. 17)? What do you think the mosquito's 'bit of
filthy magic' is (l. 20)? In what sense has it 'invisibility'
and what does 'anaesthetic' mean here (l. 21)? Explain
'streaky sorcerer' (l. 23) and 'enveloping me' (l. 25). Why
does he repeat 'Winged Victory' and what is the tone of
'you speck' (ll. 29–30)? When does the mosquito seem
aware of the human being? Where does the poet seem
to feel confidence in his power to defeat the mosquito?
What is a 'sly game of bluff' (l. 34)? Where is the poet's
attempt to ignore the mosquito shaken? What is 'your
hateful little trump' (l. 39) and what does the poem say
about this trump (ll. 38–48)? What do you think the
mosquito is doing by l. 49, and what do you picture the
poet doing in ll. 49–59? Why does the insect 'stagger/
As well as you may' (ll. 60–61), what gesture does the
poet make in ll. 60–65, and why does it fail? What is the
mosquito doing in ll. 65–66, and why is it described as 'a
winged blood-drop'? Explain what is meant by 'Am I
not mosquito enough to out-mosquito you?' (l. 70), and
what do you think has happened in the last verse of all?
Do you think Lawrence feels for the mosquito affection,
disgust, horror, bewilderment, a rueful amusement? Do
you think free verse of this kind is really 'chopped-up'
prose? What features of the language, structure, and
rhythms of this poem seem to you to *belong* to poetry
rather than prose?

(B) Write, this time in 'Lawrentian' verse, about an animal,
insect, or bird you feel you know intimately; remember
that your 'relationship' with the animal is important,
and your attitude to it as well as its appearance, movement, etc.

Baby Tortoise (p. 191)

In some ways this is very similar to the last poem; it has
the same sensitive description and awareness of the

physical being of the animal—but its stress is mainly on the heroic adventure of a single and tiny organism facing its first experience of life.

l. 21 *indomitable:* unyielding, persistent.

l. 23 *wimple:* head covering for nuns, etc., arranged in folds about the neck; here the bony 'folded' structure of the shell from which the head emerges.

l. 33 *impervious:* not open, firmly closed—the way it looked before it opened.

l. 39 *laconic:* literally brief, short—hence uncommunicative.

l. 55 *Ulysses:* the great hero of Homer's *Odyssey:* here a symbol for a heroic wanderer.

l. 57 *Buon viaggio:* (have a) good journey.

l. 59 *Titan:* race of giant gods: hence, creature of great strength or courage.

l. 60 *preponderate:* heavy, heavier—therefore more 'resistant'.

l. 64 *stoic:* here, showing fortitude or courage.

(A) A baby tortoise is apparently very small (how big does the poem tell us it is?); point out the words and phrases in the first twenty lines which stress this. In what way is it like a 'bean' (l. 7)? Why 'some *dim* bit of herbage' (l. 12)? What contrast is there between l. 14 and l. 15? What picture do you get from 'four-pinned toes' (l. 24)? What physical characteristics apart from smallness are stressed? Consider especially movement. Describe a tortoise's 'wimple' (l. 23). Why does he call it 'insect' (l. 13) and 'bird' (l. 26)? Describe the mouth and jaws of the tortoise in your own words (l. 10 and ll. 33–35). Why 'little mountain front' (l. 36)? Why might sleep be coming over it 'again' (l. 40), why is this called 'the non-life' (l. 41), and what is the meaning of the next line ('You are so hard to wake')? What 'inertia' (l. 46) is the tortoise 'pitching itself against', and what expression in the next verse has a similar meaning? Discuss the verb 'row' (l. 52) as a description of the tortoise's movement, and how does this connect with Ulysses? In what sense is it a 'challenger' (ll. 50 and 54) and a 'pioneer' (l. 62)? What voyage is it setting out on, and how could it be little *and* a Titan (l. 59)? What is its 'battle-shield' (l. 59) and what expression in the verse ll. 66–72 corresponds to it? What is the effect of the joke in the last

verse but one, and how is the whole poem summarized
in the last verse?

(B)   Write (again in 'Lawrentian' verse) about any baby
animal.

Bavarian Gentians (p. 198)

Gentians are only rarely seen in England, except occasionally in gardens: Lawrence has a bunch of one of the
varieties which grows on mountain slopes and alpine
meadows in central Europe, and flowers in the autumn.
It is a dwarf plant with relatively huge blue trumpet-
shaped flowers looking upwards: the blue is an astonish-
ing colour, and we say 'gentian blue' for an almost
electric brilliance of pure dark blue. The poem comes
from a volume called *Last Poems*, and can be thought of
partly as a flower poem—in the sense that he reaches the
essence of the flower just as he does of the mosquito and
the baby tortoise. But it is much more than this: Lawrence was ill and his poems at this time show him contemplating death—and thus the dark blue flower becomes
in his imagination a torch leading him into the underworld.

The beautiful story of Pluto and Persephone is an
essential part of this poem. In classical mythology Pluto
was god of the underworld (his other names include Dis
and Hades); after an earthquake he saw Persephone
(also called Proserpine), daughter of Ceres, gathering
flowers in the plains of Enna, fell in love with her, and
carried her away to the underworld in a chariot through
a cleft in the earth, where she became the Queen of Hell.
Her mother Ceres (also called Demeter), goddess of
harvests and agriculture, sought her throughout the
world, and during this time neglected the cultivation of
the earth, and this period became the first winter; in due
course Proserpine was allowed to rejoin her mother for
part of each year when Ceres was happy and the earth
fruitful, but had to return to her husband for the rest,
which became the period of winter.

ll. 5–   A description of the pointed cup of the flower.
6

(A) What sound contributes to the effect of l. 2? What is the
effect of the repetition of 'dark' and 'blue', and how do
they imply the oblivion of death? Where in the second
verse is the darkness contrasted, and with what? Can
you imagine a torch giving off darkness? Show how the
poet suggests this. What 'darker and darker stairs' does
he imagine himself going down (l. 13)? Why does
Persephone go 'just now' (l. 14) down these stairs?
Explain 'sightless realm' (l. 15) and 'dense gloom' (l. 18).
Who is the 'lost bride' (l. 19) and who her 'groom'?
In what sense does the last line summarize the poem?

The Oxford Voice (p. 199)

The rest of the poems in this brief selection come from a
volume called *Pansies* (from *Pensées*, 'thoughts') and show
a very different side of the poet. They are mostly short
poems, obviously 'dashed off' for the most part, and
reflecting moods, ideas, and fragments of experience.
They are often repetitive in the sense that he writes a
number of variations on one theme, as you will see if you
look up the collected poems. In Lawrence's introduction
he writes: 'This little bunch of fragments is offered as a
bunch of *pensées*, *anglicé* pansies, a handful of thoughts . . .
each little piece is a thought, not a bare idea or an
opinion or a didactic statement, but a true thought. . . .
Live and let live, and each little pansy will tip you its
separate wink.' Many of these little poems are sardonic
or satirical in one way or another, and you might try
writing your own, in whatever rhythm seems to suit
them.

The Oxford Voice has a target which is rather less
dominant now than in the twenties—the accent and
manner of speech associated with Oxford University.
For Lawrence this kind of voice expresses a conviction
that it is by definition superior—and the imitation
('the would-be Oxford voice') is 'worse still'.

(A) Describe in your own words the sound effects described
in ll. 1–2. What do 'self-effacingly' and 'deprecatingly'
mean (ll. 11–12)? Who is imagined as speaking the last
five lines, and how does he show himself both 'modest'

and certain of his own superiority? What do the rhythms of the last five lines remind you of?

Let us be Men— *(p. 199)*

(A) Is this a fair comment on modern industrial society, its work and its recreation? What would you add now to l. 4? What is added to the picture by the last line?

Good Husbands make Unhappy Wives— *(p. 200)*

(A) What do you think this *pensée* means? Is there any truth in it?

The Mosquito Knows— *(p. 200)*

(A) What is the target here? (By 'bank' the poet means of course a bank account; since his day there has been invented a 'blood bank' in which human blood *is* actually saved for emergency operations, etc., and one reader at least took this meaning, which ruins the poem.) What sort of 'beasts of prey' is he thinking of that are *not* satisfied with a mere 'bellyful'? Does a reading of *Mosquito* (p. 191) help with this poem?

Many Mansions *(p. 200)*

Here Lawrence characteristically expresses admiration and envy for the natural creature that is not concerned with property and bank accounts.

(A) Describe the bird's movement in your own words. What can he mean by 'a nest with a bathroom'? Why *can't* people 'be gay like that'?

Riches *(p. 201)*

(A) Lawrence was always happy with a modest standard of life and enjoyed things like scrubbing floors and living simply; how does this little poem illustrate this? Relate this to the two previous poems and show how the ideas of all three are related.

To Women, as far as I'm Concerned (p. 201)

(A) Try reading this aloud in a flat Midlands accent of the kind Lawrence to some extent retained throughout his life. He is protesting against the tendency to parade and analyse feelings, especially those of love, that was so prevalent then and perhaps still is.

Paltry-looking People (p. 201)

(A) What aspect of human life is contrasted with that of nature in the first verse? Show how the *sound* of l. 2 contrasts with that of l. 3. How do verses 2 and 3 go together, in terms of what activity? Which words contrast with 'trot with splendour' (l. 4)? Examine the adjectives in l. 7, explain them, and say whether you think they are a fair description of 'modern man', or do you think that things have improved in this respect since the 'twenties? Why 'rag garments' (l. 8)? Why 'stuck' in the last line? What sound echoes are there in this line, and what do they add to the effect?

(B) Having read this small collection of *Pansies*, try writing one yourself, say every day for a week, on anything that strikes you as a target; you may find that some of them turn out better than more elaborate attempts at verse-writing.

FURTHER READING

Selected Poems (Penguin: a good selection).

Collected Poems (two vols, Heinemann).

Short stories. There are various volumes in Penguins and elsewhere: try *The Virgin and the Gipsy* and *England, my England*.

Sons and Lovers (the most accessible of the novels; later you must read *The Rainbow*).

Selected Essays (Penguin).

Selected Letters (Penguin).

CRITICAL WRITING

A. Alvarez. *The Shaping Spirit* (Chatto and Windus) (contains an essay on the poetry).

C. Carswell. *The Savage Pilgrimage* (Secker and Warburg).

E. T. (Jessie Chambers). *D. H. Lawrence: A Personal Record* (Cassell). The last two are biographies.

T. S. Eliot

T. S. ELIOT, poet, critic, and dramatist, was born in St Louis, Missouri, in 1888. He was educated at two academies and at Harvard University, and later at the Paris Sorbonne, where he studied French literature and philosophy. He was awarded a travelling fellowship from Harvard, and on the outbreak of war went from Germany to Merton College, Oxford, to read philosophy. His first published poems appeared in 1915, when he also married. He taught for a year at Highgate, and then worked in Lloyds Bank for eight years; in 1919 he published *Poems*. He edited and contributed to various periodicals and established his own quarterly *The Criterion* in 1922. *The Waste Land* (1922) firmly established his reputation as a poet. In 1927 he became a British subject, and joined the Church of England. *Ash Wednesday* appeared in 1930. In 1932 he was appointed Professor of Poetry at Harvard. He published his first full-length verse play *Murder in the Cathedral* in 1935, and this was followed by four other plays, *The Family Reunion* (1939), *The Cocktail Party* (1949), *The Confidential Clerk* (1953), and *The Elder Statesman* (1958). His last and greatest work in poetry was *Four Quartets* (1935–42). Throughout this period he wrote a series of highly influential critical works, including *The Sacred Wood* (1920), *Homage to John Dryden* (1924) and *Dante* (1929), later redistributed and republished in *Selected Essays* (1932) and other volumes. He also wrote a book for children, *Old Possum's Book of Practical Cats*. He was awarded the Order of Merit and the Nobel Prize for Literature in 1948. He remarried in 1959 and died in 1965.

T. S. Eliot is usually regarded as the greatest English poet of this century; his formidable learning and scholarship, his highly influential critical writing, and above all his deeply original poetry, have won him an unrivalled reputation. His early poems were mainly urban in setting, often allusive and full of references, apparently colloquial in tone but in fact deeply calculated in their rhythms; they express an early disgust with the rootlessness of modern city life (see *Preludes* and *A Cooking Egg*, pp. 217 and 222). *The Waste Land*, written in the bitter disillusion which followed the First World War, is a highly complex poem in five movements which revealed the impotence and barrenness of a life devoid of belief; it is full of references to anthropology and quotations from the literature of many countries, and was published with detailed explanatory notes: its influence, especially on younger poets, has been enormous. Eliot's striving towards belief after the cynicism and nihilism so common in the period is seen in *Ash Wednesday*, and this logically moves towards the magnificent but appallingly difficult group of poems published in 1943 as *Four Quartets*.

It is very difficult to generalize about a poet of Eliot's range and complexity. His poems are always deeply considered, and make the highest demands on one's intelligence, as well as needing a very extensive background of reading. He commonly combines the lyrical with the matter-of-fact, or colloquial, and the movement of his poems is often determined more by emotional suggestion than logical or narrative structure. Their rhythms, in the same way, hesitate between regular patterns and 'free verse', and the rhymes, when they are used, are all the more effective by reason of their restraint. His mind frequently worked by juxtaposing apparently unconnected ideas or statements; references to the great literature of the past symbolizing past splendours are placed side by side with the squalid or the fragmentary to illustrate contrast, and tags of vulgar, shoddy, commonplace, or apparently casual speech are correlated with passages of rare lyrical beauty (see *Journey of the Magi*, p. 219, and *Triumphal March*, p. 223, for examples). The concentration of his verse and the frequent omission of connecting links make for great difficulty in understanding his more complex poems. The selection here does not represent his most powerful work, which is beyond the limits of this anthology.

We end with three quotations from Eliot's writings *about* poetry, which cast some light on his practice, and his achievement, as a poet.

> ... Very few know when there is expression of significant emotion, emotion which has its life in the poem and not in the history of the poet. The emotion of art is impersonal. And the poet cannot reach this impersonality without surrendering himself wholly to the work to be done.

He expresses elsewhere the wish to write

> poetry so transparent that we should not see the poetry, but that which we are meant to see through the poetry, poetry so transparent that in reading it we are intent on what the poem *points at*, and not on the poetry ...

Finally, he wrote, in words which fit well the poet himself, commending the great French philosopher Pascal

> to those who doubt, but who have the mind to conceive, and the sensibility to feel, the disorder, the futility, the meaninglessness, the mystery of life and suffering, and who can only find peace through a satisfaction of the whole being.

Preludes

I

The winter evening settles down
With smell of steaks in passageways.
Six o'clock.
The burnt-out ends of smoky days.
And now a gusty shower wraps   5
The grimy scraps
Of withered leaves about your feet
And newspapers from vacant lots;
The showers beat
On broken blinds and chimney-pots,   10
And at the corner of the street
A lonely cab-horse steams and stamps.

And then the lighting of the lamps.

II

The morning comes to consciousness
Of faint stale smells of beer
From the sawdust-trampled street
With all its muddy feet that press
To early coffee-stands.   5

With the other masquerades
That time resumes,
One thinks of all the hands
That are raising dingy shades
In a thousand furnished rooms.   10

III

You tossed a blanket from the bed,
You lay upon your back, and waited;
You dozed, and watched the night revealing
The thousand sordid images
Of which your soul was constituted;   5
They flickered against the ceiling.
And when all the world came back
And the light crept up between the shutters
And you heard the sparrows in the gutters,
You had such a vision of the street   10
As the street hardly understands;
Sitting along the bed's edge, where
You curled the papers from your hair,
Or clasped the yellow soles of feet
In the palms of both soiled hands.   15

IV

His soul stretched tight across the skies
That fade behind a city block,
Or trampled by insistent feet
At four and five and six o'clock;
And short square fingers stuffing pipes,   5
And evening newspapers, and eyes
Assured of certain certainties,
The conscience of a blackened street
Impatient to assume the world.

I am moved by fancies that are curled   10
Around these images, and cling:
The notion of some infinitely gentle
Infinitely suffering thing.

Wipe your hand across your mouth, and laugh;
The worlds revolve like ancient women   15
Gathering fuel in vacant lots.

Morning at the Window

They are rattling breakfast plates in basement kitchens,
And along the trampled edges of the street
I am aware of the damp souls of housemaids
Sprouting despondently at area gates.   4

The brown waves of fog toss up to me
Twisted faces from the bottom of the street,
And tear from a passer-by with muddy skirts
An aimless smile that hovers in the air   8
And vanishes along the level of the roofs.

Journey of the Magi

"A cold coming we had of it,
Just the worst time of the year
For a journey, and such a long journey:
The ways deep and the weather sharp,
The very dead of winter."   5
And the camels galled, sore-footed, refractory,
Lying down in the melting snow.
There were times we regretted
The summer palaces on slopes, the terraces,
And the silken girls bringing sherbet.   10
Then the camel men cursing and grumbling
And running away, and wanting their liquor and women,

And the night-fires going out, and the lack of shelters,
And the cities hostile and the towns unfriendly
And the villages dirty and charging high prices: 15
A hard time we had of it.
At the end we preferred to travel all night,
Sleeping in snatches,
With the voices singing in our ears, saying
That this was all folly.   20

Then at dawn we came down to a temperate valley,
Wet, below the snow line, smelling of vegetation,
With a running stream and a water-mill beating the
     darkness,
And three trees on the low sky,
And an old white horse galloped away in the meadow.   25
Then we came to a tavern with vine-leaves over the lintel,
Six hands at an open door dicing for pieces of silver,
And feet kicking the empty wine-skins.
But there was no information, and so we continued
And arrived at evening, not a moment too soon   30
Finding the place; it was (you may say) satisfactory.

All this was a long time ago, I remember,
And I would do it again, but set down
This set down
This: were we led all the way for   35
Birth or Death? There was a Birth, certainly,
We had evidence and no doubt. I had seen birth and death
But had thought they were different; this Birth was
Hard and bitter agony for us, like Death, our death.
We returned to our places, these Kingdoms,   40
But no longer at ease here, in the old dispensation,
With an alien people clutching their gods.
I should be glad of another death.

Rannoch, by Glencoe

Here the crow starves, here the patient stag
Breeds for the rifle. Between the soft moor
And the soft sky, scarcely room
To leap or soar. Substance crumbles, in the thin air
Moon cold or moon hot. The road winds in   5
Listlessness of ancient war,
Languor of broken steel,
Clamour of confused wrong, apt
In silence. Memory is strong
Beyond the bone. Pride snapped,   10
Shadow of pride is long, in the long pass
No concurrence of bone.

Usk

Do not suddenly break the branch, or
Hope to find
The white hart behind the white well.
Glance aside, not for lance, do not spell
Old enchantments. Let them sleep.   5
"Gently dip, but not too deep",
Lift your eyes
Where the roads dip and where the roads rise
Seek only there
Where the grey light meets the green air   10
The hermit's chapel, the pilgrim's prayer.

A Cooking Egg

En l'an trentiesme de mon aage
Que toutes mes hontes j'ay beues . . .

Pipit sat upright in her chair
　　Some distance from where I was sitting;
Views of the Oxford Colleges
　　Lay on the table, with the knitting.

Daguerreotypes and silhouettes,
　　Her grandfather and great great aunts,
Supported on the mantelpiece
　　An *Invitation to the Dance.*

· · · · · · · ·

I shall not want Honour in Heaven
　　For I shall meet Sir Philip Sidney
And have talk with Coriolanus
　　And other heroes of that kidney.

I shall not want Capital in Heaven
　　For I shall meet Sir Alfred Mond.
We two shall lie together, lapt
　　In a five per cent. Exchequer Bond.

I shall not want Society in Heaven,
　　Lucretia Borgia shall be my Bride;
Her anecdotes will be more amusing
　　Than Pipit's experience could provide.

I shall not want Pipit in Heaven:
　　Madame Blavatsky will instruct me
In the Seven Sacred Trances;
　　Piccarda de Donati will conduct me.

· · · · · · · ·

But where is the penny world I bought
    To eat with Pipit behind the screen?
The red-eyed scavengers are creeping
    From Kentish Town and Golder's Green;

Where are the eagles and the trumpets?

    Buried beneath some snow-deep Alps.
Over buttered scones and crumpets
    Weeping, weeping multitudes
Droop in a hundred ABC's.

Triumphal March

Stone, bronze, stone, steel, stone, oakleaves, horses' heels
Over the paving.
And the flags. And the trumpets. And so many eagles.
How many? Count them. And such a press of people.
We hardly knew ourselves that day, or knew the City.   5
This is the way to the temple, and we so many crowding
    the way.
So many waiting, how many waiting? what did it matter,
    on such a day?
Are they coming? No, not yet. You can see some eagles.
  And hear the trumpets.
Here they come. Is he coming?   10
The natural wakeful life of our Ego is a perceiving.
We can wait with our stools and our sausages.
What comes first? Can you see? Tell us. It is

    5,800,000 rifles and carbines,
      102,000 machine guns,   15

    28,000 trench mortars,
    53,000 field and heavy guns,
I cannot tell how many projectiles, mines and fuses,
    13,000 aeroplanes,
    24,000 aeroplane engines,   20
    50,000 ammunition waggons,
now 55,000 army waggons,
    11,000 field kitchens,
    1,150 field bakeries.

What a time that took. Will it be he now? No,   25
Those are the golf club Captains, these the Scouts,
And now the *société gymnastique de Poissy*
And now come the Mayor and the Liverymen. Look
There he is now, look:
There is no interrogation in his eyes   30
Or in the hands, quiet over the horse's neck,
And the eyes watchful, waiting, perceiving, indifferent.
O hidden under the dove's wing, hidden in the turtle's
    breast,
Under the palmtree at noon, under the running water
At the still point of the turning world. O hidden.   35

Now they go up to the temple. Then the sacrifice.
Now come the virgins bearing urns, urns containing
Dust
Dust
Dust of dust, and now   40
Stone, bronze, stone, steel, stone, oakleaves, horses' heels
Over the paving.

That is all we could see. But how many eagles! and how
    many trumpets!
(And Easter Day, we didn't get to the country,

So we took young Cyril to church. And they rang a bell 45
And he said right out loud, *crumpets*.)
     Don't throw away that sausage,
It'll come in handy. He's artful. Please, will you
Give us a light?
Light   50
Light
Et les soldats faisaient la haie? ILS FA FAISAIENT.

Macavity : The Mystery Cat

Macavity's a Mystery Cat: he's called the Hidden Paw—
For he's the master criminal who can defy the Law.
He's the bafflement of Scotland Yard, The Flying Squad's
 despair:
For when they reach the scene of crime—"Macavity's not
 there!"

Macavity, Macavity, there's no one like Macavity, 5
He's broken every human law, he breaks the law of gravity.
His powers of levitation would make a fakir stare,
And when you reach the scene of crime—"Macavity's not
 there!"
You may seek him in the basement, you may look up in
 the air—
But I tell you once and once again, "Macavity's not
 there!"   10

Macavity's a ginger cat; he's very tall and thin;
You would know him if you saw him, for his eyes are
 sunken in.
His brow is deeply lined with thought, his head is highly
 domed;

His coat is dusty from neglect, his whiskers are uncombed.
He sways his head from side to side, with movements like
    a snake;   15
And when you think he's half asleep, he's always wide
    awake.

Macavity, Macavity, there's no one like Macavity.
For he's a fiend in feline shape, a monster of depravity.
You may meet him in a by-street, you may see him in the
    square—
But when the crime's discovered, then "Macavity's not
    there!"   20

He's outwardly respectable. (They say he cheats at cards.)
And his footprints are not found in any file of Scotland
    Yard's.
And when the larder's looted, or the jewel-case is rifled,
Or when the milk is missing, or another Peke's been stifled,
Or the greenhouse glass is broken, and the trellis past
    repair—   25
Ay, there's the wonder of the thing! "Macavity's not
    there!"
And when the Foreign Office find a Treaty's gone astray,
Or the Admiralty lose some plans and drawings by the
    way,
There may be a scrap of paper in the hall or on the stair—
But it's useless to investigate—"Macavity's not there!" 30
And when the loss has been disclosed, the Secret Service
    say:
"It MUST have been Macavity!"—but he's half a mile
    away.

You'll be sure to find him resting, or a-licking of his
    thumbs,
Or engaged in doing complicated long division sums.

Macavity, Macavity, there's no one like Macavity,   35
There never was a Cat of such deceitfulness and suavity.
He always has an alibi, and one or two to spare:
At whatever time the deed took place—MACAVITY
    WASN'T THERE!
And they say that all the Cats whose wicked deeds are
    widely known
(I might mention Mungojerrie, I might mention Griddle-
    bone)   40
Are nothing more than agents for the Cat who all the time
Just controls their operations: the Napoleon of Crime!

Notes

Preludes (p. 217)

This group of four short poems and the closely related one which follows have two chief characteristics. First, they are urban poems, set in the life of a great city; secondly, they each evoke a mood—usually a sad or despondent mood which shows how the poet feels about the life of rented rooms and bed-sitters. The title may be modelled on Chopin's *Preludes*, twenty-four short piano pieces which might also be called 'mood-pieces'.

I *vacant lots:* (from allotment) a vacant plot of land in the
l. 8 city, often used as a dump for rubbish.

(A) Suggest a meaning for l. 4. What features of the poem tell us that the scene is forty or more years ago? Which words or phrases make the scene sordid or squalid? Why should the leaves be 'grimy' (l. 6) and why does the cab-horse 'steam' and 'stamp'? What picture do you get from the last line, remembering the date?

II *coffee-stands:* probably a coffee-stall with canvas top and
l. 5 open counter, serving late revellers from all-night parties and early workers, before cafés or restaurants are open.

l. 6 *masquerade:* literally, a false show or pretence; here the empty and futile activities of the town-dweller.

l. 9 *shades:* what we call window-blinds.

(A) Again, pick out the words or phrases which suggest squalor. How does the morning itself 'come to consciousness' (l. 1)? What corresponds to 'feet' (l. 4) in the second verse, and is there any significance in this 'disembodiment'?

III Again the note of urban squalor is dominant, with an additional distaste for the physical nature of man (could she help the soles of her feet being yellow, even if she might have washed her hands?)

(A) How did the 'thousand sordid images' flicker against the ceiling (ll. 4–6)? What draws the sleeper's attention back to the real world? Explain ll. 10–11. Does this poem show sympathy, or just distaste?

IV   This is perhaps the most powerful of the four Preludes. It implies ⁺hat there is no room for tenderness or sensitivity in the city world.

l. 4   *conscience:* consciousness.

l. 9   *assume:* take charge of—perhaps usurp.

(A)   Suggest what is meant by the first two lines; how is his 'soul stretched tight' and how 'trampled by insistent feet' (l. 3)? Why are the times mentioned in l. 4? What is the relationship between ll. 5, 6, and 7? What change of mood occurs at l. 10? Is the poet in this verse expressing pity for the town-dwellers? What is the response of the town to the 'fancies' and 'the notion'? In what sense do 'the worlds revolve/Like ancient women', and what are women actually doing (for 'lots' see note p. 228).

Morning at the Window (*p. 219*)

(A)   What sort of house will have a basement kitchen? Where is there a wry touch of humour in the first verse? What do you think the housemaids are doing? Where exactly is the poet when observing this scene? What makes the passer-by's smile 'hover' and 'vanish'?

(B)   Having read and studied all the last five poems, attempt a similar impression of some aspect of town life in prose or verse. The piece of writing should be short and the material carefully selected to belong specifically to the city—especially its anonymity and the sense of loneliness when you are surrounded by people you won't ever know.

Journey of the Magi (*p. 219*)

The Magi were the three wise men who visited the infant Christ in the stable. The opening lines come from a sermon by a seventeenth-century writer, Lancelot Andrewes. The first two verses give an apparently casual but in fact extremely precise and vivid account of the journey to Bethlehem, spoken by one of the Magi, now an old man (see l. 32). The third verse is the difficult one, and expresses the idea of ruination of the old order by the revolution of Christianity, the birth of which has meant the death of the life of the narrator's kingdom 'with an alien people clutching their gods', and the narrator awaiting the release of his own death. Two features deserve special note: the intense significance of the journey contrasted with the understatement of its narrative ('the villages dirty', 'there was no information', 'it was (you may say) satisfactory'); and the frequent images during the journey which foretell events in Christ's life.

l. 6   *refractory*: stubborn, resistant.

l. 10   *sherbet*: here, a cooling drink of dilute fruit-juices.

l. 26   *lintel*: stone over the doorway.

l. 27   *dicing*: betting or drawing lots.

l. 41   *dispensation*: order, especially a religious order.

(A)   From the evidence of the first verse, what sort of country did the narrator come from? Which line echoes the first? Explain ll. 19–20 ('With the voices . . . folly'). What picture do you get from 'a water-mill beating the darkness' (l. 23)? What events in Christ's life might be forecast or hinted at by ll. 24 and 27? What is meant by 'not a moment too soon' (l. 30)? Explain ll. 38 and 39 ('this Birth was . . . our death'), and say what picture comes to mind in l. 42 ('With an alien people clutching their gods').

Rannoch, by Glencoe (p. 221)

This and the following poem form part of a group of five short poems called 'Landscapes'. They are more than mere landscapes, however, and associate particular places with historical or legendary events; their rhythms and rhymes are particularly subtle, and deserve study. This one refers to the wild landscape of North Argyll, where in the Pass of Glencoe a large number of the MacDonald clan were massacred in 1692 by the Campbells.

l. 12   *concurrence*: mutual existence, co-operation; even centuries later the bones of the dead cannot 'concur'.

(A)   In what sense does the stag nowadays 'breed for the rifle' (l. 2)? What two nouns are the implied subjects of 'leap and soar' (l. 4)? Suggest a meaning for 'moon cold or moon hot' (l. 5). What picture emerges from ll. 5–9 (attend especially to 'listlessness', 'languor', 'confused wrong', 'apt in silence')? Which sentence is echoed by the last phrase ('in the long pass/No concurrence of bone')?

Usk (p. 221)

A small town on the river Usk in central Monmouth-shire, which passes close to Caerleon, long associated with the legends of King Arthur. There is a ruined Norman castle, and parts of the church date from 1100.

(A) Which expressions suggest that you could easily 'disturb' this legendary landscape? When do you find internal rhymes or echoes in the poem? What does the poet suggest we *should* do in this landscape instead of 'hoping to find' and 'spelling old enchantments'?

(B) Having studied these two poems, write *briefly* in prose or free verse about a place you know which has strong historical or legendary associations.

A Cooking Egg (p. 222)

This is one sample of an extensive and impressive series of early poems in which Eliot depicts the sense of failure and emptiness of modern life, especially, perhaps, urban life. The quotation which heads the poem is the opening of François Villon's 'Great Testament', and means 'In the thirtieth year of my age, when I have drunk all my shame.' This ties in with the title; a cooking egg is one which isn't really fresh. The poem divides into three sections—the first representing a scene in the present, the second his (unrealized) hopes, and the third a lamenta-tion for the hopeless actuality of life.

v. 1 We do not know who Pipit is: she could be an old nurse
& 2 or even his wife; certainly she is prim and old-fashioned. Notice the cosy rhyme 'sitting', 'with the knitting'. A daguerreotype is an early kind of photograph and in Victorian times silhouettes were taken as portraits. She has a touch of old-fashioned romance in the picture on her mantelpiece.

v. 3– His wants as a human being and his early ambitions,
7 now never to be fulfilled, are deferred to 'heaven'. Verse 3 pictures him talking to the heroes of the past;

verse 4 refers to a leading financier of the time; verse 5 points to even more exaggerated dreams: Lucretia Borgia was a formidable and beautiful member of her notorious Renaissance family, contrasted strongly with the dull reality of Pipit's conversation; in verse 6 Madame Blavatsky is a Russian theosophist, an expert in exotic states of spiritual being, and Piccarda de Donati is one of the spiritual guides in Dante's *Paradiso*.

v. 8 & 9 He easily bought in his youth, or thought he had, a 'penny world' to experience or consume in private with Pipit; but in reality the 'red-eyed scavengers' who collect the remnants of such hopes are creeping from their dreary suburbs to the city (perhaps to their daily work as clerks). 'The eagles and the trumpets', his early hopes, are vanished and buried for ever. The people whose hopes, like his, have been defeated, weep silently over snacks in a teashop (ABC is the 'Aerated Bread Company').

Triumphal March (p. 223)

This powerful poem is one of a pair called 'Coriolan', in reference to Shakespeare's play which deals with the problems of statesmanship and the dangers of dictatorship. Its chief effect is satirical: a huge parade to honour a dictator is seen by members of a holiday crowd, and the whole poem is a comment on the essential unreality of the occasion, interspersed by what one critic usefully calls 'slides of the focus, or shiftings of the plane', so that philosophical thought (l. 11 for example) and commonplace absurdities (l. 12, ll. 45–46) exist side by side and comment on the event.

l. 52 *Et les soldats faisaient la haie? ILS LA FAISAIENT:* And did the soldiers line the streets? I'LL SAY THEY DID!

(A) Suggest what effect is made by the opening three lines and whose viewpoint they illustrate. (The 'trumpets and the eagles' echo *A Cooking Egg* p. 222). What is the effect of the ludicrous and horrifying list of weapons and armaments in ll. 14–25? Where is there a sense of anti-climax after this? Where is 'the leader' described, and what is the significance of 'no interrogation' (l. 30) and 'indifferent' (l. 32)? Describe him in your own words. Where does the poem 'shift' to eternal realities as contrasting with the dictator's kind of reality (rifles, machine guns, etc.)? How does the poet avoid our feeling that he is describing a particular period of history or a particular military dictator (consider ll. 26–28, 37, and 44–46). Why is the word 'dust 'repeated in l. 38–40 and why is the opening line repeated here (think again of *who* is seeing the procession)? What is the point of ll. 44–46, and what reminded Cyril of 'crumpets' in church? What meaning in addition to asking for a light for a cigarette do you see in ll. 48–50? Finally, say in general terms how effective an attack on the pretensions of political and military leaders you find this poem. By what means is the whole thing made absurd?

(B)   Write a satirical account of a public occasion like *Triumphal March*, making use of some of Eliot's devices as well as your own.

Macavity: the Mystery Cat (*p. 225*)

This is perhaps the most famous of the comic poems about cats which Eliot wrote as a relaxation from his serious poetry and plays, and called *Old Possum's Book of Practical Cats*. It can perhaps act also as a relaxation for us. It doesn't need any solemn or detailed analysis; its charm comes from its neat rhymes and galloping rhythm as well as the comic effect of a master-criminal who is in fact a cat.

l. 7   He can raise himself magically into the air so skilfully as to make a Mohammedan devotee (who would be very skilled at such tricks) stare in wonder.

l. 36   *suavity*: blandness of manner; he is deceitful but conceals it with great skill and elegance.

FURTHER READING

Selected Poems (Penguin). Very good on early and middle poems, but doesn't include the later ones.

Collected Poems (Faber). Many of these are very difficult, but you could follow some of the easier ones without help.

Murder in the Cathedral (Faber). Probably the finest of his plays; about the murder of Thomas à Becket.

CRITICAL WRITING

F. R. Leavis. *New Bearings in English Poetry*. Rather advanced but very helpful on what Eliot has contributed that is new to English poetry. Dr Leavis was almost the first critic to recognize Eliot's importance.

L. G. Salinger. "T. S. Eliot, Poet and Critic" (in *Pelican Guide to English Literature*, Vol. 7).

W. H. Auden

W. H. AUDEN was born at York in 1907, the son of a doctor. He was educated at Gresham's School at Holt, Norfolk, and at Christ Church, Oxford. After his university career he spent some time in Germany, and then taught in England and Scotland for a time. *Poems* appeared in 1930, and *The Orators* in 1932. Later he worked on documentary films—for example he wrote the verse commentary to a film called *Night Mail*, made by the GPO Film Unit. He met Christopher Isherwood and wrote a number of plays with him (*e.g.* *The Dog Beneath the Skin* (1935), *The Ascent of F6* (1936)). During the Spanish Civil War he served as stretcher-bearer with the Republicans. He travelled widely in Europe and paid visits to Iceland (*Letters from Iceland* (1937)) and China, on which he published a travel book. In 1938 he went to the United States, and there he held several posts as lecturer in schools and universities; he remained in America and became a naturalized citizen of the USA. In 1956 he was elected Professor of Poetry at Oxford. Among his volumes of verse are *Look Stranger* (1936), *Another Time* (1940), *New Year Letter* (1941), *For the Time Being* (1945), *The Age of Anxiety* (1948), *Nones* (1952), and *The Shield of Achilles* (1955) as well as the frequently revised *Collected Shorter Poems*. He died in 1973.

Auden's reputation was made in the 'thirties, a period not easily understood by students today. From 1930 onwards there was a series of crises, international and national, and everyone was conscious of the rising menace of war in Europe: more specifically, the rise of fascism and the economic crises in the West (*e.g.* more than two million unemployed in Britain) made it an intensely political period, when even the most reluctant were driven into political involvement. Auden early identified himself with the left wing in opposition to the rise of dictatorship in Europe, and to those in England who tolerated or even co-operated with fascism. Thus his first volume (*Poems* (1930)) is strongly political in content or implication, and this basic attitude remained, in spite of inconsistencies, at least till the Second World War.

He had from the beginning a formidable talent and brilliance, though his prolific poetry has always been uneven; the first few volumes were original, lively, and vigorously committed to the real issues of his time. They show also a very wide range of reference, to science, psychology, philosophy, even geology, and—more disconcerting—an excessive use of purely personal symbols and private jokes, which sometimes seemed to point backwards to adolescence; their liveliness, frequent gaiety, often fresh and colloquial language were often counterbalanced by wilful obscurity, over-ingenuity, and a kind of 'free-wheeling'. Auden showed a deep interest in language and metaphor, and much of his early imagery—derelict landscape, ruined industrial scenes, slagheaps, glaciers, guerrilla warfare with its maps, spies, outposts, frontiers ('Making gunpowder in the top room')—was immediately adopted by imitators. Two volumes with a high proportion of good poems belong to this period, *Look Stranger* (1936) and *Another Time* (1940). He showed throughout an extraordinary facility in various verse forms —he can write very effective light verse as well—a facility that sometimes deteriorates into slickness. He wrote interesting and sometimes fine elegiac verse on writers and thinkers (Yeats and Freud, for example); simple and direct love poems (*e.g. That Night when Joy Began*, p. 239); satire and parody, often dazzling, sometimes cruel; very uneven but often interesting verse plays; sonnet sequences, verse letters, loose and strict forms, with equal apparent ease. He can use, in fact, a remarkable variety of patterns and tones, and only a very small part of his range can be represented here. He is almost always lively and provocative, skilled and ingenious, and these are valuable and not common qualities; but many critics feel that he did not fulfil the great promise of his first book, and that he never wrote a major poem.

O What is that Sound?

O what is that sound which so thrills the ear
    Down in the valley drumming, drumming?
Only the scarlet soldiers, dear,
    The soldiers coming.

O what is that light I see flashing so clear
    Over the distance brightly, brightly?
Only the sun on their weapons, dear,
    As they step lightly.

O what are they doing with all that gear,
    What are they doing this morning, this morning?
Only their usual manœuvres, dear,
    Or perhaps a warning.

O why have they left the road down there,
    Why are they suddenly wheeling, wheeling?
Perhaps a change in their orders, dear.
    Why are you kneeling?

O haven't they stopped for the doctor's care,
    Haven't they reined their horses, their horses?
Why, they are none of them wounded, dear,
    None of these forces.

O is it the parson they want, with white hair,
    Is it the parson, is it, is it?
No, they are passing his gateway, dear,
    Without a visit.

O it must be the farmer who lives so near.
   It must be the farmer so cunning, so cunning?
They have passed the farmyard already, dear,
   And now they are running.

O where are you going? Stay with me here!
   Were the vows you swore deceiving, deceiving?
No, I promised to love you, dear,
   But I must be leaving.

O it's broken the lock and splintered the door,
   O it's the gate where they're turning, turning;
Their boots are heavy on the floor
   And their eyes are burning.

O Where are You Going?

"O where are you going?" said reader to rider,
"That valley is fatal when furnaces burn,
Yonder's the midden whose odours will madden,
That gap is the grave where the tall return."

"O do you imagine," said fearer to farer,
"That dusk will delay on your path to the pass,
Your diligent looking discover the lacking
Your footsteps feel from granite to grass?"

"O what was that bird," said horror to hearer,
"Did you see that shape in the twisted trees?
Behind you swiftly the figure comes softly,
The spot on your skin is a shocking disease?"

"Out of this house"—said rider to reader,
"Yours never will"—said farer to fearer,
"They're looking for you"—said hearer to horror,
As he left them there, as he left them there.

Epitaph on a Tyrant

Perfection, of a kind, was what he was after,
And the poetry he invented was easy to understand;
He knew human folly like the back of his hand,
And was greatly interested in armies and fleets;
When he laughed, respectable senators burst with
    laughter,   5
And when he cried the little children died in the streets.

That Night When Joy Began . . .

That night when joy began
Our narrowest veins to flush,
We waited for the flash
Of morning's levelled gun.   4

But morning let us pass
And day by day relief
Outgrows his nervous laugh,
Grows credulous of peace,   8

As mile by mile is seen
No trespasser's reproach,
And love's best glasses reach
No fields but are his own.   12

Now the Leaves are Falling Fast

Now the leaves are falling fast,
Nurse's flowers will not last;
Nurses to the graves are gone,
And the prams go rolling on.   4

Whispering neighbours, left and right,
Pluck us from the real delight;
And the active hands must freeze
Lonely on the separate knees.   8

Dead in hundreds at the back
Follow wooden in our track,
Arms raised stiffly to reprove
In false attitudes of love.   12

Starving through the leafless wood
Trolls run scolding for their food;
And the nightingale is dumb,
And the angel will not come.   16

Cold, impossible, ahead
Lifts the mountain's lovely head
Whose white waterfall could bless
Travellers in their last distress.   20

Who's Who

A shilling life will give you all the facts:
How Father beat him, how he ran away,
What were the struggles of his youth, what acts
Made him the greatest figure of his day:
Of how he fought, fished, hunted, worked all night, 5
Though giddy, climbed new mountains; named a
  sea:
Some of the last researchers even write
Love made him weep pints like you and me.

With all his honours on, he sighed for one
Who, say astonished critics, lived at home;   10
Did little jobs about the house with skill
And nothing else; could whistle, would sit still
Or potter round the garden; answered some
Of his long marvellous letters but kept none.

The Novelist

Encased in talent like a uniform,
The rank of every poet is well known;
They can amaze us like a thunderstorm,
Or die so young, or live for years alone.   4

They can dash forward like hussars; but he
Must struggle out of his boyish gift and learn
How to be plain and awkward, how to be
One after whom none think it worth to turn.   8

For, to achieve his lightest wish, he must
Become the whole of boredom, subject to
Vulgar complaints like love, among the Just

Be just, among the Filthy filthy too,   12
And in his own weak person, if he can,
Must suffer dully all the wrongs of Man.

Over the Heather the Wet Wind Blows

Over the heather the wet wind blows,
I've lice in my tunic and a cold in my nose.

The rain comes pattering out of the sky,
I'm a Wall soldier, I don't know why.

The mist creeps over the hard grey stone,
My girl's in Tungria; I sleep alone.   6

Aulus goes hanging around her place,
I don't like his manners, I don't like his face.

Piso's a Christian, he worships a fish;
There'd be no kissing if he had his wish.

She gave me a ring but I diced it away;
I want my girl and I want my pay.   12

When I'm a veteran with only one eye
I shall do nothing but look at the sky.

On This Island

Look, stranger, on this island now
The leaping light for your delight discovers,
Stand stable here
And silent be,
That through the channels of the ear   5
May wander like a river
The swaying sound of the sea.

Here at the small field's ending pause
When the chalk wall falls to the foam and its tall
ledges
Oppose the pluck   10
And knock of the tide,
And the shingle scrambles after the suck-
ing surf,
And the gull lodges
A moment on its sheer side.

Far off like floating seeds the ships   15
Diverge on urgent voluntary errands,
And the full view
Indeed may enter
And move in memory as now these clouds do,
That pass the harbour mirror   20
And all the summer through the water saunter.

The Unknown Citizen

(To JS/07/M/378
This Marble Monument
Is Erected by the State)

He was found by the Bureau of Statistics to be
One against whom there was no official complaint,
And all the reports on his conduct agree
That, in the modern sense of an old-fashioned word, he
    was a saint,
For in everything he did he served the Greater
    Community.   5
Except for the War till the day he retired
He worked in a factory and never got fired,
But satisfied his employers, Fudge Motors Inc.
Yet he wasn't a scab or odd in his views,
For his Union reports that he paid his dues,   10
(Our report on his Union shows it was sound)
And our Social Psychology workers found
That he was popular with his mates and liked a drink.
The Press are convinced that he bought a paper every day
And that his reactions to advertisements were normal in
    every way.   15
Policies taken out in his name prove that he was fully
    insured,
And his Health-card shows he was once in hospital but left
    it cured.
Both Producers Research and High-Grade Living declare
He was fully sensible to the advantages of the Instalment
    Plan
And had everything necessary to the Modern Man,   20
A phonograph, a radio, a car and a frigidaire.

Our researchers into Public Opinion are content
That he held the proper opinions for the time of year,
When there was peace, he was for peace; when there was
        war, he went.
He was married and added five children to the
        population,   25
Which our Eugenist says was the right number for a parent
        of his generation,
And our teachers report that he never interfered with their
        education.
Was he free? Was he happy? The question is absurd:
Had anything been wrong, we should certainly have heard.

A Permanent Way

Self-drivers may curse their luck,
Stuck on new-fangled trails,
But the good old train will jog
To the dogma of the rails

And steam so straight ahead
That I cannot be led astray
By tempting scenes which occur
Along any permanent way.

Intriguing dales escape
Into hills of the shape I like,
Though, were I actually put
Where a foot-path leaves the pike

For some steep romantic spot,
I should ask what chance there is
Of at least a ten-dollar cheque
Or a family peck of a kiss:

But, forcibly held to my tracks,
I can safely relax and dream
Of a love and a livelihood
To fit that wood or stream;

And what could be greater fun
Once one has chosen and paid,
Than the inexpensive delight
Of the choice one might have made.

Notes

O What is that Sound? (p. 237)

This poem is called *The Quarry* in some editions. It is an early poem in ballad form, and there are two voices—an innocent and naïve one who asks the questions and an 'experienced' one who answers them. In one sense it is merely a ballad, though with a powerful building-up of tension; but if you know that it was written in the 'thirties when most people were conscious of the immediate menace of war or attack, you will see that it is also a kind of allegory. In this interpretation, if the questioner is the ordinary citizen, who might the person who answers be?

(A) What indication is there in the first two verses that the soldiers seem glamorous to the questioner, and which repeated word particularly suggests that the answering voice is pretending that they aren't dangerous? Where does an air of real menace first appear? Why are 'none of them wounded' (verse 5)? Which three people does the questioner hope the soldiers are 'aiming at'? Suggest what difference there is between the phrasing of the questions in verses 5–7, and why? What happens to the 'answerer' in verse 8, and what light does this cast on his or her previous answers? What final answer to all the questions is given in the last verse, what is the final 'quarry' of the soldiers, and why is there no question and answer in this verse?

(B) Write in prose or verse a narrative which depends on an increasing air of quiet menace.

O Where are You Going? (p. 238)

This fine early poem has something in common with the previous one. In each of the first three verses fears and dangers are stated or hinted at by unnamed speakers; in the last verse the fears are answered by the person they try to frighten.

[247]

(A) To understand the structure of the poem, find the 'names' of the three questioners and the person they are addressing; the first is 'reader to rider'. Then ask yourself what the three questioners' names, and what the three 'answerers'' have in common. What contrast is there between these three pairs of names, and what relationship is there in the sounds of the pairs? What kinds of danger are described in the first verse and how are they appropriate warnings to a 'rider'? Then answer the same questions about verses 2 and 3. Which of the fears and dangers seem real ones, and which are more like nightmares? Which question exactly is answered in the first line of the fourth verse, which in the second, and which in the third? What does the *rhythm* of the last line suggest that the 'rider' or 'farer' is doing after his answers? What general moral do you think the poet is offering, and how is it applicable to us all?

Epitaph on a Tyrant (p. 239)

A sketch of a potential dictator; you might perhaps think of Hitler or Mussolini, or perhaps some pettier dictator in South America or the Caribbean. (It can usefully be compared with the much more powerful *Triumphal March* of T. S. Eliot, p. 223.)

(A) In what sense was the tyrant 'after perfection' and what is added by 'of a kind' (l. 1)? Why did the 'respectable senators' laugh, and what is the force of the word 'respectable' here (l. 5)? Explain carefully the exact meaning of the last line.

(B) Write an epitaph, in prose or verse, to go on the tombstone of a tyrant you know or know of.

That Night when Joy Began . . . (p. 239)

A short love poem.

(A) In the first verse, what is meant by l. 2, and what suggests that the lovers believe their love will not last? In what sense would morning seem like a 'levelled gun', and how does the word 'flash' link 'morning' with 'gun'?

In verse 2 what implies that the love survives this danger, why has relief at first a 'nervous laugh', and what does 'credulous' mean? In the third verse what 'landscape' are the lovers looking at, and what is meant by 'trespasser's reproach'? What sort of 'glasses' are referred to in l. 11, and what is the significance of the last line? Point out anything notable about the kind of rhymes in this poem, and if you have read Owen's poems (pp. 153–161) say what such rhymes are called.

Now the Leaves are Falling Fast (p. 240)

One critic has said that this poem echoes the work of Housman and Blake (see pp. 33–49). One way of looking at it is as a summary of the frustrations inherent in human life, the aspirations that are not fulfilled, the sense in which each of us lives and dies alone. But there is also some typical mystification in some of the images.

v. 4   *trolls*: mischievous dwarfs (from Norse mythology).

(A)   What features in the poem suggest that life is a journey? In verse 1 where is mortality stressed, and where the continuity of life? How do the 'whispering neighbours' 'pluck us from the real delight' (verse 2), and where are the gestures of love frustrated? How does verse 3 suggest the dead hand of tradition and the past? What earlier line is referred to by 'leafless wood' in l. 4, and why is 'scolding' a better word than (say) 'howling'? What kinds of emotion are symbolized by 'nightingale' and 'angel' (verse 4), and what by the mountain and the waterfall of verse 5? How specifically could the waterfall 'bless' distressed travellers, and what is the force of the word 'impossible' applied to the mountain?

Who's Who (p. 241)

This is a sonnet, and it draws a contrast between the publicly known facts of a famous man's life (in the octave or first eight lines) and the private truth about his emotional life and the humble person he loved.

(A)   What is a 'shilling life', and what do you find ironic about 'all the facts' (l. 1)? Is there any significance in his father beating him and his running away? Which lines describe acts and which (in the octave) make him like other human beings? Why were the critics 'astonished' to learn that he loved the person he did (ll. 9–10)? Describe the person he loved in your own words; why did she 'answer some' of his 'long marvellous letters' but not keep any (ll. 13–14)? Who are the 'critics' and the 'researchers', why are they concerned with his life, and what would *their* attitude be to the destruction of his letters? Explain the meaning of the title.

(B) Write a short piece about the contrast of public and private life of a great person.

The Novelist (p. 241)

Another sonnet, one of a series about various kinds of writers and artists.

(A) Exactly which part of the poem deals with the poet, and which images describe him as 'romantic'? Suggest names of poets who 'died young' or 'lived for years alone' (l. 4). What might the novelist's 'boyish gift' be (l. 5) and why must he be 'plain and awkward' and 'become the whole of boredom'? Why must the novelist, as distinct from the poet, be 'just among the Just' and 'filthy among the Filthy' (ll. 11–12)?

What is the novelist's 'lightest wish' (l. 9)? Why must he suffer 'all the wrongs of Man' (l. 14)? Do you think Auden's view of the novelist's work applies to all novelists, or few? Make some suggestions if you can. Do you think Auden, as a poet, feels pity for the responsibilities of the novelist?

Over the Heather the Wet Wind Blows (p. 242)

A clever little poem with a 'blues rhythm'; the title suggests that a Roman soldier is guarding one of the walls the Romans built to keep out invaders.

l. 6 *Tungria:* presumably a Roman province.

l. 9 *fish:* the fish was an early Christian secret symbol, because its Greek name (*ichthus*) was believed to conceal a statement about Christ.

(A) Suggest which wall the soldier is guarding on the evidence of l. 1. Why should a Roman soldier especially catch cold there (l. 2)? Where is the 'wet wind' echoed? Which verses or lines express his loneliness and which his anxieties? Suggest who 'Aulus' (l. 7) might be, and what the soldier fears about him. Explain l. 10 about Piso the Christian; how do you know that he doesn't understand the early Christians? What is meant by 'veteran', and why does he expect to have 'only one eye' (l. 13)? How will the sky he then looks at differ from the one he's looking at now? Why are the blues rhythm and title appropriate to this poem?

(B) Write a 'blues' for a modern soldier far away from home, or write a tune for this one.

On this Island (p. 243)

This is one of Auden's few pieces of natural description, perhaps of a coastal scene in the West Country. It is a poem of place and scene, and suffers from none of the strain of some of his poems; here there is no display of learning, but a delight in the scene for itself, and a delicate movement that fits the subject.

(A) What might cause the light to 'leap' (l. 2)? What alliteration and echoes of sound do you detect in the first verse? What is compared to 'the channels of the ear'? Suggest what might be meant on a small island by 'the small field's ending pause' (l. 8). How do the ledges of the chalk wall 'oppose' the movement of the tide? Which two words describe the dragging and the pounding of the waves and how do they express sound as well as movement? What effect is added by splitting the word 'suck-ing'; is this a flow or ebb of the wave? Where do you find true rhymes and where half-rhymes in this verse? In what sense are the distant ships like 'seeds' (l. 16)—consider their shape as seen from above and what their function is. How do they diverge (l. 17), and why 'voluntary'? Find in the last four lines half-rhymes and echoing words, and show how these fit the subject— how in fact echoes in the memory are like reflections in the water.

(B) Write a sketch of a coastal landscape, aiming at brevity and precision.

The Unknown Citizen (p. 244)

This bitterly satirical poem was written after Auden became an American citizen. The title echoes the name on the grave of 'the Unknown Soldier' buried ceremonially after the First World War. The picture is that of an average citizen who has been analysed by computer and statistics but whose individuality is still unknown.

l. 26 *Eugenist:* scientist, or pseudo-scientist, concerned with breeding a fine race, in this case of human beings.

(A) Why the reference number under the title? What does it tell us about the State's attitude to the dead man? What role is played in the satirical point of the poem by 'Bureau of Statistics' and 'Greater Community' (ll. 1 and 5)? Make a list of the other capitalized bodies for whom this man was only a number. Where is the irony in 'everything necessary to the Modern Man' (l. 20)? Where are his opinions described apart from ll. 23–24? Comment on these opinions, and explain the satirical force of ll. 23, 26, and 27. In what way is the bitterness of the poem concentrated in the last two lines?

(B) Write some satirical verses on the Unknown Citizen of your country.

A Permanent Way (p. 245)

This poem is closely related in theme to Robert Graves's *Here Live your Life out!* (p. 261) and should be compared with it in some detail. Consider what double meaning the title has, and the exact meaning of the last verse.

FURTHER READING

Selected Poems (Penguin).
Collected Shorter Poems (Faber).

CRITICAL WRITING

R. G. Cox. "The Poetry of W. H. Auden" (an essay in *Pelican Guide to English Literature*, Vol. 7).
R. Hoggart. *Auden: an Introductory Essay* (Chatto and Windus).

Robert Graves

ROBERT GRAVES, poet, critic, and novelist, was born in Wimbledon, London, in 1895, the son of a poet, A. P. Graves. He was educated at Charterhouse, joined the army straight from school, and served throughout the First World War, during which he published two small volumes of poetry. He went back to complete his education at St John's College, Oxford, and worked in Cairo for one year (1926) as Professor of English Literature. He has lived in Majorca in the Balearic Isles off Spain since the Second World War. He produced a large output of fiction (*I, Claudius* was awarded two literary prizes in 1934), criticism, translation, etc., but his chief concern has been with poetry, in which he has continued to write from 1914 to the present day. He was elected Professor of Poetry at Oxford in 1961.

Robert Graves has been throughout his life a dedicated poet, though he has done important work in many other kinds of writing. *Goodbye to All That* (1929) is a notable piece of autobiography as well as a fine personal account of trench warfare in the First World War; he has written distinguished novels, the result of scholarship combined with imaginative power (some titles are suggested in 'Further Reading', p. 271). He has written some highly individual and powerful criticism, especially of poetry (*A Survey of Modernist Poetry* (with Laura Riding, 1927), *The Common Asphodel* (1949)), collections of essays (*Steps* (1958)), an interesting compilation about reading, *The Reader Over your Shoulder* (with Alan Ross), translations of classical works, notably *The Golden Ass*, and a valuable reference book with a highly personal tone, *Greek Myths* (Penguin, 1955). In spite of this large output his major work throughout his life has been poetry, and he tends to regard his novels as pot-boilers in comparison.

His poems are fairly few in number and nearly all

lyrical in form. He is very much of a perfectionist in relation to his own poems; he has continually repressed poems which in his view 'no longer pass muster', and the result, he writes, is that

> Collected Poems 1959 is not much longer than Collected Poems 1926. Critics may decide that the benefit of the doubt is being too generously conceded. They will be right, of course. At any rate, I can promise that no silver spoons have been thrown out with the refuse, and that I have been fair to my younger, middle, and elder selves. The survival rate has kept fairly even throughout the period, at five poems a year.

Though his range is large, there is an increasing emphasis on love poems, especially where the loved person is almost identified with the White Goddess he half believes in—the archetypal, partly maternal, partly mistress figure of so many primitive religions—on whom he has written a long and learned book (*The White Goddess* (1948)).

Because most of his love poems are difficult, only one is included here (*Mid-winter Waking*, p. 261). But he has many other subjects, and there is always a play of subtle intelligence and grace of form; he is fascinated by oddity or mysteries and writes of them with a strong element of fantasy and humour (*Lost Acres*, p. 255, *Flying Crooked*, p. 256, *Warning to Children*, p. 257)—these are essentially poems about ideas; he is moved by certain landscapes which he sees with remarkable vividness (*Rocky Acres*, p. 258, *Here Live Your Life Out!*, p. 261); he can write charming and original poems about the simple day-to-day domesticities, sometimes directly (*The China Plate*, p. 264), sometimes in terms of an invented myth (*Lollocks*, p. 262). Robert Graves's poetry is never modish and seems timeless; his work is not really at all like that of his contemporaries. Perhaps what really distinguishes his poetry is the clash his sparkling intelligence and passionate feelings make against the cool skilled measured rhythms and patterns of his verse forms.

Lost Acres

These acres, always again lost
    By every new ordnance-survey
And searched for at exhausting cost
    Of time and thought, are still away.   4

They have their paper-substitute—
    Intercalation of an inch
At the so-many-thousandth foot:
    And no one parish feels the pinch.   8

But lost they are, despite all care,
    And perhaps likely to be bound
Together in a piece somewhere,
    A plot of undiscovered ground.   12

Invisible, they have the spite
    To swerve the tautest measuring-chain
And the exact theodolite
    Perched every side of them in vain.   16

Yet, be assured, we have no need
    To plot these acres of the mind
With prehistoric fern and reed
    And monsters such as heroes find.   20

Maybe they have their flowers, their birds,
    Their trees behind the phantom fence,
But of a substance without words:
    To walk there would be loss of sense.   24

Love Without Hope

Love without hope, as when the young bird-catcher
Swept off his tall hat to the Squire's own daughter,
So let the imprisoned larks escape and fly
Singing about her head, as she rode by.

Flying Crooked

The butterfly, a cabbage-white,
(His honest idiocy of flight)
Will never now, it is too late,
Master the art of flying straight,   4
Yet has—who knows so well as I?—
A just sense of how not to fly:
He lurches here and here by guess
And God and hope and hopelessness.   8
Even the aerobatic swift
Has not his flying-crooked gift.

The Bards

The bards falter in shame, their running verse
Stumbles, with marrow-bones the drunken diners
Pelt them for their delay.
It is a something fearful in the song
Plagues them—an unknown grief that like a churl   5
Goes commonplace in cowskin
And bursts unheralded, crowing and coughing,

An unpilled holly-club twirled in his hand,
Into their many-shielded, samite-curtained,
Jewel-bright hall where twelve kings sit at chess   10
Over the white-bronze pieces and the gold;
And by a gross enchantment
Flails down the rafters and leads off the queens—
The wild-swan-breasted, the rose-ruddy-cheeked
Raven-haired daughters of their admiration —   15
To stir his black pots and to bed on straw.

Warning to Children

Children, if you dare to think
Of the greatness, rareness, muchness,
Fewness of this precious only
Endless world in which you say
You live, you think of things like this: 5
Blocks of slate enclosing dappled
Red and green, enclosing tawny
Yellow nets, enclosing white
And black acres of dominoes,
Where a neat brown paper parcel   10
Tempts you to untie the string.
In the parcel a small island,
On the island a large tree,
On the tree a husky fruit.
Strip the husk and pare the rind off: 15
In the kernel you will see
Blocks of slate enclosed by dappled
Red and green, enclosed by tawny
Yellow nets, enclosed by white
And black acres of dominoes,   20

Where the same brown paper parcel —
Children, leave the string untied!
For who dares undo the parcel
Finds himself at once inside it,
On the island, in the fruit,   25
Blocks of slate about his head,
Finds himself enclosed by dappled
Green and red, enclosed by yellow
Tawny nets, enclosed by black
And white acres of dominoes,   30
With the same brown paper parcel
Still untied upon his knee.
And, if he then should dare to think
Of the fewness, muchness, rareness,
Greatness of this endless only   35
Precious world in which he says
He lives—he then unties the string.

Rocky Acres

This is a wild land, country of my choice,
With harsh craggy mountain, moor ample and bare.
Seldom in these acres is heard any voice
But voice of cold water that runs here and there
Through rocks and lank heather growing without care. 5
No mice in the heath run, no song-birds fly
For fear of the buzzard that floats in the sky.

He soars and he hovers, rocking on his wings,
He scans his wide parish with a sharp eye,
He catches the trembling of small hidden things,   10
He tears them in pieces, dropping them from the sky;

Tenderness and pity the heart will deny,
Where life is but nourished by water and rock —
A hardy adventure, full of fear and shock.

Time has never journeyed to this lost land,   15
Crakeberry and heather bloom out of date,
The rocks jut, the streams flow singing on either hand,
Careless if the season be early or late,
The skies wander overhead, now blue, now slate;
Winter would be known by his cutting snow   20
If June did not borrow his armour also.

Yet this is my country, beloved by me best,
The first land that rose from Chaos and the Flood,
Nursing no valleys for comfort and rest,
Trampled by no shod hooves, bought with no blood.   25
Sempiternal country whose barrows have stood
Stronghold for demigods when on earth they go,
Terror for fat burghers on far plains below.

Song : Lift boy

Let me tell you the story of how I began:
I began as the knife-boy and ended as the boot-man,
With nothing in my pockets but a jack-knife and a button,
With nothing in my pockets but a jack-knife and a button,
With nothing in my pockets.   5

Let me tell you the story of how I went on:
I began as the lift-boy and ended as the lift-man,
With nothing in my pockets but a jack-knife and a button,
With nothing in my pockets but a jack-knife and a button,
With nothing in my pockets.   10

I found it very easy to whistle and play
With nothing in my head or my pockets all day,
With nothing in my pockets.

But along came Old Eagle, like Moses or David,
He stopped at the fourth floor and preached me
     Damnation: 15
"Not a soul shall be saved, not one shall be saved.
The whole First Creation shall forfeit salvation:
From knife-boy to lift-boy, from ragged to regal,
Not one shall be saved, not you, not Old Eagle,
No soul on earth escapeth, even if all repent—"   20
So I cut the cords of the lift and down we went,
With nothing in our pockets.

In Broken Images

He is quick, thinking in clear images;
I am slow, thinking in broken images.

He becomes dull, trusting to his clear images;
I become sharp, mistrusting my broken images.   4

Trusting his images, he assumes their relevance;
Mistrusting my images, I question their relevance.

Assuming their relevance, he assumes the fact;
Questioning their relevance, I question the fact.   8

When the fact fails him, he questions his senses;
When the fact fails me, I approve my senses.

He continues quick and dull in his clear images;
I continue slow and sharp in my broken images.   12

He in a new confusion of his understanding;
I in a new understanding of my confusion.

Mid-winter Waking

Stirring suddenly from long hibernation,
I knew myself once more a poet
Guarded by timeless principalities
Against the worm of death, this hillside haunting;
And presently dared open both my eyes.   5

O gracious, lofty, shone against from under,
Back-of-the-mind-far clouds like towers;
And you, sudden warm airs that blow
Before the expected season of new blossom,
While sheep still gnaw at roots and lambless go—   10

Be witness that on waking, this mid-winter,
I found her hand in mine laid closely
Who shall watch out the Spring with me.
We stared in silence all around us
But found no winter anywhere to see.   15

Here Live your Life out!

Window-gazing, at one time or another
In the course of travel, you must have startled at
Some coign of true felicity. "Stay!" it beckoned,
"Here live your life out!" If you were simple-hearted

The village rose, perhaps, from a broad stream   5
Lined with alders and gold-flowering flags—
Hills, mills, hay-fields, orchards—and, plain to see,
The very house behind its mulberry-tree
Stood, by a miracle, untenanted!

Alas, you could not alight, found yourself jolted   10
Viciously on. Public conveyances
Are not amenable to casual halts
Except in sternly drawn emergencies—
Bandits, floods, landslides, earthquakes or the like—
Nor could you muster resolution enough   15
To shout: "This is emergency, let me out!",
Rushing to grasp their brakes; so the whole scene
Withdrew for ever. Once at the terminus
(As your internal mentor will have told you),
It would have been pure folly to engage   20
A private car, drive back, sue for possession.
Too far, too late:
Already bolder tenants were at the gate.

Lollocks

By sloth on sorrow fathered,
These dusty-featured Lollocks
Have their nativity in all disordered
Backs of cupboard drawers.   4

They play hide and seek
Among collars and novels
And empty medicine bottles,
And letters from abroad   8
That never will be answered.

Every sultry night
They plague little children,
Gurgling from the cistern,   12
Humming from the air,
Skewing up the bed-clothes,
Twitching the blind.

When the imbecile agèd   16
Are over-long in dying
And the nurse drowses,
Lollocks come skipping
Up the tattered stairs   20
And are nasty together
In the bed's shadow.

The signs of their presence
Are boils on the neck,   24
Dreams of vexation suddenly recalled
In the middle of the morning,
Languor after food.

Men cannot see them,   28
Men cannot hear them,
Do not believe in them—
But suffer the more,
Both in neck and belly.   32

Women can see them—
O those naughty wives
Who sit by the fireside
Munching bread and honey,   36
Watching them in mischief
From corners of their eyes,
Slily allowing them to lick
Honey-sticky fingers.   40

Sovereign against Lollocks
Are hard broom and soft broom,
To well comb the hair,
To well brush the shoe,   44
And to pay every debt
As it falls due.

The China Plate

From a crowded barrow in a street-market
The plate was ransomed for a few coppers,
Was brought gleefully home, given a place
On a commanding shelf.   4

"Quite a museum-piece", an expert cries
(Eyeing it through the ready pocket-lens)—
As though a glass case would be less sepulchral
Than the barrow-hearse!   8

For weeks this plate retells the history
Whenever an eye runs in that direction:
"Near perdition I was, in a street-market
With rags and old shoes".   12

"A few coppers"—here once again
The purchaser's proud hand lifts down
The bargain, displays the pot-bank sign
Scrawled raggedly underneath.   16

Enough, permit the treasure to forget
The emotion of that providential purchase,
Becoming a good citizen of the house
Like its fellow-crockery.   20

Let it dispense sandwiches at a party
And not be noticed in the drunken buzz,
Or little cakes at afternoon tea
When cakes are in demand.   24

Let it regain a lost habit of life,
Foreseeing death in honourable breakage
Somewhere between the kitchen and the shelf
To be sincerely mourned.   28

Leaving the Rest Unsaid

Finis, apparent on an earlier page,
With fallen obelisk for colophon
Must this be here repeated?

Death has been ruefully announced
And to die once is death enough,   5
Be sure, for any life-time.

Must the book end, as you would end it,
With testamentary appendices
And graveyard indices?

But no, I will not lay me down   10
To let your tearful music mar
The decent mystery of my progress.

So now, my solemn ones, leaving the rest unsaid,
Rising in air as on a gander's wing
At a careless comma,   15

Notes

Lost Acres (p. 255)

This strange and fascinating poem, typical of Graves's early work, is not easy: it expresses the idea that there may be minor errors in surveying which correspond to the 'intercalary' day inserted into the calendar (Feb. 29 in leap years) to make the solar and calendar years correspond.

v. 1   Surveyors try to find the lost acres without success.

v. 2   Maps are distorted very slightly so that 'no one parish feels the pinch'—*i.e.*, misses the small area.

v. 3   Perhaps these missing 'bits' are all together in one place.

v. 4   No one can measure or find them. *Theodolite:* surveyor's measuring instrument.

v. 5   They are 'acres of the mind' beyond the power of words
–6   or understanding.

(A)   Has this poem a kind of logic? Can you imagine the 'lost acres' or at least the idea of them? What sort of appeal does a poem of this kind make?

(B)   Write a story or poem about finding a small area 'behind the phantom fence' of which no one knows, and what happened there.

Love without Hope (p. 256)

(A)   What was significant in the bird-catcher's gesture, and where did he keep his birds? What kind of compliment to the Squire's daughter is suggested? Why the title?

Flying Crooked (p. 256)

Another charming small poem, which suggests that the cabbage-white's apparently idiotic way of flying may be right for him; at least he is very skilled at 'flying crooked'!

(A)   What is meant by 'who knows as well as I' (l. 5)? Give, or guess, the meaning of 'aerobatic'. What is the bird called a swift like, and why is its name appropriate? What general thought does this poem promote?

(B) Write a poem about another animal, bird, or insect which might be commended for doing something that is apparently unskilful or clumsy.

The Bards (p. 256)

Another strange poem, this time with a medieval setting. An elaborate and decadent society has its tame poets who are haunted by 'an unknown grief' that bursts in upon them like a peasant and, stealing the beautiful ladies of the court, takes them back to his hovel.

l. 8 *unpilled:* unpeeled.

l. 9 *samite:* silk dress fabric, often interwoven with gold.

(A) How are the faltering poets treated? Describe the 'churl' —his clothing, weapon, and actions—in your own words. What are we told about the hall, and what about the women?

Warning to Children (p. 257)

This poem is about an idea which must have haunted most of us, especially in childhood—the idea that philosophers call 'Infinite Regress'; in my own childhood the idea took the form of a sauce-bottle with a label showing a man serving a sauce-bottle with a label showing a man . . ., etc. It perhaps implies that you can never reach to the real essence of anything.

ll. 2– The mysterious world of childhood, in which all the
5 qualities of things are strange and new.

(A) Why is the poem so titled? Can you remember anything as a child which gave you this sensation?

Rocky Acres (p. 258)

A picture of a harsh, hilly, and lonely landscape dominated by hawks, which the poet loves best. The last verse relates this scene to the first emerging landscapes of the world; it is completely untamed and uninhabited save by the old gods living in the barrows, who are imagined making raids on the civilized people in the plains.

l. 7   *buzzard*: a hawk mostly seen on moor or mountain.

l. 16   *Crakeberry*: perhaps cranberry, a small shrub bearing acid berries and growing in wild places.

l. 26   *sempiternal*: eternal.

(A)   Express the description of the buzzard (ll. 7–11) in your own words; what is 'his wide parish'? Explain ll. 20–21. What is the meaning of ll. 24 and 25? What are 'burghers' and why are they fat?

(B)   Write a description in verse or prose of a wild landscape you know or imagine, bringing out its harshness and indifference to cosiness and 'the life of the plains'.

Song: Lift-boy (p. 259)

l. 14   *Old Eagle*: some kind of a religious maniac, who preaches that all mankind are damned.

(A)   What might a 'knife-boy' and a 'boot-man' have to do in, say, a hotel? What is the purpose of the repeated chorus 'With nothing in my pockets'? What has happened in the last two lines, and why? The whole poem may be a satirical comment—on what?

(B)   Write a poem with a chorus about a modern boy or young man (this one is perhaps Edwardian) in a 'deadend' job.

In Broken Images (p. 260)

ll. 1   *images*: something like 'ideas' or 'conceptions'—or per-
–2   haps, for the poet, figures of speech like simile or metaphor—*i.e.*, ways of expressing himself, especially in poetry.

(A)   Suggest what contrast the poem shows between 'he' and 'I'. In ll. 11–12, some words are picked up from earlier in the poem: what are they? In what ways is the poet ('I') better off than 'he', and in what ways worse off? What is meant by the last two lines?

Mid-winter Waking (p. 261)

A relatively straightforward poem in which the writer comes back to his work as a poet sensing 'warm airs' in midwinter, and with his lover's hand in his (or perhaps the hand of his 'muse' or inspiration) it seems like midsummer.

ll. 3– As a poet he is immortal; *principalities*: perhaps here,
4 angels, or powers.

ll. 6– The grammar here is not easy: it is the beautiful clouds
11 and the 'warm airs' that are to be witness that the lovers had, as it were, defeated winter.

(A) Suggest what else 'midwinter' suggests beyond a mere season, and then apply your idea to 'the season of new blossom' (l. 9) and 'Spring' (l. 13). Describe the clouds (ll. 6–7) in your own words. What is the purpose of l. 10?

Here Live your Life out! (*p. 261*)

l. 3   *coign*: place giving a good view; *felicity*: happiness.

l. 19   *mentor*: trusted adviser.

(A) This poem has a meaning well beyond the problems of house-hunting. Suggest what the railway train, or bus or coach, is a symbol or metaphor for, and then ask yourself what 'the house' stands for. Why does the vehicle jolt '*viciously*' on? Who might the 'bolder tenants' be? Then write a paragraph saying what you take to be the meaning of the whole poem.

(B) Write a story or poem on the theme 'Missed Opportunities'.

Lollocks (*p. 262*)

This is a light poem, subtle but not profound, and intended mainly to amuse. 'Lollocks' is a coined word, and one critic called the poem "a small, perfectly acceptable example of myth-making". Lollocks relate to domestic life rather as 'gremlins' were said to relate to aircraft by pilots during the last war; find out about gremlins, and you will be some way towards understanding Lollocks.

l. 27   *languor*: inertia, boredom.

l. 41   *sovereign*: as in 'a sovereign remedy': thus 'a perfect cure'.

(A) Where are lollocks born, and why? Explain the reference to medicine bottles and letters from abroad (ll. 7–9). How do they annoy children by noises and movement? How do the 'imbecile agèd' connect the things mentioned in the previous verse? Why is 'tattered stairs' appropriate and what picture do you get from 'are nasty together'? How do we recognize the presence of lollocks? Why can't men see them, while women can? What is the attitude of 'wives' to lollocks? How can one get rid of them? Now try to define what you think lollocks are.

(B) Write a poem about mythical little monsters that haunt the classroom, or the dining-hall, or the science labs, and give them a suitable name.

The China Plate (p. 264)

A rare or valuable plate is bought cheaply from a street stall, and is much admired; the poet advocates that it should not be kept on a shelf for display, but used, even though it will in due time be broken.

l. 15 *pot-bank sign:* mark on the back of the plate showing its rarity.

(A) Explain in your own words how the people who bought the plate show their pride in it. Which lines suggest that it's no better on display than on the street barrow? Where in the poem does Graves first show what he thinks should be done with the plate? Why is he willing to risk its breakage in spite of its value?

(B) Write a short composition on 'Display *v.* Use'; you might like to discuss books or best crockery or cutlery canteens, or even rooms that are seldom used.

Leaving the Rest Unsaid (p. 265)

This is the last poem in several of Robert Graves's collections of verse; the clue to its meaning lies in the title and in its ending with a comma.

l. 2 *obelisk:* usually a tapering stone monument, but also a mark on old manuscripts to show that a passage is spurious; *colophon:* ornamental tailpiece, usually in old books.

ll. 8– *appendices:* containing lists of things left in a will; *indices* (plural of 'index'): alphabetical list at the end of books— 'graveyard' because it suggests that the work, and the poet, is dead and finished.

l. 14 *gander:* male goose, with a fine flight.

(A)   What do you think the poet intends by putting this poem
      last, and especially by ending it as he does?

FURTHER READING

(1) *Poetry*
Robert Graves, selected by himself (Penguin).
Collected Poems (Cassell: various editions).

(2) *Other Writing*
I, Claudius.
Claudius the King.
Wife to Mr Milton.
King Jesus.
Steps (essays).
The Common Asphodel (criticism).

CRITICAL WRITING

J. M. Cohen. *Robert Graves* (Oliver and Boyd).

Robert Frost

ROBERT FROST was born in San Francisco in 1875 and went at the age of ten to live in New England, the area which inspired almost all of his poetry. He was educated at Dartmouth College, New England, and Harvard University, became a schoolmaster for a short time, and then a farm labourer. During this period he wrote poetry but with little recognition. From 1912 to 1915 he lived in England, where he became friendly with several poets, including Edward Thomas, and published *A Boy's Will* (1913) and *North of Boston* (1914). In America his poetry was soon admired, and he was awarded the Pulitzer Prize on four occasions between 1924 and 1943. He went on writing verse throughout his life, publishing *Steeple Bush* (1947) at the age of seventy-two. He died in 1963.

Robert Frost's first volume was reviewed by Edward Thomas (see pp. 167–177), who wrote:

> These poems are revolutionary because they lack the exaggeration of rhetoric, and even at first sight appear to lack the intensity of which rhetoric is an imitation. . . . Many, if not most, of the separate lines and separate sentences are plain and in themselves nothing. But they are bound together and made elements of beauty by a calm eagerness of emotion.

This last phrase makes an excellent starting point for the reading of Robert Frost. Again and again he transforms an apparently commonplace scene or situation and apparently casual and colloquial tone and phrasing by his art into something deeply convincing—most often by the delight with which his close observant eye and touch renders the daily activities of farming and the landscape which is their background—mowing, apple-picking, mending a wall. These poems reflect a humane quiet concern and satisfaction in their rhythms and their gentle lyricism, a

[273]

homely philosophy closely related to the New England
character. There is a hint that the pioneering spirit has
not yet died—that nature can still be inimical:

> Something there is that doesn't love a wall

or again,

> All out-of-doors looked darkly in on him.

He wrote a large number of dramatic dialogues in verse,
many of which are very fine, and only omitted here because they are too long. Often there is mystery or pathos
just be   d the corner of the eye. Often there is an explicit
or near-explicit 'moral', though sometimes this is hinted
at rather than stated, and frequently there is an almost
proverbial tone—a countryman's store of wisdom and
experience:

> Home is the place where, when you have to go there
> They have to take you in.

> Earth's the right place for love.

Alongside the relish for traditional experience goes a
sensitivity and delicate observation that comes sharply in
the context of the slow, quiet, ruminative, ironic tone:

> . . . The earnest love that laid the swale in rows
> Not without feeble-pointed spikes of flowers
> (Pale orchises) . . .

> Magnified apples appear and disappear
> Stem end and blossom end,
> And every fleck of russet showing clear.

> The only other sound's the sweep
> Of easy wind and downy flake.

We learn to trust Robert Frost; his characteristic voice
is an undertone, almost absent-minded, but behind it we
sense a 'lifetime of devotion—devotion to his own craft
and to the investigating of reality' (C. Day Lewis). The
very lack of glamour or display gives his poems a stability
and well-weathered honesty, like seasoned timber or a
finely-balanced tool smooth and sturdy from use. In

contrast to the other two American or partly American poets represented in this book (Eliot, American-born and living in England, Auden English-born and living in America), Frost gives us a continual sense of the regional America behind the skyscrapers and the big cities, close to the earth and engaged in its immemorial activities, patient and stoical—a picture of man totally committed to his own daily life.

The Pasture

I'm going out to clean the pasture spring;
I'll only stop to rake the leaves away
(And wait to watch the water clear, I may):
I shan't be gone long.—You come too.

I'm going out to fetch the little calf
That's standing by the mother. It's so young
It totters when she licks it with her tongue.
I shan't be gone long.—You come too.

Mowing

There was never a sound beside the wood but one,
And that was my long scythe whispering to the ground.
What was it it whispered? I knew not well myself;
Perhaps it was something about the heat of the sun,
Something, perhaps, about the lack of sound—   5
And that was why it whispered and did not speak.
It was no dream of the gift of idle hours
Or easy gold at the hand of fay or elf:
Anything more than the truth would have seemed too
    weak
To the earnest love that laid the swale in rows,   10
Not without feeble-pointed spikes of flowers
(Pale orchises), and scared a bright green snake.
The fact is the sweetest dream that labour knows.
My long scythe whispered and left the hay to make.

Mending Wall

Something there is that doesn't love a wall,
That sends the frozen-ground-swell under it,
And spills the upper boulders in the sun;
And makes gaps even two can pass abreast.
The work of hunters is another thing: 5
I have come after them and made repair
Where they have left not one stone on a stone,
But they would have the rabbit out of hiding,
To please the yelping dogs. The gaps I mean,
No one has seen them made or heard them made,   10
But at spring mending-time we find them there.
I let my neighbour know beyond the hill;
And on a day we meet to walk the line
And set the wall between us once again.
We keep the wall between us as we go.   15
To each the boulders that have fallen to each.
And some are loaves and some so nearly balls
We have to use a spell to make them balance:
"Stay where you are until our backs are turned!"
We wear our fingers rough with handling them.   20
Oh, just another kind of outdoor game,
One on a side. It comes to little more:
There where it is we do not need the wall:
He is all pine and I am apple orchard.
My apple trees will never get across   25
And eat the cones under his pines, I tell him.
He only says, "Good fences make good neighbours."
Spring is the mischief in me, and I wonder
If I could put a notion in his head:
"*Why* do they make good neighbours? Isn't it   30
Where there are cows? But here there are no cows.

Before I built a wall I'd ask to know
What I was walling in or walling out,
And to whom I was like to give offence.
Something there is that doesn't love a wall,   35
That wants it down." I could say "Elves" to him,
But it's not elves exactly, and I'd rather
He said it for himself. I see him there
Bringing a stone grasped firmly by the top
In each hand, like an old-stone savage armed.   40
He moves in darkness as it seems to me,
Not of woods only and the shade of trees.
He will not go behind his father's saying,
And he likes having thought of it so well
He says again, "Good fences make good neighbours."   45

After Apple-picking

My long two-pointed ladder's sticking through a tree
Toward heaven still,
And there's a barrel that I didn't fill
Beside it, and there may be two or three
Apples I didn't pick upon some bough.   5
But I am done with apple-picking now.
Essence of winter sleep is on the night,
The scent of apples: I am drowsing off.
I cannot rub the strangeness from my sight
I got from looking through a pane of glass   10
I skimmed this morning from the drinking trough
And held against the world of hoary grass.
It melted, and I let it fall and break.
But I was well
Upon my way to sleep before it fell,   15
And I could tell

What form my dreaming was about to take.
Magnified apples appear and disappear,
Stem end and blossom end,
And every fleck of russet showing clear.   20
My instep arch not only keeps the ache,
It keeps the pressure of a ladder-round.
I feel the ladder sway as the boughs bend.
And I keep hearing from the cellar bin
The rumbling sound   25
Of load on load of apples coming in.
For I have had too much
Of apple-picking: I am overtired
Of the great harvest I myself desired.
There were ten thousand thousand fruit to touch,   30
Cherish in hand, lift down, and not let fall.
For all
That struck the earth,
No matter if not bruised or spiked with stubble,
Went sure to the cider-apple heap   35
As of no worth.
One can see what will trouble
This sleep of mine, whatever sleep it is.
Were he not gone,
The woodchuck could say whether it's like his   40
Long sleep, as I describe its coming on,
Or just some human sleep.

An Old Man's Winter Night

All out-of-doors looked darkly in at him
Through the thin frost, almost in separate stars,
That gathers on the pane in empty rooms.
What kept his eyes from giving back the gaze

Was the lamp tilted near them in his hand.   5
What kept him from remembering what it was
That brought him to that creaking room was age.
He stood with barrels round him—at a loss.
And having scared the cellar under him
In clomping here, he scared it once again   10
In clomping off;—and scared the outer night,
Which has its sounds, familiar, like the roar
Of trees and crack of branches, common things,
But nothing so like beating on a box.
A light he was to no one but himself   15
Where now he sat, concerned with he knew what,
A quiet light, and then not even that.
He consigned to the moon, such as she was,
So late-arising, to the broken moon
As better than the sun in any case   20
For such a charge, his snow upon the roof,
His icicles along the wall to keep;
And slept. The log that shifted with a jolt
Once in the stove, disturbed him and he shifted,
And eased his heavy breathing, but still slept.   25
One aged man—one man—can't keep a house,
A farm, a countryside, or if he can,
It's thus he does it of a winter night.

Birches

When I see birches bend to left and right
Across the lines of straighter darker trees,
I like to think some boy's been swinging them.
But swinging doesn't bend them down to stay
As ice-storms do. Often you must have seen them   5
Loaded with ice a sunny winter morning

After a rain. They click upon themselves
As the breeze rises, and turn many-coloured
As the stir cracks and crazes their enamel.
Soon the sun's warmth makes them shed crystal shells 10
Shattering and avalanching on the snow-crust—
Such heaps of broken glass to sweep away
You'd think the inner dome of heaven had fallen.
They are dragged to the withered bracken by the load,
And they seem not to break; though once they are
      bowed   15
So low for long, they never right themselves:
You may see their trunks arching in the woods
Years afterwards, trailing their leaves on the ground
Like girls on hands and knees that throw their hair
Before them over their heads to dry in the sun.   20
But I was going to say when Truth broke in
With all her matter-of-fact about the ice-storm
I should prefer to have some boy bend them
As he went out and in to fetch the cows—
Some boy too far from town to learn baseball,   25
Whose only play was what he found himself,
Summer or winter, and could play alone.
One by one he subdued his father's trees
By riding them down over and over again
Until he took the stiffness out of them,   30
And not one but hung limp, not one was left
For him to conquer. He learned all there was
To learn about not launching out too soon
And so not carrying the tree away
Clear to the ground. He always kept his poise   35
To the top branches, climbing carefully
With the same pains you use to fill a cup
Up to the brim, and even above the brim.
Then he flung outward, feet first, with a swish,
Kicking his way down through the air to the ground.   40

So was I once myself a swinger of birches.
And so I dream of going back to be.
It's when I'm weary of considerations,
And life is too much like a pathless wood
Where your face burns and tickles with the cobwebs   45
Broken across it, and one eye is weeping
From a twig's having lashed across it open.
I'd like to get away from earth awhile
And then come back to it and begin over.
May no fate wilfully misunderstand me   50
And half grant what I wish and snatch me away
Not to return. Earth's the right place for love:
I don't know where it's likely to go better.
I'd like to go by climbing a birch tree,
And climb black branches up a snow-white trunk   55
Toward heaven, till the tree could bear no more,
But dipped its top and set me down again.
That would be good both going and coming back.
One could do worse than be a swinger of birches.

Dust of Snow

The way a crow
Shook down on me
The dust of snow
From a hemlock tree   4

Has given my heart
A change of mood
And saved some part
Of a day I had rued.   8

Stopping by Woods on a Snowy Evening

Whose woods these are I think I know.
His house is in the village though;
He will not see me stopping here
To watch his woods fill up with snow.   4

My little horse must think it queer
To stop without a farmhouse near
Between the woods and frozen lake
The darkest evening of the year.   8

He gives his harness bells a shake
To ask if there is some mistake.
The only other sound's the sweep
Of easy wind and downy flake.   12

The woods are lovely, dark and deep,
But I have promises to keep,
And miles to go before I sleep,
And miles to go before I sleep.   16

Two Look at Two

Love and forgetting might have carried them
A little further up the mountainside
With night so near, but not much further up.
They must have halted soon in any case
With thoughts of the path back, how rough it was   5
With rock and washout, and unsafe in darkness;
When they were halted by a tumbled wall

With barbed-wire binding. They stood facing this,
Spending what onward impulse they still had
In one last look the way they must not go,   10
On up the failing path, where, if a stone
Or earthslide moved at night, it moved itself;
No footstep moved it. "This is all", they sighed,
"Good-night to woods." But not so; there was more.
A doe from round a spruce stood looking at them   15
Across the wall, as near the wall as they.
She saw them in their field, they her in hers.
The difficulty of seeing what stood still,
Like some up-ended boulder split in two,
Was in her clouded eyes: they saw no fear there.   20
She seemed to think that two thus they were safe.
Then, as if they were something that, though strange,
She could not trouble her mind with too long,
She sighed and passed unscared along the wall.
"*This*, then, is all. What more is there to ask?"   25
But no, not yet. A snort to bid them wait.
A buck from round the spruce stood looking at them
Across the wall as near the wall as they.
This was an antlered buck of lusty nostril,
Not the same doe come back into her place.   30
He viewed them quizzically with jerks of head,
As if to ask, "Why don't you make some motion?
Or give some sign of life? Because you can't.
I doubt as if you're as living as you look."
Thus till he had them almost feeling dared   35
To stretch a proffering hand—and a spell-breaking.
Then he too passed unscared along the wall.
Two had seen two, whichever side you spoke from.
"This *must* be all." It was all. Still they stood,
A great wave from it going over them,   40
As if the earth in one unlooked-for favour
Had made them certain earth returned their love.

Tree at My Window

Tree at my window, window tree,
My sash is lowered when night comes on;
But let there never be curtain drawn
Between you and me.   4

Vague dream-head lifted out of the ground,
And thing next most diffuse to cloud,
Not all your light tongues talking aloud
Could be profound.   8

But, tree, I have seen you taken and tossed,
And if you have seen me when I slept,
You have seen me when I was taken and swept
And all but lost.   12

That day she put our heads together,
Fate had her imagination about her,
Your head so much concerned with outer,
Mine with inner, weather.   16

Unharvested

A scent of ripeness from over a wall.
And come to leave the routine road
And look for what had made me stall,
There sure enough was an apple tree
That had eased itself of its summer load,   5
And of all but its trivial foliage free,
Now breathed as light as a lady's fan.

For there there had been an apple fall
As complete as the apple had given man.
The ground was one circle of solid red.   10

May something go always unharvested!
May much stay out of our stated plan,
Apples or something forgotten and left,
So smelling their sweetness would be no theft.

The Silken Tent

She is as in a field a silken tent
At midday when a sunny summer breeze
Has dried the dew and all its ropes relent,
So that in guys it gently sways at ease,
And its supporting central cedar pole,   5
That is its pinnacle to heavenward
And signifies the sureness of the soul,
Seems to owe naught to any single cord,
But strictly held by none, is loosely bound
By countless silken ties of love and thought   10
To everything on earth the compass round,
And only by one's going slightly taut
In the capriciousness of summer air
Is of the slightest bondage made aware.

Notes

The Pasture (p. 277)

This is one of Frost's earliest poems, dealing calmly with the daily duties of a farmer, and stressing companionability.

(A) What picture do you get from ll. 2 and 3? Is it necessary to stay and 'watch the water clear' and why is he unsure whether he will? Who do you think he's speaking to ('you'), and what is the effect of the repeated invitation 'You come too'?

Mowing (p. 277)

A subtle poem about one of the basic activities of farming in the past—mowing with a scythe; the poet asks what the scythe's whisper can mean, and answers the question obliquely in the course of the poem.

l. 8 *fay:* fairy; fairy gold is supposed to melt in one's hand.

l. 10 *swale:* presumably the same as swathe—grass or corn laid in rows as it falls from the scythe.

(A) Have you ever seen mowing with a scythe or even better heard the whispering sound it makes as the blade goes through the stems and the grass falls? Why does he imagine it whispering 'to the ground' (l. 2)? What time of the year do you think this is? (Suggest a month or months—and compare with the haycocks in Edward Thomas's *Adlestrop* (p. 169). What is the first suggested answer to the question in l. 3? Where is there a gentle touch of humour? Where does he reject a 'romantic' attitude to the work and which word suggests its unreality? Why '*more* than the truth' (l. 9)? Whose 'earnest love' is he speaking of in l. 10? What is cut down with the grass and how does this relate to Keats's 'spares the next swathe and all its twinèd flowers' (*Ode to Autumn*, p. 66)? l. 13 is the key line: which words contrast in the line, how can a 'fact' be a 'dream', and how does labour know this?

What relationship has this line with ll. 7–8? What, then, *was* the scythe whispering—has he answered his question? What is the effect of the last line ('make', used intransitively here, means something like 'to mature')?

(B) Write freely in verse or prose about any continuous piece of labour (gardening, housework, carpentry) which is in your experience its own reward.

Mending Wall (p. 278)

Again the subject is one of the regular duties of a farmer —keeping his stone walls in good shape. It is important to understand that this is dry stone walling, of the kind common in Wales and the north country, where there is plenty of stone and no need to grow hedges, even if they would survive in hilly country.

(A) Give two instances of the 'something' that 'doesn't love a wall'; what do you understand by 'frozen-ground-swell' (l. 2)? How do you suppose the hunters damaged the wall, and what were they hunting (ll. 5–9)? Describe how the two neighbours repair the wall and where they walk while doing so (ll. 11–15). Which are the most awkward stones to replace, how does the poet suggest they can be persuaded to stay in position, and for how long probably (ll. 17–19)? Why is the wall not strictly necessary, and how does the poet express this (ll. 21–26)? What does his neighbour say about this, and what is the poet tempted to say in reply (ll. 27–36)? Why would he rather the neighbour 'said it for himself' (l. 38)? Describe the neighbour carrying stones and say why the sight reminds the poet of 'an old-stone savage armed' (what is the learned word for the Old Stone Age?). What other 'darkness' does this neighbour move in as well as that of 'woods only and the shade of trees' (ll. 41–42)? Is there anything significant in his being compared with a stone-age man? Does the wall suggest anything else to you but a wall—any other kind of division? Who is the neighbour quoting in "Good fences make good neighbours" and what does the last line but one mean? Finally, what conflict do you see between the two 'theme-statements' of the poem—the first line and the last line?

After Apple-picking (p. 279)

This poem, like *Mending Wall* and *Mowing*, concerns itself with the 'daily work of gaining a livelihood'—here the activity of the fruit-farmer—or rather with the sensations of fatigue and fulfilment after the work is done.

l. 40   *woodchuck*: an American rodent, not unlike a squirrel.

(A)   What indications are there at the beginning that the task is unfinished, and does the rest of the poem suggest why? What time of year is this, and how do you know? Point out the indications that the poet is tired after his labours, and that the emotions are those of someone between waking and sleep. Consider carefully ll. 9–13; what is the 'pane of glass', what did he do with it, and why was the grass 'hoary' at this time of the morning? How could he tell 'what form my dreaming was about to take' (l. 17)? Why do you suppose the 'magnified apples' 'appear and disappear' in his half-sleep, what is the 'blossom end' of an apple (the line should tell you), and why does he see such minute detail as 'every speck of russet showing clear' (l. 20)? (Think of falling to sleep yourself after any long repetitive task.) What physical sensations are described in ll. 21–23, and why is he still having them? What sound does he chiefly remember, and how do the lines describing it reinforce the memory of the sound? Where does he show signs of having 'overdone it'? Show how the careful movements of the apple-picker are 'enacted' in the rhythm and language of ll. 30–31. Why were all the apples that fell on the earth put on the cider-apple heap, even if not visibly bruised, and what do you think 'spiked with stubble' (l. 34) means? What will trouble his sleep (ll. 37–38)? Why has the woodchuck 'gone' and what is his 'long sleep' (l. 40)?

(B)   Write about your sensations and half-dreams after any demanding physical job.

An Old Man's Winter Night (p. 280)

A quietly touching poem describing a solitary old man who goes at night to his cellar, forgets what for, and returns to sleep by his stove.

(A) In what sense is 'all out-of-doors' looking at the old man (l. 1), and which other parts of the poem refer to the out-door scene? Describe the effect of the thin frost on the window in your own words (ll. 2–3).

What 'gaze' was he unable to give back (l. 4) and why? Which word in l. 7 corresponds to 'lamp' in l. 5 and what are they each 'keeping him from'? What might be in the barrels (l. 8)? In what sense did he 'scare' the cellar (ll. 10–11), and what do you picture happening between 'clomping here' and 'clomping off'? What familiar sounds outside does he disturb (ll. 11–14)? Explain carefully what you think l. 15 means; why does he now know what he's concerned with, and what has happened by the time the poet says 'and then not even that'? In what sense does he consign 'his snow' and 'his icicles' to the moon, and why is it described as 'broken' (ll. 18–22)? Describe how his sleeping was disturbed. What is meant by the last three lines, where is his age and solitude emphasized, and why should he be expected to 'keep a countryside' (l. 27)?

(B) Write in any form you like of an old man or woman living in solitude (you may find it helpful to refer to R. S. Thomas's *An Old Man*, *The Hill Farmer Speaks*, and *Lore*, pp. 302, 309, and 311).

Birches (p. 281)

This attractive and varied poem deals with one of the leisure activities of rural children in New England. It is beautifully varied in tone and rhythm, and Mr Day Lewis says of it: "Like all Mr Frost's best poems, this has worn well and weathered well, and will go on doing so, because it is soundly constructed of seasoned materials, is carefully sited, is shapely, and because a spirit of sober joy inhabits it." The birch tree (you will know the English silver birch) is slender; the lower part of its trunk will be quite firm for climbing but the upper part is pliable, and apparently you can swing the tree-top to the ground if you climb carefully, and if you do this often enough the tree becomes permanently misshapen.

(A) The first two sentences (ll. 1–5) state the theme: put it in your own words. What is the topic of the long passage from l. 5 to l. 20? Describe in your own words the effect on such a slender tree of being 'loaded with ice', explaining 'crazes their enamel' (l. 9); what is the 'broken glass' (l. 12) and the 'dome of heaven' (l. 13)? What *shape* is the tree in l. 14–16? In what sense has the poet let 'Truth break in' (l. 21), and what is contrasted with 'Truth'? Why didn't the boy play more conventional games than swinging birches (ll. 25–27)? Describe in your own words the mistake (in 'birch-swinging') the boy learned about (ll. 32–35), and what is the point of the simile about the cup (ll. 37–38)? How does the rhythm help the meaning of l. 39? What common wish is implied in l. 42; what is the point of 'considerations' (l. 43)? Show in detail how the metaphor in ll. 44–47 fits the problems and frustrations of adult life; is it a suitable one for this poem? What is the English equivalent of 'begin over' (l. 49)? Where does he contradict the wish to 'get away from the earth awhile' (l. 48), and what fear does he express in ll. 50–52? Examine the uses of 'go' (ll. 53 and 54) and 'going' (l. 58). How does the rhythm of l. 55 fit the meaning? What, finally, is the meaning and the implication of the last line?

(B) Write about any solitary game or pursuit from your own childhood.

Dust of Snow (p. 283)

This tiny and delicate poem shows the consolations that nature offers to human anxiety or misery.

l. 4   *hemlock:* a coniferous North American tree (in England the name is used for a poisonous plant).

l. 8   *rued:* regretted, thought a failure.

Stopping by Woods on a Snowy Evening (p. 284)

This poem records a moment of pure delight in mid-winter—a transitory moment of contemplation of the beauty of snow-covered woods before he must go on with his duties.

(A) Why does it matter whose woods they are (ll. 1–2)? What has he just done before verse 2 opens? Examine closely the third verse, and say what it adds to the poem; consider especially the adjectives 'easy' and 'downy' in l. 12. What shows that he would like to stay longer, and what prevents him? What effects do you think are made by the repetition of l. 15?

Two Look at Two (p. 284)

Two lovers walk on a mountainside at dusk, reluctant to go back to 'civilization', when they see a female deer staring at them; this, they feel, makes the walk perfect but there is more to come—an antlered buck. This becomes an almost mystical experience, as the end of the poem implies—a blessing of their love from nature itself.

l. 15   *spruce:* the spruce fir-tree.
l. 31   *quizzically:* with curiosity.
(A)   Forgetting what (l. 1)? What do you think is meant by 'washout' (l. 6) and 'binding' (l. 8)? Explain how they used their last 'onward impulse' (l. 9) and what this means. Why 'failing' path (l. 11), and why did 'no foot-step' move a stone there at night (l. 13)? Why did they 'sigh' (l. 13) and why did they feel "This is all"? Is there anything significant in the distance of the doe from the wall being the same as the lovers' (ll. 15–16)? Explain l. 17. Describe what the lovers looked like to the deer, and who is 'they' in l. 20? Why did the deer think that 'two thus' would be safe (l. 21) and what does the poet wish us to understand by this? Describe the deer's attitude in another word or phrase than 'unscared' (l. 24). Describe in your own words the 'antlered buck of lusty nostril' (l. 29). Why *don't* the lovers 'make some motion/or give some sign of life' (ll. 32–33)? What made the lovers feel they should offer to shake hands, and why would this be a 'spell-breaking' (l. 36)? Explain 'whichever side you spoke from' (l. 38). What was 'the great wave' and from *what* exactly (l. 40)? Explain the last two lines. What significance do you attach to there being a buck as well as a doe, and relate this to the title. Do you see any connexion between this poem and *Dust of Snow* or *Birches*?

Tree at my Window (p. 286)

This is a fairly straightforward lyric, expressing an imaginative relationship between the poet and the tree outside his window.

(A) Why does he shut the window but not draw the curtains (verse 1)? In what way is the tree a 'vague dream-head' (l. 5) and only less 'diffuse' than a cloud (l. 6)? What is meant by the tree's 'tongues' and in what two senses could they be called 'light' (l. 7)? Why not profound? (l. 8: compare with Edward Thomas's *Aspens* here). In verse 3 what is meant by 'I have seen you taken and tossed'? (Think especially about 'taken'.) How can the tree see him sleeping and why might he then be 'taken and swept/And all but lost'? How did fate 'put our heads together' (l. 13), what meaning do you attach to 'head' here, and what is meant by 'outer' and 'inner' weather in the last two lines?

Unharvested (p. 286)

A quiet and subtle poem with a strong 'moral'.

(A) How does he first know of the apple-tree? Is there any significance in '*routine* road' (l. 2)? What does 'stall' mean in l. 37? What picture do you get from 'trivial foliage' (l. 6) and in what way is the tree now like 'a lady's fan' (l. 7)? Explain the double meaning of 'fall' and 'apple' in ll. 8–9. What picture do you get from l. 10? The last four lines are the 'key' of the poem; why does he hope that not everything will be harvested and how does he generalize this in l. 12? Explain carefully the last two lines.

(B) Write freely in verse or prose about some delight or pleasure in your experience that was out of your 'stated plan' or off your 'routine road'.

The Silken Tent (p. 287)

This delicate and beautiful but rather difficult poem is a sort of extended metaphor, comparing a woman, most improbably but convincingly, to a large tent gently blowing in a summer breeze.

(A) In what sense do the tent's ropes 'relent' (l. 3)? Are they
looser or tighter than usual? What is symbolized by 'the
central cedar pole' (l. 5)—the poem tells you—and what
by the 'silken ties' (l. 10)? Why, then, does the pole look
'heavenward' and why is it 'loosely bound' by '. . . love
and thought' *to the earth*? (Look at Wordsworth's *Skylark*,
p. 25, for a similar idea.) Is it true that the tent is
'strictly held by none' (l. 9), and what two meanings
might be present in 'strictly'? Give another phrase for
'everything on earth the compass round' (l. 11). What
sort of 'capriciousness' might make one of the ropes
'slightly taut' (ll. 12–13)? What do you think of the whole
poem as a metaphor for someone both 'free' and 'bound'?

FURTHER READING

Selected Poems, with an introduction by C. Day Lewis (Penguin).
A very substantial collection, drawn from about ten published
volumes.

CRITICAL WRITING

J. G. Southworth. *Some Modern Poets* (Blackwell): includes an
essay on Robert Frost.
C. Day Lewis's introduction to the Penguin selection: a fine
summary.

R. S. Thomas

R. S. THOMAS was born in Cardiff in 1913. For more than twenty years he has been a parish priest in Wales. He was Rector of Manafon from 1942–54, a hilly isolated area, much of it uninhabited; vicar of Eglwysfach 1954–67; and since 1967 vicar of St Hywyn, Aberdaron, with St Mary, Bodferin. He taught himself the Welsh language as an adult, in order to understand the remote hill farmers who were under his care. He published his first slim volume of poetry in Carmarthenshire with the poet Keidrych Rhys's Druid Press and then with the Montgomery Printing Co., Newtown. The BBC broadcast a verse dialogue in dramatic form called *The Minister* in 1952. He received an Arts Council Award for *Song at the Year's Turning*, as the best book of verse between July 1953 and June 1956, and the same volume received the Heinemann Award of the Royal Society of Literature 1956. *Poetry for Supper*, a book of short poems, was recommended by the Book Society and the Poetry Book Society, and judged by *The Observer* to be the best book of poems published in 1958.

R. S. Thomas (not to be confused with either Edward Thomas or Dylan Thomas) is the most recent of the poets in this anthology, with a fairly recently established reputation. His body of work is already considerable, and though selections of previous volumes have been published together, there is not yet at the time of writing a collected edition. He is rapidly emerging as one of the best poets now writing in the language. His subjects are at first sight narrow in range: he writes almost exclusively about the people and landscape of the Welsh hill country—sometimes a number of poems about one person, so that we get to know him (or occasionally her) in several guises; but the emotional range is far wider than this description suggests. Though he writes firmly and convincingly about a particular parish in a particular kind of country, his treatment of his themes and the play of his imagination give them (as perhaps in all good poems) a universality which makes them reflect the human condition itself. They are utterly lacking in sentimentality—indeed their tone is often stern and bare—but they never lack tenderness or compassion for the hard-working, narrow, parochial, yet deeply human farmers he knows so well. The grimness of the landscape echoes and reinforces the grimness of the men's lives; as he writes in *The Minister*:

> In the high marginal land
> No names last longer than the wind
> And the rain lets them on the cold tombstone . . .
> But man remains summer and winter through
> Rooting in vain within his dwindling acre.

Thus the life of the people is never sweetened or romanticized, and the poet has no illusions about its harshness; yet there is a deep sympathy and understanding of the forces that have made them what they are. He has a superb ear and a rhythm all of his own, which John Betjeman says he guards carefully:

> He thinks that poetry should be read to oneself not out loud and that it is heard by an inner ear. He does not read nineteenth-century poems because he thinks that their obvious and jingly rhythms might upset his own sense of metre.

He is constantly aware that his parish is a metaphor for the whole of human life, as in *The Village*:

> So little happens; the black dog
> Cracking his fleas in the hot sun
> Is history. Yet the girl who crosses
> From door to door moves to a scale
> Beyond the bland day's two dimensions.

"His imagery," Kingsley Amis writes, "thickly clustered as it frequently is, and made to proliferate with great brilliance, is built upon a simple foundation of earth, trees, snow, stars and wild creatures"; another critic writes: "The poems . . . come cleanly off the page,

sniffing of cold and ploughed earth and leafless branches."
He is capable of very 'unparsonical' thoughts: a thrush
sings, using the minister's bush as 'its pulpit', and the
minister reflects:

> Its singing troubled my young mind
> With strange theories, pagan but sweet,
> That made the Book's black letters dance
> To a tune John Calvin never heard.

R. S. Thomas is close to Robert Frost in some of his moods,
but far less 'domesticated', and occasionally reminiscent
of Edward Thomas, but far starker and more impersonal;
he is really only like himself—a poet of deep quiet strength,
memorable, 'gritty', and powerful.

Tramp

A knock at the door
And he stands there,
A tramp with his can
Asking for tea,
Strong for a poor man
On his way—where?   6

He looks at his feet,
I look at the sky;
Over us the planes build
The shining rafters
Of that new world
We have sworn by.   12

I sleep in my bed,
He sleeps in the old,
Dead leaves of a ditch.
My dreams are haunted;
Are his dreams rich?
If I wake early,   18
He wakes cold.

Song

Wandering, wandering, hoping to find
The ring of mushrooms with the wet rind,
Cold to the touch, but bright with dew,
A green asylum from time's range.   4

And finding instead the harsh ways
Of the ruinous wind and the clawed rain;
The storm's hysteria in the bush;
The wild creatures and their pain.   8

Abersoch

There was that headland, asleep on the sea,
The air full of thunder and the far air
Brittle with lightning; there was that girl
Riding her cycle, hair at half-mast,
And the men smoking, the dinghies at rest
On the calm tide. There were people going
About their business, while the storm grew
Louder and nearer and did not break.

Why do I remember these few things,
That were rumours of life, not life itself
That was being lived fiercely, where the storm raged?
Was it just that the girl smiled,
Though not at me, and the men smoking
Had the look of those who have come safely home?

An Old Man

Look at him there on the wet road,
Muffled with smoke, an old man trying
Time's treacherous ice with a slow foot.
Tears on his cheek are the last glitter

On bare branches of the long storm   5
That shook him once leaving him bowed
And destitute as a tree stripped
Of foliage under a bald sky.

Come, then, winter, build with your cold
Hands a bridge over those depths   10
His mind balks at; let him go on,
Confident still; let the hard hammer
Of pain fall with as light a blow
On the brow's anvil as the sun does now.

The Evacuee

She woke up under a loose quilt
Of leaf patterns, woven by the light
At the small window, busy with the boughs
Of a young cherry; but wearily she lay,
Waiting for the siren, slow to trust   5
Nature's deceptive peace, and then afraid
Of the long silence, she would have crept
Uneasily from the bedroom with its frieze
Of fresh sunlight, had not a cock crowed,
Shattering the surface of that limpid pool   10
Of stillness, and before the ripples died
One by one in the field's shallows,
The farm woke with uninhibited din.

And now the noise and not the silence drew her
Down the bare stairs at great speed.   15
The sounds and voices were a rough sheet
Waiting to catch her, as though she leaped
From a scorched storey of the charred past.

And there the table and the gallery
Of farm faces trying to be kind   20
Beckoned her nearer, and she sat down
Under an awning of salt hams.

And so she grew, a small bird in the nest
Of welcome that was built about her,
Home now after so long away   25
In the flowerless streets of the drab town.
The men watched her busy with the hens,
The soft flesh ripening warm as corn
On the sticks of limbs, the grey eyes clear,
Rinsed with dew of their long dread.   30
The men watched her, and, nodding, smiled
With earth's charity, patient and strong.

Farm Child

Look at this village boy, his head is stuffed
With all the nests he knows, his pockets with flowers,
Snail-shells and bits of glass, the fruit of hours
Spent in the fields by thorn and thistle tuft.
Look at his eyes, see the harebell hiding there;   5
Mark how the sun has freckled his smooth face
Like a finch's egg under that bush of hair
That dares the wind, and in the mixen now
Notice his poise; from such unconscious grace
Earth breeds and beckons to the stubborn plough.   10

Soil

A field with tall hedges and a young
Moon in the branches and one star
Declining westward set the scene
Where he works slowly astride the rows
Of red mangolds and green swedes   5
Plying mechanically his cold blade.

This is his world, the hedge defines
The mind's limits; only the sky
Is boundless, and he never looks up;
His gaze is deep in the dark soil,   10
As are his feet. The soil is all;
His hands fondle it, and his bones
Are formed out of it with the swedes.
And if sometimes the knife errs,
Burying itself in his shocked flesh,   15
Then out of the wound the blood seeps home
To the warm soil from which it came.

Children's Song

We live in our own world,
A world that is too small
For you to stoop and enter
Even on hands and knees,
The adult subterfuge.   5
And though you probe and pry
With analytic eye,
And eavesdrop all our talk

With an amused look,
You cannot find the centre   10
Where we dance, where we play,
Where life is still asleep
Under the closed flower,
Under the smooth shell
Of eggs in the cupped nest   15
That mock the faded blue
Of your remoter heaven.

The Village

Scarcely a street, too few houses
To merit the title; just a way between
The one tavern and the one shop
That leads nowhere and fails at the top
Of the short hill, eaten away   5
By the long erosion of the green tide
Of grass creeping perpetually nearer
This last outpost of time past.

So little happens; the black dog
Cracking his fleas in the hot sun   10
Is history. Yet the girl who crosses
From door to door moves to a scale
Beyond the bland day's two dimensions.

Stay, then, village, for round you spins
On slow axis a world as vast   15
And meaningful as any poised
By great Plato's solitary mind.

The Poacher

Turning aside, never meeting
In the still lanes, fly infested,
Our frank greeting with quick smile,
You are the wind that set the bramble
Aimlessly clawing the void air.   5
The fox knows you, the sly weasel
Feels always the steel comb
Of eyes parting like sharp rain
Among the grasses its smooth fur.
No smoke haunting the cold chimney   10
Over your hearth betrays your dwelling
In blue writing above the trees.
The robed night, your dark familiar,
Covers your movements; the slick sun,
A dawn accomplice, removes your tracks   15
One by one from the bright dew.

Cynddylan on a Tractor

Ah, you should see Cynddylan on a tractor.
Gone the old look that yoked him to the soil;
He's a new man now, part of the machine,
His nerves of metal and his blood oil.
The clutch curses, but the gears obey   5
His least bidding, and lo, he's away
Out of the farmyard, scattering hens.
Riding to work now as a great man should,
He is the knight at arms breaking the fields'

Mirror of silence, emptying the wood   10
Of foxes and squirrels and bright jays.
The sun comes over the tall trees
Kindling all the hedges, but not for him
Who runs his engine on a different fuel.
And all the birds are singing, bills wide in vain,   15
As Cynddylan passes proudly up the lane.

Evans

Evans? Yes, many a time
I came down his bare flight
Of stairs into the gaunt kitchen
With its wood fire, where crickets sang
Accompaniment to the black kettle's   5
Whine, and so into the cold
Dark to smother in the thick tide
Of night that drifted about the walls
Of his stark farm on the hill ridge.

It was not the dark filling my eyes   10
And mouth appalled me; not even the drip
Of rain like blood from the one tree
Weather-tortured. It was the dark
Silting the veins of that sick man
I left stranded upon the vast   15
And lonely shore of his bleak bed.

A Day in Autumn

It will not always be like this,
The air windless, a few last
Leaves adding their decoration
To the trees' shoulders, braiding the cuffs
Of the boughs with gold; a bird preening   5
In the lawn's mirror. Having looked up
From the day's chores, pause a minute,
Let the mind take its photograph
Of the bright scene, something to wear
Against the heart in the long cold.   10

The Hill Farmer Speaks

I am the farmer, stripped of love
And thought and grace by the land's hardness;
But what I am saying over the fields'
Desolate acres, rough with dew,
Is, Listen, listen, I am a man like you.   5

The wind goes over the hill pastures
Year after year, and the ewes starve,
Milkless, for want of the new grass.
And I starve, too, for something the spring
Can never foster in veins run dry.   10

The pig is a friend, the cattle's breath
Mingles with mine in the still lanes;
I wear it willingly like a cloak
To shelter me from your curious gaze.

The hens go in and out at the door   15
From sun to shadow, as stray thoughts pass
Over the floor of my wide skull.
The dirt is under my cracked nails;
The tale of my life is smirched with dung;
The phlegm rattles. But what I am saying   20
Over the grasses rough with dew
Is, Listen, listen, I am a man like you.

A Blackbird Singing

It seems wrong that out of this bird,
Black, bold, a suggestion of dark
Places about it, there yet should come
Such rich music, as though the notes'
Ore were changed to a rare metal   5
At one touch of that bright bill.

You have heard it often, alone at your desk
In a green April, your mind drawn
Away from its work by sweet disturbance
Of the mild evening outside your room.   10

A slow singer, but loading each phrase
With history's overtones, love, joy
And grief learned by his dark tribe
In other orchards and passed on
Instinctively as they are now,   15
But fresh always with new tears.

Lore

Job Davies, eighty-five
Winters old, and still alive
After the slow poison
And treachery of the seasons.   4

Miserable? Kick my arse!
It needs more than the rain's hearse,
Wind-drawn, to pull me off
The great perch of my laugh.   8

What's living but courage?
Paunch full of hot porridge,
Nerves strengthened with tea,
Peat-black, dawn found me   12

Mowing where the grass grew,
Bearded with golden dew.
Rhythm of the long scythe
Kept this tall frame lithe.   16

What to do? Stay green.
Never mind the machine,
Whose fuel is human souls.
Live large, man, and dream small.   20

Notes

Tramp (p. 301)

(A) Why doesn't the tramp make his own tea? What is his can like, and what does l. 5 mean? Where is the tramp going? In what sense do the planes 'build/The shining rafters' of a new world, and in what sense have we 'sworn by' that world? Suggest what the poet's dreams might be 'haunted' by from the evidence of the poem and why he 'wakes early'. What evidence is there that the tramp's will not be similar? In what four ways are poet and tramp contrasted, and in what ways is each better off than the other?

(B) Write in prose or verse about a chance encounter with a tramp or pedlar or gipsy.

Song (p. 301)

(A) Suggest a time of year and a time of day for this poem. What connexion is there between dew and mushrooms? Why 'ring' and 'wet rind' (l. 2)? Explain the fourth line, remembering that 'asylum' can mean a place of refuge or sanctuary. Pick out words in the first verse which suggest peace and calm, and corresponding words in verse two suggesting violence. What picture do you get from l. 7, and what is its connexion with the last line? Then show how the two verses embody two contrasting aspects of nature.

Abersoch (p. 302)

Abersoch is a small fishing town on the Lleyn peninsula in Caernarvonshire (North Wales). The poet describes vividly a scene there that has remained in his mind, and asks why this should be so.

(A) What indications are there that the storm was in the distance? Show what features made the scene normal and undramatic, and where life was 'being lived fiercely'. Where is there a touch of wry humour? What were the 'men smoking' likely to do for a living, and what does the last line mean? Summarize the poet's possible reasons for having remembered the scene.

An Old Man (p. 302)

(A) How could the road be wet and also icy (l. 3)? In what sense is it 'time's treacherous ice' and how does one 'try' ice with 'a slow foot'? In the second sentence (ll. 4–8) try to explain why the old man might be weeping, why this is the 'last glitter', what might be symbolized by 'the long storm/That shook him once', and why he was left 'bowed and destitute'. Having established these meanings, suggest what is meant by 'these depths/His mind balks at' (ll. 10–11), and 'the hard hammer of pain'; how will the latter fall 'on the brow's anvil', and what does this metaphor remind you of? Summarize, finally, what the poet wishes for the old man. How does this poem compare with another priest's poem about an old man (Hopkins's *Felix Randal*, p. 114)?

The Evacuee (p. 303)

As most students will know, many children during the Second World War were evacuated into rural districts to avoid the bombing of large towns; often their parents had to remain behind to work or were in the armed forces.

l. 5   *siren*: the air-raid warning.

l. 13 *uninhibited*: not restrained, therefore loud and cheerful.

l. 22 *awning*: literally a canvas roof; here the kitchen ceiling from which cured hams are hanging.

(A) Explain ll. 1–4; in what senses does the child lie 'under a quilt'? Relate this to 'frieze' (l. 8). Why is she 'waiting for the siren', what then frightens her, and what sound relieves this 'waiting'? Suggest what makes the 'uninhibited din' (l. 13). What finally brings her downstairs, and how are the 'sounds and voices' like 'a rough sheet' (l. 16)? How does this image connect with the child's past experience or sight, and why is her past called 'charred' (l. 18)? Why '*trying* to be kind' (l. 20)? What is odd about l. 25, and what earlier in the poem contrasts with 'flowerless' (l. 26)? Put in your own words the description of the child as she settled into the life of the farm (ll. 27–30). Comment on the last two lines.

(B) Write an imaginative story in prose or verse about being evacuated, or ask parents or relatives what it was like.

Farm Child (p. 304)

A sketch of a child who, unlike the evacuee, was brought up on a farm.

l. 5   *harebell:* a clear blue bell-shaped flower.
l. 8   *mixen:* dung-heap.

(A) How do the two lines describing the farm child's eyes and skin connect with earlier lines of the poem? How is his head 'stuffed' (l. 1), and how does his hair 'dare the wind' (l. 8)? What contrast is implied in ll. 8–9 'and in the mixen now/Notice his poise'? What will he do for a living, and why?

(B) Compare in any form you like the leisure activities of the farm child with those of a town boy. Which do you prefer, and what can be said in favour of either?

Soil (p. 305)

The farm worker in this poem is 'topping' root-crops, probably for cattle; the swedes or mangolds (see Edward Thomas's poem *Swedes*, p. 175) have their green tops sliced off with a knife; the roots may then be clamped for winter feed, and the tops fed to cattle. The farm worker here is probably using a knife with a curved blade, rather like some kinds of chopper.

(A) The poem starts with 'tall hedges'; where is this referred to later and what is its significance? Why is he working after dark? Why does he never look up?

In what ways is his body connected with the soil? What is meant by 'the knife errs' (l. 14), and what is the impact of 'shocked flesh' (l. 15)? Explain the last two lines and show how they account for the title.

Children's Song (p. 305)

This delicate little poem shows imaginatively the world

of children as utterly remote and incomprehensible to parents and adults, though they pretend to understand and even patronize it.

l. 5   *subterfuge*: a device for evading an issue.

(A)   Express in your own words how adults try to enter physically the child's world (ll. 4–5). In what sense is the world of childhood 'too small' (l. 2)? Which lines show the adults patronizing the child's world? What is the relationship between 'the closed flower' (l. 13), 'the eggs' (l. 15), and the child's world? What colour are 'the eggs in the cupped nest' and how do they 'mock the faded blue/Of your remoter heaven'? Who is referred to in 'your' (l. 17)? You might find it useful to compare this idea with a similar one in Hopkins's *Spring* (p. 115).

(B)   Write in prose or verse about a game or activity you vividly remember from your own childhood, which adults failed to understand.

The Village (p. 306)

A small and insignificant village is seen by the poet as a 'microcosm' (small-scale version) of the universe itself.

l. 17   *Plato*: the great Greek philosopher, who pictured the universe in his writings.

(A)   What features of the first ten lines suggest that the village is isolated? Small? In a state of decay and gradually suffering depopulation? Quiet and inactive? What do you think is meant by 'the black dog . . . is history' (ll. 9–11)? What are the two dimensions of the 'bland day' (l. 13), and in what sense is the girl moving to a scale 'beyond' this (l. 12)? How can one say that the world spins round the village, and which expression echoes 'poised' in l. 16?

(B)   Write about any isolated and insignificant place which seems to 'embody' history.

The Poacher (p. 307)

A vivid account of a poacher, emphasizing his secretiveness and the way he melts into the landscape and becomes almost part of it.

l. 13 *familiar:* intimate friend—but it also implies a witch's familiar or diabolic agent.

(A) Say in your own words how the poacher behaves when he is greeted (ll. 1–3). In what sense is the poacher 'the wind', and what does the wind do (ll. 4–5)? What is the weasel's knowledge of the poacher, and to what is it compared (ll. 6–9)? In what sense would smoke betray his dwelling, and why is it like 'blue writing' (l. 12)? Why is the sun called 'slick' and 'a dawn accomplice' (ll. 14–15)? What two natural agents seem to work for the poacher, and how do they imply his secrecy?

Cynddylan on a Tractor (p. 307)

A cheerful poem, though perhaps with an undertone of bitterness, about the invasion of machinery into the old peasant ways of the Welsh countryside. The tractor-driver's name is pronounced (roughly) 'Cun-thullan'.

(A) Which lines contrast the Cynddylan of the past with the present? What sound do you imagine when 'the clutch curses' (l. 5)? How does his arrival break the field's 'mirror of silence' and empty the wood (ll. 10–11)? On what 'different fuel' does he run his engine—different from what (ll. 12–14)? Why are the birds' bills 'wide in vain' (l. 15)? Do you think the poet resents Cynddylan's tractor and its effect on the landscape?

(B) Write in prose or verse about someone in a car, lorry, or farm vehicle breaking the peace of a country scene.

Evans (p. 308)

We remember here that R. S. Thomas is a priest, one of whose duties is visiting the sick. The whole poem can usefully be compared with Hopkins's *Felix Randal* (p. 114).

(A) At what time of the day and what time of the year does the poet visit Evans? Consider why the poem starts with a question 'Evans?' (compare this with the opening of Edward Thomas's *Adlestrop*). How do we guess that the farm is isolated? Where is the word 'dark' in l. 10 echoed, and what is the significance of this echo? Why did the drip of rain seem like blood and the one tree 'weather-tortured'? What does 'silting' mean in l. 14, and how does it connect with the last two lines. In what sense is Evans 'stranded' on his bed?

A Day in Autumn (p. 309)

(A) Explain the description of the autumn tree in your own words (ll. 2–5), and the bird 'preening' (trimming its feathers) in 'the lawn's mirror'. Suggest why he says 'Having looked up/From the day's chores', and connect this with the poem *Soil* (p. 305). How can 'the mind' take 'a photograph', and why would it be appropriate to 'wear it/Against the heart' (ll. 9–10)? What double meaning might there be in 'the long cold' (l. 10)?

(B) Describe *briefly* a summer or autumn scene that stays in your memory 'in the long cold'.

The Hill Farmer Speaks (p. 309)

This poem, very characteristic of R. S. Thomas, reminds us that the poorest and humblest farmer is just as much of a human being as any reader of the poem.

(A) What indications are there of the hill farmer's poverty? Consider ll. 9–10; do they imply that the farmer is literally starving? Where does he show intimacy with his animals, and shyness towards strangers? In what weather could the cattle's breath be like a cloak? Which lines suggest that he is old? Dirty? Ungraceful? Unable to think properly? What is the effect of the repetition of l. 5, and in what sense is the farmer 'saying' (ll. 3 and 20) this?

A Blackbird Singing (p. 310)

(A) Which words in the first verse contrast the bird's appearance with its song? Where else in the poem is the bird's colour referred to? In what sense is its bill 'bright' (l. 6)? Who is 'you' in l. 7, and what are 'you' doing when you hear the bird? What is meant by 'history's overtones' (l. 12) and which of the three words 'love', 'joy', and 'grief' seem to the poet dominant in the bird's song? How do you know?

(B) Compare this poem with Hardy's *The Darkling Thrush* (p. 134).

Lore (p. 311)

The last poem in this small collection is a shout of defiance and life from an old hard-working farm labourer.

(A) Why 'winters old' (l. 2), and why have the seasons brought him 'slow poison/And treachery' (ll. 3–4)? What picture do you get from 'the rain's hearse,/Wind drawn' (ll. 6–7)? What does Job Davis have for breakfast, and what keeps him fit? The last verse is difficult and profound: which of the old man's activities contrast with 'the machine', what sort of machine is he thinking of, and how could its fuel be 'human souls' (l. 19)? Explain what you think is meant by 'stay green' (l. 17) and the last line. The title, 'Lore', means a body of traditions or beliefs; how does it fit the poem?

(B) Write about an old person you know who keeps cheerful, and discuss his or her outlook on life (refer back, if you wish, also to *An Old Man*, p. 302).

FURTHER READING

Penguin Modern Poets No. 1 (a short but good selection of R. S. Thomas).

The Bread of Truth.

Tares.

Poetry for Supper.

Song at the Year's Turning.

These volumes contain R. S. Thomas's poems; at the time of publishing this anthology there was not yet a collected edition.